JUNE'S OLD MILL
ER GROUND MEAL
GOOD

Greater *A Shared Destiny* Atlanta

By Darlene Roth

Dedication

To the staff members of the Atlanta
History Center, past, present and future

First Edition
Copyright©2000
by Heritage Media Corporation
All rights reserved. No part of this book may be reproduced
in any form or by any means, electronic or mechanical,
including photocopying, without permission in
writing from the publisher. All inquiries should be
addressed to Heritage Media Corp.

ISBN: 1-886483-28-0

Library of Congress Card Catalog Number: 98-073491

Publisher: C.E. Parks

Editor-in-Chief: Lori M. Parks

Author: Darlene Roth

Photography Assistant: Riley Hayes

Vice President of Sales: Jill DeLeary

VP/Corporate Development: Bart Barica

CFO: Randall Peterson

Production Manager: Deborah Sherwood

Managing Editor: Betsy Baxter Blondin

Art Director: Gina Mancini

Project Editor: Sara Rufner

Assistant Art Director: Susie Passons

Graphic Designer: Marianne Mackey

Coordinating Editors: Renee Kim, Betsy Lelja, Elizabeth Lex,
Mary Ann Stabile, Adriane Wessels, John Woodward

Production Staff: Astrit Bushi, Jeff Caton, Dave Hermstead,
Jay Kennedy, Vincent Kornegay, John Leyva, Gavin Rattmann, Charlie Silvia

Profile Writers: Helen Cauley, Mickey Goodman, David Nordan, Laura Raines,
Darlene Roth, Erica Stephens, Rich Tewell, Curtis Zanone

Human Resources Manager: Ellen Ruby

Administration: Juan Diaz, Debbie Hunter, Azalea Maes, Majka Penner,
Scott Reid, Patrick Rucker, Cory Sottek

Produced in cooperation with the Atlanta History Center
www.atlantahistorycenter.com

Published by

Heritage Media Corp.
1954 Kellogg Avenue
Carlsbad, California 92008
www.heritagemedia.com

Printed by Heritage Media Corp. in the United States of America

All maps were produced for the author

Table of Contents

Preface

The metropolitan Atlanta region encompasses approximately one-fifth of the territory of Georgia, yet fully half of all Georgians live within commuting distance of the city of Atlanta. Whether they ever visit Atlanta, shop there, or take in any of the city's many entertainments, they are influenced by its presence.

By the same token, the city has grown by taking on the characteristics of its neighbors and their (once) rural environment. In the name of Atlanta, suburban growth has swallowed up more than 20 counties, according to the United States census, and growth is not stopping. Sprawl, air pollution, water shortages, traffic — all have begun to threaten the quality of living in the region in the last 20 years.

According to the governor and many others, the future of Atlanta now lies in some kind of regional planning — planning that recognizes the synergy of the parts that make up the whole — whereby public services and major systems for transportation, water, and air quality control can be provided without the loss of local authority that is so dear to the citizenry and so important to the continuance of democracy. "Smart growth" is the current buzz word for controlling development so it does not outpace local resources.

Yet thinking regionally and growing "smart" require a broad understanding of how Atlanta came to be, not only as a city, but also as a region. To support this greater consciousness of Atlanta's development, this history provides a look at Atlanta as the region it is and seeks to show what has held the region together since its inception in the first half of the 19th century.

"Greater Atlanta: A Shared Destiny" focuses on seven of the primary counties that compose the metropolitan area — Fulton, DeKalb, Cobb, Gwinnett, Clayton, Henry and Fayette — to demonstrate the shared aspirations, experiences and real connections that have held the people of the counties together as well as the tensions and differences that have often distinguished the city of Atlanta from its surrounding, and always supporting, environs. The story frustrates, fascinates and inspires.

Acknowledgments

Both Rick Beard, director of the Atlanta Historical Society, and Greg Paxton, director of the Georgia Trust for Historic Preservation, recommended to Heritage Media that I write this book, and I thank the two of them for the opportunity it has given me to stretch my knowledge and write about something I love — local history.

Since the coverage in the book reached well beyond the city limits of Atlanta, many local libraries and historical societies contributed to the preparation of the book with photographs and images, resource materials and suggestions. I wish to thank the staffs of the Fayette County Historical Society, the McDonough and Marietta public libraries, and the Henry County Genealogical Society for their assistance. Among the local agencies, the Gwinnett Historical Society and the folks at the tourism office in Jonesboro were especially helpful. Vivian Price in Chamblee contributed a key image and so did my colleague of many years, Randy Roark.

Special thanks go to Greg Eow of the DeKalb Historical Society, who scanned images for the book not once, but twice, and with generous good nature. It was a source of great comfort to know how much I could rely on the staff at the Atlanta History Center, especially Helen Matthews, Mike Brubaker and Michael Rose, who extended interest and extra support at every turn of this book's progress.

The book would not have been possible, however, without the assistance of Riley Hayes, who came along at just the right time and sustained the effort in so many ways, not the least of which came through his good eye, his good sense and his sense of humor.

Chapter 1

LONG BEFORE THERE WAS AN ATLANTA, INDIGENOUS PEOPLES KNOWN AS THE MOUND BUILDERS INHABITED THE REGION, MAINTAINING A VAST TERRITORY OF OCCUPATION THAT EXTENDED AS FAR SOUTH AS WHAT IS NOW SOUTH GEORGIA AND AS FAR NORTH AS WHAT IS NOW TENNESSEE. THEIR LANDS WERE CRISS-CROSSED BY HUNTING TRAILS AND TRADE ROUTES. EIGHT THOUSAND YEARS AGO, THE PEOPLE WHO CARVED BOWLS OUT OF THE ROCKS ALONG SOAPSTONE RIDGE IN DEKALB COUNTY TRADED THOSE BOWLS FOR OTHER GOODS WITH PEOPLE AS FAR AWAY AS THE MISSISSIPPI RIVER AND THE GULF OF MEXICO.

Before Atlanta

The Creek Indians, descendants of the ancient mound-building Muskogee peoples, maintained a nucleus of towns and villages in and around what is now Columbus, Georgia, but their lands extended throughout middle Georgia and into Alabama. They also occupied much of north Georgia until 1755 when the Cherokees defeated them in battle near what is now Canton (known as the Battle of Taliwa).

After that, the Chattahoochee River served as a boundary between the two Indian tribes, with the Cherokees controlling lands north and west of the river and the Creeks the lands south and east of the river. Twenty years later, both tribes sided with the British during the Revolutionary War, a fact used against them by resentful Georgia colonials who raided their towns and villages in brutal retaliation. Relations between Georgians and the Indians were hardly harmonious at this time, and over the next half-century they grew worse as the State of Georgia sought to exercise eminent domain over Indian lands.

In 1802 Georgia ceded its title to the Alabama and Mississippi territories (they were not yet states) to the federal government, setting in place the present state line. In return, the federal government agreed to void the remaining Indian titles to lands within the new state boundaries. Over the course of the ensuing decades, the federal government wrested a series of land cessions from the Indians that vaulted across the

Georgia map from river to river until the cessions stopped midstate at the Ocmulgee River. In 1815 Gen. Andrew Jackson pushed a settlement with the Creeks, obtaining from them 2 million acres of land in Georgia, but thereafter, Creek resistance to ceding land increased and precipitated a crisis in the tribe that ultimately engulfed all of northwest Georgia and came to a head in 1825.

The first Indian cession affecting this section of the state had actually come from the Cherokee Indians, not the Creeks, in 1817. In this treaty the Cherokees lost their ancestral capital in eastern Tennessee and certain other lands in Georgia. In 1819 the Cherokees established a new national capital in northwest Georgia at New Echota (near present-day Calhoun) — site of a bicameral legislature, stores, businesses, schools and a bilingual newspaper. They created a republican form of government in order to follow official U.S. counsel that if they assimilated, they could stay on these lands. The Cherokees adopted white farming techniques, white marriage customs, schooling, even white religion, as evidenced by their invitation to accept Christian missions in their territories. Spring Place near New Echota contained one such mission station. Members of the Cherokee governing body effectively negotiated terms for themselves, and on occasion even represented the Creeks in the U.S. Congress and the Georgia Legislature. The Cherokees in this part of Georgia tried assimilation; the Creeks took another path.

In 1819 the Creeks added some of their territory to the Cherokee land cession, which Georgia quickly laid out into Hall, Habersham, Walton and Gwinnett counties. Two years later, in 1821, the Creeks were asked for another piece of land lying between the Ocmulgee and Flint rivers, the Hightower Trail and the Chattahoochee River. Creek Chief William McIntosh, along with a handful of other leaders of the Lower Creeks (the Georgia Creeks) signed the proposed treaty, but

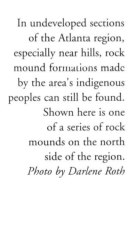

In undeveloped sections of the Atlanta region, especially near hills, rock mound formations made by the area's indigenous peoples can still be found. Shown here is one of a series of rock mounds on the north side of the region.
Photo by Darlene Roth

the Upper Creeks (the Alabama Creeks) would not sign. The U.S. government wanted a treaty that reflected tribal consensus, so the federal agents continued negotiations with the Indians for the land. Acting on its own, Georgia went ahead anyway and divided up the territory into five new counties, including Henry and Fayette. The Creeks, unable to come to terms among themselves, entered into a divisive and costly civil war over the treaty.

It took three more years to straighten matters out. In Council in May 1824, the Creeks, with Cherokee Chiefs John Ridge and David Vann in attendance, voted to reunite. They wished to become a single nation in order to keep their land in common, "as it always [had] been" and to "follow the pattern of the Cherokees," i.e., to begin to assimilate. It was too late. Agents for the federal government were told by none other than Secretary of War John C. Calhoun (the same man who had told the Indians they could stay if they assimilated) to respect the "feelings and wishes of the state of Georgia" in the dispute.

The U.S. Indian agents pressed for the Indians to withdraw. The two commissioners for the state of Georgia, who acted with even greater resolution, would not take no for an answer, resorted to threats and bribery and met secretly with Creek Chief William McIntosh. McIntosh continued to maintain a public position against the treaty among his fellow chieftains while he negotiated for a providential settlement for himself. McIntosh, a half-breed Indian and first cousin to Governor George M. Troup, was already living an assimilated existence on a large plantation on the Chattahoochee with an inn, a ferry, hundreds of cultivated acres including 150 acres of good bottomland and, reputedly, 100 black slaves. He spoke the best English of any of the Creek councilmen, and he sensed — or knew outright — that the Creeks would have to sell out now or would be removed later.

On February 12, 1825, William McIntosh, who had also signed treaties in 1805, 1818, 1821 and 1824, signed the Treaty of Indian Springs that effectively led to the removal of Creek Indians from the state of Georgia. When he did so, McIntosh was seated at a table in his own residence on land that was to be exempted from the treaty. He had been warned under threat of death by Opothle Yoholo — second in command to Big Warrior, the most important Creek Chief and leader of the Alabama Creeks — that he could not agree to sell Creek land without full council consideration and the consent of the nation as a whole. McIntosh signed anyway, knowing his life was at stake.

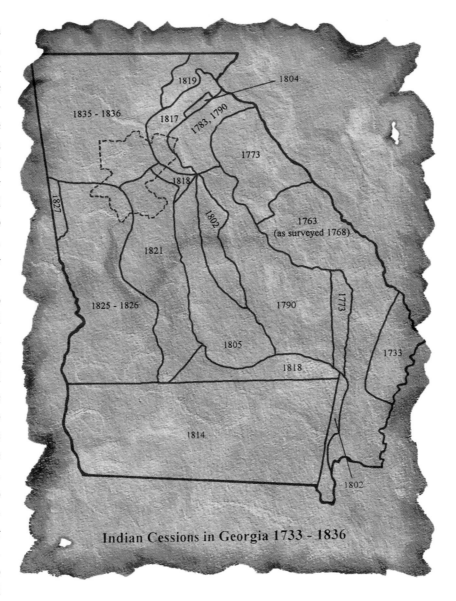

Indian Cessions in Georgia 1733 - 1836

In a dramatic moment Opothle Yoholo, watching from outside the inn where the treaty party met, declaimed on the duplicity inside: "Brothers," he said to assembled Creeks, "our lands are gone...We are deceived by the double-tongue of the pale-face Chief McIntosh." As a demonstration to the U.S. government of their new national unity and an assertion of their desire to stay on their lands, the Creek Council sent a party of Creeks to assassinate Chief McIntosh on April 25, 1925. The Creeks reiterated to the U.S. Commissioners that they considered the treaty to be counterfeit, but to show goodwill they ceded some lands east of the Chattahoochee.

In a poignant speech to the Georgia Legislature in his personal farewell to the state (just two weeks before his murder), McIntosh had invoked the feeling of loss for the whole tribe, pleading for his own protection: "You are like the mighty storm; we are like the tender & bending tree, we must bow before you, you have tore [sic] us up by the root, but still, you are our Brothers and friends, you have promised to replant us in a better soil, and to watch over us, and nurse us... [As] We are about to take our final leave of you..."

The matter remained unsettled (in all but Georgia's eyes) until President John Quincy Adams negotiated a new treaty with the Creeks in 1826, by which all Creek lands were finally ceded in Georgia. The Creeks, politically weakened and scattered, retained some of their lands in Alabama, but after 1826 only Cherokees remained inside Georgia.

The 14,000 acres of land known as "Cherokee Georgia" constituted only a part of the Cherokee territory that coursed over the mountains of North Carolina, Tennessee and Alabama, but because of the capital at New Echota, it was an important part. Cherokee Georgia was the Cherokee showcase for assimilation, where tribal advancement toward "civilization" was most obvious. The land was dotted with comfortable houses, villages, large farms, trade centers, mission schools, mills

William McIntosh was both hero and villain in the last Indian land cessions to the state of Georgia. As a mixed breed, McIntosh faced an impossible set of choices, finally giving way to what he saw as inevitable.
The Atlanta Historical Society, Inc.

and household industries. The population totaled 15,060, of which 1,277 were enslaved African-Americans. In addition, more than 200 white people lived on Cherokee lands as part of the Indian nation.

Between 1821 and 1835 the Cherokees lived a politically precarious existence, under pressure to sell their lands and move west. Georgia, still operating out of its 1802 agreement with the U.S. government, pushed for removing the Indians by force if they would not peaceably depart. The Georgia Legislature took matters into its own hands in 1828 by annexing Cherokee lands within the assigned state borders. The legislators nullified Cherokee charters and contracts and stripped the Indians of all authority in a series of laws that also prevented white persons from living or working on Indian properties or for the Indians' welfare. Then they physically removed from Indian control certain "improvements" on their lands — chiefly ferries, toll roads and several profitable farms.

Joseph Vann, son of Chief James Vann, who had set the Cherokees on their course of assimilation and whose 1805 house still stands in north Georgia (today it is a museum), hired a white overseer to run his plantation, though it had become illegal to do so. To retaliate for his "insubordination," the state confiscated his property and turned him and his family out. The Vanns relocated to Tennessee, leaving behind their 800 acres, brick home, 42 slave cabins, six barns, five smokehouses, grist and sawmills, blacksmith shop, peach kiln, trading post, orchards and other property. Decades later the United States was to compensate the family for their loss, but by that time the remaining family members were far away in Oklahoma.

In 1830 the U.S. Congress passed the Indian Removal Act, spearheaded by the Georgia delegation, to remove — once and for all — the Indians still living on lands east of the Mississippi, most of them in the

Southern states, and relocate them in the West. The Indians were given one last opportunity to move voluntarily, and a few did, selling their property off at bargain prices. Most simply clung to their homelands.

Georgia took matters into its own hands again by ordering a survey of Cherokee lands in 1831 so they could be redistributed by lottery to new settlers. Georgia was impatient to settle Cherokee territory with its own citizenry, for the state had an Indian frontier within its borders that lay across a network of Anglo-American migratory routes, future transportation passages, productive agricultural regions, and most important, iron and gold deposits. The populations in the young counties (Gwinnett, DeKalb and Henry) were now pressing up against the Indian populations, seeking expansion, and Georgia wanted to eliminate its Indian frontier as well as the animosity, the "foreign" dealings and the federal intervention that tended to go with it.

The state was in competition for population growth with the developing regions to the west. All roads led to the West, to the Alabama territory and beyond, and Georgia was the natural passage for migrants coming from the east and circumnavigating the mountains. The roads to Alabama followed and paralleled the Indian trading paths among the Creeks, Chickasaws and Cherokees, criss-crossing and branching out into many arteries. A steady stream of migrants from Virginia and the Carolinas moved daily over these roads, passing through Indian territory, often with incidents that were impossible to police or correct. Though some, like George Waters of Gwinnett County, stayed to live in peace with their Indian neighbors, most settlers moved on, understandably reluctant to live as squatters in Indian territory. There were many "Alabama Roads" cutting across the state through Indian and non-Indian territory, remnants of which still exist in the region and evoke the migratory current that poured through northwest Georgia and sometimes left white settlement in its wake.

Aside from wanting to encourage settlement, Georgia also wanted to extend its trade and commerce through Indian territory, without hindrance, into the interior of the United States. The northeast section of the state was uniquely situated to accommodate this expansion. Traders could trek overland from the Eastern seaboard cities of Savannah, Georgia, and Charleston, South Carolina, proceed to the base of the Blue Ridge, pass around the mountains, turn north toward

Migrating settlers moved across the region on a set of roads all called "Alabama" because they headed west toward the Alabama territory. Such routes depended on "flat shoals," such as those shown, for safe crossing over the region's rivers. These are now a favorite part of the state park at Indian Springs.
Photo by Darlene Roth

in the region and gave Georgia legislators the rationale they needed, they thought, finally to exercise eminent domain through the gold lottery of 1831.

The old gold region in Georgia was rich and extensive, forming an east-west belt nearly 20 miles wide along the base of the Blue Ridge. The 1831 survey parceled Cherokee lands into 40-acre gold lots and 100-acre farm lots. Unmarried white males could draw one ticket; married males with children could draw two; certain officers and soldiers of the late revolution, their widows and orphans could also draw. The gold lottery included all of the Atlanta metro areas north and east of the Chattahoochee. A corner of Gwinnett County actually saw some gold mining at this time, but the center of the gold rush lay farther north in Dawson County, at Dahlonega, where the United States ultimately built a mint. What the gold lottery signaled for the region was that the "right" white citizens could now claim to move into Cherokee lands and settle on them, whether or not there were Indians already living there.

By 1833 the lands in Cherokee Georgia had been absorbed into the state, subdivided into Cherokee, Cobb, Forsyth and seven other counties. The cessions of the Treaty of New Echota that had been signed by a faction of Cherokees in 1830, yet opposed by the preponderance of the Indian nation, were rendered superfluous by the state's actions. The Cherokees appealed to the U.S. Supreme Court, but in a twist of legal precedent Justice John Marshall and his peers ruled that the Cherokees, while a separate people, were not a foreign nation and therefore had no right to sue Georgia for compensation or redress, no matter how just their cause. The Cherokees won a moral victory but lost their land.

After several more years of futile delays, postponements and much resistance, 16,000 Cherokees

Tennessee and from there gain entrance to the vast markets of the Tennessee, Ohio and Mississippi valleys. For decades Georgians debated where the best route to the interior lay and what means (railroad or canal) would be most profitable in making the potential connection stronger.

In a few years they would decide on railroads, but before they could get a foot of track planned, they had to turn their attentions instead to a matter that completely changed their circumstances: in 1829 gold was discovered in the Cherokee hills. A gold rush, America's first, exploded before their eyes, and nothing the legislature did could keep out the squatters, miners, prospectors and thieves from "them thar hills." The ensuing chaos threatened what tenuous stability existed with their slaves and children were rounded up and organized for forced departure. Gen. Winfield Scott oversaw the removal, setting up his headquarters at New Echota, cruelly twisting the promise of democracy the capital had once symbolized. Many of the Indians were forced to leave their homes so quickly that they had only the clothes on their back with them. Others carried what they could — a few household implements, some sacred objects, extra clothing or a favorite child's possession. A very few escaped farther into the hills and passed out of history altogether. Refugee camps, removal forts set up in different locations in northwest Georgia, kept the Indians imprisoned until they could be moved out, contingent by contingent, under armed military escorts.

The earliest march in June 1838 proved to be such a disaster in the excessive heat of that summer that the remaining marches were postponed until the weather cooled down. Still, more than 4,000 died en route to the Oklahoma Territories. The armed forces were inadequately supplied with food and medicine for the Indians' benefit. The very young died. The sick expired. The old walked too sorrowfully, too slowly, to keep up and dropped from exhaustion. As one escorting soldier wrote, "they lay down by the roadside . . .[and] They died of broken hearts." The Trail of Tears, as the removal has been remembered in history, fulfilled a haunting prophecy of Cherokee Chief Dragging Canoe nearly a century earlier, who presaged in 1768 that when white men "passed the mountains" and settled on Cherokee lands, "the whole country, which the Cherokees and their fathers have so long occupied, will be demanded, and the remnant of the Ani-Yunwiya, 'the Real People,' once so great and formidable, will be obliged to seek refuge in some distant wilderness..."

The Indians left legacies behind — trails (which became roadways for the white civilization), town and village sites (many taken over for white villages and towns), farms, orchards, sacred grounds (such as at Etowah and Stone Mountain), ferries, communal ball fields and Indian names on rivers and land (adopted by the whites). The names Chattahoochee, Oconee, Coosa and Alabama come from the Creeks; Kennesaw, Tallulah and Dahlonega from the Cherokees.

The Hightower (Etowah) Trail — from the Creek "italwa" and the Cherokee "itawa" — was the most important route in north Georgia that connected the Coosa River in the northwest across the state to the Savannah River near what is now Augusta. The section of it running from High Shoals on the Appalachee River to the Shallow Ford on the Chattahoochee below Roswell forms much of the boundary between present-day DeKalb and Gwinnett counties.

The Hightower Trail connected with another route, later a stage road between Decatur, Panthersville, Morrow, Jonesboro, Fayetteville and Columbus, which had originally connected the Etowah Mounds with the Indian villages on the lower Chattahoochee. The Peachtree Trail, running south of and parallel to Nancy Creek, extended from Standing Peachtree (the most important Indian town in the Atlanta area, straddling the Chattahoochee River at Peachtree Creek) to Hog Mountain in what is now Gwinnett County.

The Peachtree Trail also crossed the Sandtown path, portions of which are still marked in southwest Atlanta and Cobb County. Marietta Road, Decatur,

Throughout the Atlanta region, Sandtown Road signs, markers to Indian trails, and the words Hightower and Etowah evoke the complex network of trade paths and migration routes carved out of the area by the American Indians. *Photo by Riley Hayes*

Peachtree Street SW (originally Whitehall Road), and Peachtree Street owe their origins to Indian pathways. What is now Fulton County was clearly a convergence point for Indians in much the same way it was for white migratory traffic that flowed from east and west in the early 19th century between the eastern coastal and river towns (Augusta and Savannah, Georgia, and Charleston, South Carolina) and the West.

The White Settlers

White settlement in northwestern Georgia was sparse until the Indians were removed. Once the lands were ceded, settlement raced ahead, spurred on by Georgia's unique lottery system and an ambitious legislature. Gwinnett County was formed from the Cherokee Cession of 1817 and the Creek Cession of 1818 and is the oldest county in the immediate Atlanta metropolitan area. The 42nd county in Georgia, Gwinnett was named for Button Gwinnett, a signer of the Declaration of Independence. Fayette and Henry counties were formed from the Creek Cession of 1821, and were the 49th and 50th counties to be formed in Georgia, named for the Marquis de LaFayette and Patrick Henry, respectively.

Henry County map

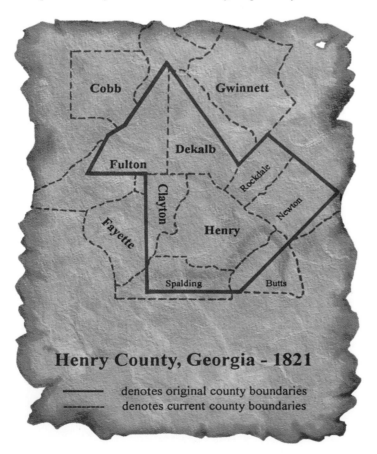

Henry County, Georgia - 1821

——— denotes original county boundaries
--------- denotes current county boundaries

At that time the northwest boundary of Henry County lay at the Chattahoochee River. DeKalb County was formed in 1822 from Fayette, Henry and Gwinnett counties, and named for Baron de Kalb, a Revolutionary War hero from Germany. Campbell County (now Fulton), named for Col. Duncan G. Campbell, negotiator of the Indian Springs treaty of 1823, was created in 1828 from DeKalb, Fayette, Coweta and Carroll counties, the latter two having been established from the Creek Cession of 1826. Cobb County was the last local county to be formed in the pioneer period (1832); it was carved from Cherokee County, which originally corresponded with all of Cherokee Georgia. Cherokee, the 79th county, required three acts of legislation between 1830 and 1831 to complete its definition. Fulton (1854) and Clayton (1858) counties were formed later out of the other existing counties, Campbell and DeKalb counties, and Henry and Fayette counties, respectively. Much later still, Milton County, created in 1857 from Cherokee, Cobb and Forsyth counties, was merged into Fulton County in 1932. In order of creation, then, the local counties appeared in this sequence: Gwinnett, Fayette, Henry, DeKalb, Campbell, Cherokee, Cobb, Fulton (from Campbell), Milton (merged into Fulton) and Clayton.

Except for a small section of the Etowah and Coosa rivers around Rome, Georgia, the rivers in this section of the state were not navigable — no steamboats here! Settlers moved in over land, crossing the rivers as they came. Ferries across these rivers — the Ocmulgee, the Appalachee, the Flint, the Chattahoochee and others — were as essential to sectional growth as they were lucrative to their early owners.

The ferries were connected by roads to the county seats and in some instances to each other, giving rise to the first transportation nexus in the area. Thus, Keys Ferry in Henry County on the Ocmulgee tied directly to McDonough by Keys Ferry Road. Montgomery Ferry Road (in present-day Ansley Park) led to DeFoors Ferry Road (in northwest Atlanta), which ran to Standing Peachtree, though the connection between them today has been lost in a century of development.

The road from Lawrenceville to Isom's (or Heard's) Ferry ran through Dunwoody and Sandy Springs; Isom's was also connected to Johnson's Ferry and Power's Ferry. The Martin's Ferry Road followed exactly the Hightower Trail leading from eastern Georgia to western Georgia between the sixth district of Fulton County and the eighteenth of DeKalb.

Fulton County, then as now, was the converging point for almost all of the east and west traffic that flowed across the state between the southern port cities and the western lands. It was also in what was to become Fulton County that the east-west routes crossed the one primary north-south route, which has had many incarnations and routes, but is now most heavily traveled by the snowbirds and trucks going south into Florida along Interstate 75.

Some of the ferries that accommodated the migrations across the state were established by the Indians and taken over by the settlers. Atlantans have long since abandoned or replaced the ferry crossings with bridges, but their names remain — Paces Ferry, Isoms, Powers, Grogans, Bakers, Greensferry, Nelsons, Martins, Bells and, later but most important of all, the Mayson-Turner Ferry (the road to that ferry is now Bankhead Highway), across which the Federal party came to receive the surrender of Atlanta during the Civil War. Most of the ferries were established in the 1820s and early 1830s, and those that lasted served the local populace until the middle of the 20th century.

Land was the key to settlement, and every time Georgia held a land lottery the state incurred a population increase. The lottery was a unique system of land dispersal among the original colonial states in the United States. Usually, land exchanged hands through headrights, crown grants or simple purchase. The Georgia lottery was supposed to discourage speculation, which it did on the first round of draws. But land speculators, who always had more money than the ticket holders, came along with the winners and bought their lands for a pittance, and could then turn around and resell them for minimal prices and still make a profit. Nonetheless, the lotteries helped establish permanent settlements.

Lottery lands were divided into sections, districts and land lots; each land lot contained 202 1/2 acres;

a district was nine square miles, and a section consisted of three districts. The normal draw gained the ticket holder one land lot (202 1/2 acres), except in the gold lotteries where the largest draw netted just 100 acres. In each lottery the state set aside land for county seats and other county uses, for schools and cemeteries; churches could easily obtain land but not entire land lots. As towns were established, the land lots were subdivided into town lots, blocks and parcels. Once established, the numbering system held; today's real estate identification numbers in metro-Atlanta emanate from those lottery surveys in the early 1800s.

In each new county the principal town was the county seat, situated in the center of the county so as to be equidistant from all its citizens. Before the center of Gwinnett County was ascertained by survey, and before the lottery was held, a temporary courthouse site was established approximately one mile west of the present courthouse in Lawrenceville. Lot 146 was finally established as the county center, and the county purchased the lot from the lottery holder for that draw, John Breedlove, and planned the courthouse that is still located on the property (though not in the same building).

As county lines changed, residents either learned to live with what seemed to be a haphazard location or tried to move the county seat to a more convenient location. None of the original county seats in the metro-Atlanta counties relocated, but their county boundaries shifted. Decatur was located in the center of original DeKalb County, but when Fulton was formed, Decatur "moved" to the western edge of DeKalb. Campbellton was left without a county entirely when Fulton was established to supersede Campbell County.

This old and rare photograph of an area ferry shows Calhoun Turner carrying Cobb Countian John Hooper across the Chattahoochee River, c. 1897. The Mayson-Turner ferry served travelers along what is now US 78/278, Bankhead Highway. *The Atlanta Historical Society, Inc.*

None of the county seats, even as centers of government, would be recognized as anything but quiet, tiny Southern towns in the 1820s. Lawrenceville, Fayetteville and Decatur were approximately the same size. Lawrenceville (fd. 1821) contained a courthouse, jail, academy, 33 houses, 16 stores and offices and 400 people; Fayetteville (fd. 1827), described by a contemporary gazetteer as a "healthy spot" and "rising in importance," contained 42 houses along with its courthouse and jail. Decatur (fd. 1823) had stores, a jail, the courthouse, an academy, 40 houses and the "fair" promise of becoming a "large town." Decatur served a county population of 10,000 people by 1830, about 10 percent of whom were enslaved.

By 1830 the local counties were growing quickly: Fayette had more than 5,000 citizens, nearly double what it had in 1825; DeKalb had more than 10,000 people, as did Henry County. African-Americans numbered no more than 10 percent of the totals in these counties. Campbell County had a population of only 3,000. Gwinnett was the most populous county by 1830 with more than 13,000 people, at least triple the number who had settled there by 1820, a quite remarkable increase given that Gwinnett gave up half its territory for the formation of new counties in the same decade. In 1825 there were 689 families in Gwinnett County, 46 of them headed by women and 21 headed by veterans of the Revolutionary War.

The Browning courthouse, relocated but still standing in Tucker, served Browning's district, named after Andrew Browning. Small extension courthouses such as these were dotted throughout the counties to dispense justice on a more convenient, localized basis. *DeKalb Historical Society*

These numbers indicate the success of the lottery in giving women and soldiers property but do not account for the speculation that also occurred in the county. Men outnumbered women by nearly 1,000 in Gwinnett, a number that suggests the frontier conditions that still prevailed. There were 920 African-American slaves in Gwinnett who had been brought with their owners and lived for the most part in family units with their white owners. Most of the slave owners had four or five slaves. The two largest slave owners in the county, David Dixon and Wilson Strickland, owned 14 slaves each, an inconsiderable number when compared with the high rates of slave ownership in the rice-growing coastal counties but also a clear indication that a slave-dependent economy moved into this area with its earliest settlers.

All three towns honored heroes of the early Republic and the Revolutionary War with their nomenclature: Commodore Stephen Decatur, Capt. James ("don't give up the ship") Lawrence, and, of course the Marquis de LaFayette. In Lawrenceville, the four streets bordering the courthouse further honored Commodore Perry (naval officer), Zebulon Pike (soldier and explorer), George Croghan (hero of the War of 1812), and Augustine Clayton (judge and congressman). Campbellton, seat of government for old Campbell County, contained a brick courthouse judged "far too large for the county," by one commentator, plus a hotel — the only one around — as well as the obligatory jail and academy. It also had two churches — all for a town population of 175 and a county population of 3,000.

In the 1820s there were other scattered towns and many small settlements, enclaves really, where collections of people succeeded in obtaining a post office or resettling an Indian village. Among the settlements were a few resort towns, usually located in conjunction with healing waters — Indian Springs, Madison Springs and Franklin Springs were among the many such places in Georgia in Wilkes, Clarke, Greene, Jefferson and other counties. Among them, Indian Springs (now in Butts County), where McIntosh had signed the treaties giving rise to the Atlanta metropolitan area, had become the most fashionable watering place in Georgia, "the Saratoga of the South" according to some, with several dozen cabins and large hotels (one of them McIntosh's old inn) where 600-800 people could stay at one time. The permanent population was not large, but the place was well known and enjoyed a high visitation. From there north, people added other locales to the list of early spas — some of them located in former Cherokee Georgia — Lithia, Powder, and Blue Springs, to name a handful.

The site of treaty signings, the Indian Springs Hotel, once the home of Chief William McIntosh, became in time Georgia's first great resort. Today the building houses the Butts County Historical Society. *Photo by Darlene Roth*

Among the other communities, Sand Town in Campbell County, once a stop on the Sandtown Trail, was in existence on the Chattahoochee long before many other localities. In Gwinnett there were Choice's Store, Demopolis, and Loughbridge; in Henry County, Pleasant Grove; and in DeKalb stood Whitehall — so called for being the only house in the area painted white — and Standing Peachtree (at the old Indian town site). In 1827 there were a handful of communities and outposts in this area, but in all of Georgia at the time there were only 165 post offices, an indication of the relative lack of development throughout the state. Oftentimes the reason for the village existence was the presence of an important institution — usually a store or a church — in the vicinity.

Two figures whose personal biographies elucidate the transition from Indian to white settlement during this early period in the Atlanta area are the Montgomery brothers, Hugh Lawson Montgomery and James McC. Montgomery. Hugh served as an Indian agent between 1825 and 1834, surveyed much of North Georgia, and at one time represented Jackson County in the legislature. Related by marriage to the Venables of Stone Mountain, James McC. Montgomery married Nancy Farlow of Hancock County, for whom Nancy's Creek is named. Describing himself as a "merchant on the frontier," Montgomery settled himself on the land lot where Fort Standing Peachtree stood, long before he was actually granted the land in 1833.

Generally regarded as one of DeKalb County's premier pioneers, James McC. Montgomery served as postmaster, census taker, clerk of the Court of Ordinary, and the first state senator from the county. Because he lived on the Chattahoochee, Montgomery's store was a way station for whites pioneering west and for Indians across the river in Cherokee Georgia. Appointed to "appraise" the value of Cherokee properties, which were to be disposed of in the Indian migrations, Montgomery tried to enroll the Indians in voluntary migrations west, but he met resistance from the Indians and obstacles from the white authorities.

The year 1834 was the last of his in service as an appraiser, and he was not directly involved in the removal. It was not, however, until 1837 when the Indians were on their way west, that he could establish a ferry across the Chattahoochee on lands, according to the Acts of Georgia, which were "his own." Montgomery was farsighted in that he sold a slave of his, Ransom

The first regional settlements grew up around institutions such as this one. Choice's Store was a combination post office, trade post, stagecoach stop and center of a militia district in Gwinnett County. *The Gwinnett County Historical Society*

The Elisha Winn House, c. 1812, is one of Gwinnett's most historical sites, having been the place where the county was organized in 1818.
Photo by Riley Hayes

Montgomery, to the state for $1,000 and the promise of emancipation, then guaranteed a right-of-way to the Western and Atlantic railroad for passage through his land. James McC. Montgomery never lived to see the railroad; and his slave Ransom died in servitude.

Settlement in the Atlanta region progressed from the eastern side of Gwinnett County to the west toward the Georgia border, from the southern part of Henry County toward the north in the direction of the Chattahoochee River and the state of Tennessee. The region did not develop village by village, so much as family by family.

Once there were enough families in a single geographic location, a militia district would be delineated for the protection of the inhabitants, a holdover concept from colonial days when a local militia unit could be called up for emergencies within the district. Militia districts were the original political subdivisions in each county, formed whenever the population density could support a military unit of 100 men — able-bodied, white and between the ages of 18 and 45. A militia district could be named for its captain, for a prominent local citizen, for a nearby town or almost anything else. Once established, the district grew in size but its geography did not change.

The local militias lasted until the Civil War when they were superseded by the Conscription Acts of the Confederacy. A few long-lived units were later absorbed into the National Guard and the Coast Guard, but most of them disappeared while the district delineations as they presently exist became voting precincts, identified by numbers and no longer by colorful names.

Some idea of how the militia districts were defined can be seen in DeKalb County, which had 13 such districts in 1830 named Dean's, Foote's, Gillis', Givens', Griffin's, Harris', Heard's, Johnson's, Latimer's, Mobley's, Morton's, Rhodes' and Says'. Says' District, for example, encompassed Stone Mountain and its vicinity (the mountain and the town); Latimer's enveloped Decatur and its environs; Dean's covered what were later designated the Buckhead, Oakgrove, Cross Keys and Shallowford post offices; Harris' District took care of the extreme northwest of the county along the Chattahoochee; and Foote's carried the areas that are now known as East Atlanta, Edgewood, Kirkwood, Oakhurst and Druid Hills neighborhoods. While DeKalb has lost all traces of its original political sectioning, Henry County's organization can still be somewhat comprehended because the militia districts bore as many geographic as personal names: McDonough (after the town), Lovejoys (the family and plantation), Bear Creek, Andersons, Millers, Browns (Browns Mill) and Holloways.

As populations increased, settlers built private roads while county officials built public ones. Roads ran in spoke-like patterns from the county seats to the edges of the counties in all directions, connecting county seat with county seat and county seats with the nearest fords, ferries, mills and bridges. In 1823 Henry County commissioners authorized roads to be built from the Henry County Courthouse to the Pike County Courthouse, to the Fayette Ferry, from Lovejoy's to Sand Town on the Chattahoochee, and in the direction of Covington as far as the county line; DeKalb Street was laid out from the Henry Courthouse in the direction of DeKalb County; and Gwinnett Street (Lawrenceville Street) was laid off from the northeast corner of the courthouse square toward Gwinnett.

The route between Lawrenceville and Augusta, 90 miles away, was a well-worn path but roads going west, south, and north from Lawrenceville had yet to be etched on the land. In the 1820s county officials had roads laid out from Lawrenceville to Bosman's Ferry and Vann's Ferry (the Indian chief's ferry) on the Chattahoochee, to Langston's Mill and Richardson's Mill, to Price's Bridge on the Appalachee, to the Jackson County Courthouse and to other existing roads such as Covington and Walton.

While roads became plentiful during the 1820s, amenities were few for the new residents. There simply were not many cultural institutions of any kind in the area. There was an occasional academy, such as the Lawrenceville Academy established in 1824 and run by the Presbyterian minister for many years. The Henry County Academy was authorized in 1826 and opened in 1827 with 104 "scholars," both male and female, between the ages of 8 and 16. It was common for the county seat to have an academy for the white males of the county, but several churches also built small schools.

There were a few taverns, of course, at the cross-roads and the ferry crossings, but they were not the foundations of community so much as they were founts of gossip and news — the place where strangers brought the outside world into the frontier. Regular stagecoach service was not well developed at first; it wasn't until the 1830s that regular service came as far as Decatur and connected Decatur with Marietta. Service ran from Augusta and Macon to Monroe, then to Covington and north. The first newspaper in the area, one of only 15 in the state at the time, appears to have been *The Jacksonian*, published at McDonough beginning in 1827.

After courthouses, the primary cultural institutions of the time were churches, which could obtain free land in the newly opening territories. Once established, churches founded missions in the newest settlements, leapfrogging the territories along with the families who founded them. Thus, the Yellow River Baptist Association created mission churches in DeKalb County from the established congregations in Gwinnett County. There were Baptists and Methodists in plentiful numbers, but since church buildings were few, their meetings often contained Presbyterians, Episcopalians and other Christians as well.

As a rule, the Baptists were the first congregations to arrive, having received land from the state — usually one acre. If the Methodists followed, they could also obtain land from the state, no more nor less than had been given the Baptists. Not more, nor better land would be given to the second group of congregants, no matter what the denomination. Among the earliest churches in the Atlanta area were Sardis Baptist (1823), Sharon Baptist (1824) and Lebanon Primitive Baptist (1824) in Henry. (More than half of the pioneer churches in Henry County were Baptist.) The Baptists were the most numerous of the denominations, with local associations for the Yellow River, the Flint River and the Chattahoochee River (the last one the newest).

Each church had its own minister, but the Methodists were serviced with a combination of ministers and circuit riders. In the entire state in the 1820s there were approximately 20,000 Baptists on the rolls, and 17,000 Methodists. The Presbyterians, the next largest Protestant denomination, had only 2,000 communicants. There were Roman Catholics in three of the older towns in Georgia, notably Savannah, Augusta and Macon, but none in northwest Georgia. Catholics did not establish a foothold in the metro-Atlanta region until years later when Irish workers came to build the Western and Atlantic and Georgia Railroads. The only Jews in Georgia at this time were located in Savannah, whose synagogue is one of the oldest in the United States.

Henry and Gwinnett were peopled almost entirely by migrants from the older counties of Georgia and other states of the Union, especially the Southern states. Some immigrants came directly from Scotland and Ireland; a handful were from Germany and France, but the great predominance were of Anglo-American stock.

A view of the original route to Decatur Courthouse, McDonough Road, c. 1900
DeKalb Historical Society

They came in family groups, leapfrogging the counties, settling for awhile one place and then moving on. For example, the Bibb, Cash, Clark, Daley, Foster, Harper, Higginbotham, Keys, Maddox, Thrasher and Turpin families all came to Henry County from Virginia via Wilkes County, Georgia. The Carrs, Duffeys, Laneys and McKibbens came from Mecklenburg County, North Carolina. The Elliott family actually consolidated their numbers in Henry County, with branches of the family coming from Georgia's Morgan, Oglethorpe and Wilkes counties to Henry County.

William Maltbie, a native of Connecticut, represents another pioneer pattern. Arriving on his own, Maltbie operated a store at Hog Mountain before Gwinnett County was formed and then moved to Lawrenceville once it was established. He settled down permanently when he married the daughter of Elisha Winn, one of the county's founders, and became the first postmaster for Gwinnett. His father-in-law sold the first slave in Gwinnett County in 1819, a 6-year-old boy named Isham, owned by James H. Kidd who lived near Hog Mountain. Slave traders came along with the land speculators in early settlements, both of whom knew not only that they had virgin territory to cultivate but also that they could plan on profiting from resales in a newly settled area.

The settlers who moved into this region came to a portion of the richest area of the state, the Piedmont Plateau, which lies between the coastal plains and the mountain chains in north Georgia. The plateau, which traverses the southern end of the Appalachians,

contains multiple creeks, rivers, small streams and fertile soils. The series of valleys along the creek beds contained forests and rich red loamy soil for the growing of all kinds of grains plus cash crops like cotton and tobacco. The forests were replete with oak, hickory, poplar, maple, walnut, sycamore, black gum, sweet gum, chestnut, dogwood, cedar, elm and ash trees. Animal life was plentiful: turkey, bear, deer, beaver, fox, squirrel, wolf, mink, coon, opossum, quail, pigeon, geese and ducks; and in the abundant streams there were fish of all kinds. It was a hunter's paradise; it was a farmer's paradise, and it became a draw for yet another kind of enterprise.

In the midst of the Piedmont Plateau, the Peachtree Ridge divides the ranges of hills along the Chattahoochee tableland. It is a watershed — water to the east of the ridge flows into the Atlantic; water to the west flows to the Gulf of Mexico. The ridge is 1,100 feet above sea level and offered what it had always offered, access around the mountains and transportation across sometimes difficult terrain to the expanses that lay west. The Peachtree Ridge converges with two other ridges, running eastward and southwestward, at a point about six miles east of the Chattahoochee.

In 1830 there was as yet nothing at this point except two settlements, one named White Hall and one named Thrashersville. But the point was to be a magnet to progress and transportation revolution: railroads follow the watershed courses. It was at this point that three railroads, following the topography, were to terminate without regard for the site as a location for a town but creating nonetheless a new center for the region, and giving rise to Atlanta.

THE BOWMAN HOUSE IN GWINNETT COUNTY, MADE OF LOGS AND CLAY CHINKING, IS REPRESENTATIVE OF EARLY SETTLEMENT HOUSES THROUGHOUT GREATER ATLANTA.
PHOTO BY RILEY HAYES

Chapter 2

Before the Civil War, Atlanta was simply the largest of the local small towns and county seats. As a byproduct of the railroads, Atlanta became a magnet for opportunism and speculation, industry and commerce. The region, tied together by a network of stagecoach lines running between the towns and seats, was forever changed by the introduction of railroads.

Like its sister states in the United States of the early 1800s, Georgia set out to establish greater transportation connections inside the state as well as with surrounding states, and even foreign countries, in order to support its populations and to extend its influence, trade and commerce. Georgia reached across the Atlantic through the seaport of Savannah on its own coast and overland from Augusta through the old colonial trade center, Charleston, South Carolina. In 1825 the Georgia Legislature created a Board of Internal Improvements, whose job it was to explore the possibilities of canal, railroad and road construction throughout the state.

At first, Georgia fostered the development of turnpikes and canals. The turnpikes were privately funded and never constituted an effective network for the state. The largest of the canal projects — the Savannah, Ogeechee and Altamaha Canal in coastal Georgia — was abandoned in favor of the railroads almost as soon as it was finished in 1831. The Board of Internal Improvements fostered two major projects to traverse the state: one from Tennessee to the Atlantic and the other from Savannah to the Flint River (in proximity to Macon, Georgia). Chief Engineer of the Board Hamilton Fulton and soon-to-be Governor Wilson Lumpkin surveyed the state, including its settled portion and the portion lying in Cherokee Georgia, to support both projects. Lumpkin and Fulton both favored building a railroad.

The first railroad in Georgia connected Charleston, South Carolina, to Augusta, Georgia, in 1833; that railroad was then continued to Athens, Georgia. Savannah, not to be outdone by Charleston, connected to Macon, Georgia, via the Central of Georgia Railroad, making the coastal trade center an easier recipient of the rich farm produce of central Georgia. Once Macon and Augusta were connected to Georgia's coast, the state focused its transportation objectives in the interior, connecting these two railroads with a third line that ran north from the Chattahoochee River to the state of Tennessee, there to secure passage through the valleys of Tennessee out to the great Mississippi and Ohio rivers. If Georgia could connect the Savannah seaport to the Memphis river port on the Mississippi River, it could trade foreign imports from anywhere in the known world and send out local products, chiefly cotton, in exchange. The promise of success held enough economic incentive to put the state of Georgia into the railroad business.

The state therefore funded the development of the Western and Atlantic Railroad (W&A) to run north from a point near the Chattahoochee River, at which point the W&A was to converge with the Georgia Railroad, running west from Augusta, and the Macon and Western Railroad (an extension

Map of pre-Civil War Georgia railroads

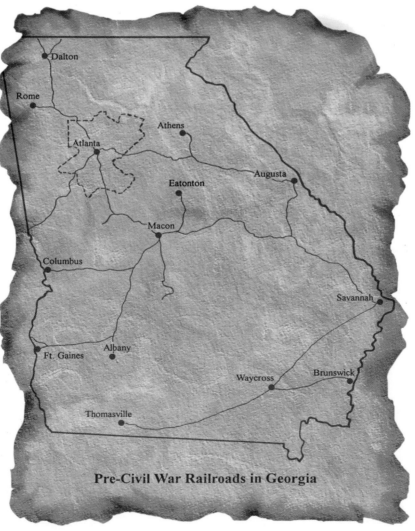

Pre-Civil War Railroads in Georgia

of the Central of Georgia) running north from Macon. That point roughly six miles from the Chattahoochee was staked out in 1837, and from it Atlanta was to emerge. This same point of land lay upon the summit of a 1,000-foot ridge that followed a gentle gradient north and west toward the northern terminus at Ross' Landing (Chattanooga), a summit connected to a set of connecting ridges that sloped easily east and south.

Topographically, the set of ridges formed perfect railroad country. The two railroads meeting the W&A's southern terminus followed the ridges that came in from the south and east and were completed by 1846, forming a "steel triangle" that characterized the heart of Atlanta until the 1920s. A fourth line, the Atlanta and West Point Railroad, connected the Atlanta junction with middle Alabama and was begun in 1845, joining the other three lines on track that came into the triangular junction from the southwest.

In 1850 the Western and Atlantic completed its through-service to Chattanooga. In 1857 Chattanooga was connected by rail to Memphis, and the original Georgia transportation dream was realized. By 1860 Georgia had more than 1,000 miles of railroad, most of it connected to the railroad "hub" at a place founded as Terminus in 1837, renamed Marthasville in 1843, and incorporated as the City of Atlanta in 1847, 10 years after its founding.

The importance of the railroads is reflected in Atlanta's early sequence of names: first Terminus, meaning the end of the rail line; then Marthasville, after the youngest daughter of Gov. Wilson Lumpkin, the Georgia politician who had pushed hardest to move the Indians out of the region and the railroads into it. Finally, the name Atlanta stemmed from the "Atlanta" Station on the Western and Atlantic Railroad, presumed to be the feminine version of Atlantic by the railroad's chief engineer, Richard Peters, who first adopted the term.

The Atlanta population in 1850 was a whopping 2,500, large enough to be enumerated as a city by the United States Bureau of the Census. Atlanta's population represented approximately 20 percent of the population of DeKalb County, which numbered 12,000 people. At that time, the county seat for DeKalb County, Decatur, had a population of about 600 people, Stone Mountain, 300. To the south, McDonough, the county seat for Henry County, numbered 500, and Campbellton, center of Campbell County, only 175. By comparison, the population of Savannah — the largest city in Georgia — was well over 10,000. (The 1850 population of New York City — the largest city in the country — was more than 700,000.)

Much of this population increase had to do with the introduction of the railroads, for the impact of the railroads on the Atlanta region was considerable. First, it provided easy long-distance travel for residents to and from the old, colonial Georgia cities (Augusta, Macon, Columbus), to the coastal ports (Charleston, Savannah, Brunswick) and to the interior markets in Tennessee and beyond. Second, the rails connected Atlanta to further destinations — Chattanooga, Nashville and Memphis, and from there to the upper Mississippi Valley that runs north into Minnesota and Illinois; to Loudon and Knoxville, Tennessee, Lynchburg, Virginia, and from there to lines running north and east to New York, Boston and Philadelphia. Atlanta was also connected to Montgomery, Alabama, and from there by water to Mobile, New Orleans, Louisiana, and the Lower Mississippi. Atlanta was connected to southwestern Georgia through Columbus, to the seaports along the Atlantic Ocean through Macon and Savannah, and to Southeastern states through Columbia, South Carolina and Charleston.

Third, the railroad allowed an influx of new commerce, new industry and new travelers. There

Martha Lumpkin Compton (1827-1917), daughter of Gov. Wilson Lumpkin, inspired Atlanta's first official name, Marthasville, and, as Martha "Atalanta" Lumpkin, claimed its final name.
The Atlanta Historical Society, Inc.

were no prominent places east, south, north or west, that could not now reach Atlanta easily. And travelers from abroad, taking the "southern tour" of the United States, were as likely now to pass through Atlanta as any other destination point in the southeast, the railroad connections were so easy. Equally true then as now, they were likely to change their connections in Atlanta, then move on to other locales in search of the most telling locations for observations on slavery, Southern cotton culture and hospitality.

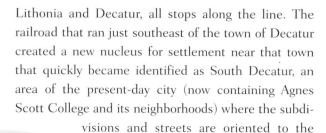

An extremely rare pre-Civil War photograph of the railroad depot at Stone Mountain
DeKalb Historical Society

Fourth, the railroads, brought into being to serve agriculture and forestry in the state, also stimulated local communication, retailing and entertainment. The railroads increased the economic growth of the state phenomenally; in the closing years of the 1850s, the wealth of the state increased from just under $500 million to nearly $700 million. In the process, the railroads reshaped the geographic relationships among the towns of the Atlanta region, moving the course of communication and commerce from the old wagon roads to the railroads, reinforcing some old connections, fostering the development of new towns along the tracks and leaving some localities altogether behind.

Some old connections between county seats were reoriented because of new ties with the railroad. For instance, the stops on the Georgia Railroad running from Augusta reinforced traffic and commerce between Social Circle, Covington, Stone Mountain,

Lithonia and Decatur, all stops along the line. The railroad that ran just southeast of the town of Decatur created a new nucleus for settlement near that town that quickly became identified as South Decatur, an area of the present-day city (now containing Agnes Scott College and its neighborhoods) where the subdivisions and streets are oriented to the railroad, a developmental pattern that was distinct from the rest of the town. The link between Decatur and McDonough was weakened by the railroad since the Georgia Railroad bypassed McDonough on the east, and the Monroe Railroad (later the Macon & Western) bypassed McDonough on the west. The towns of Griffin, Hampton and Jonesboro were founded on the Monroe line and flourished while the town of McDonough, still important as a county seat, experienced a period of commercial decline because of the absence of railroad connections.

Finally, the railroads provided new ways to structure time and public assembly in the upper Piedmont, as "market day" began to replace "court day" as the largest gathering in any of the local towns. Towns ran on "train" time, rather than on the schedules of the stagecoach and wagon lines. Stagecoaches now met the trains; stagecoach arrivals, often the "event" of the day before the railroads came, were big events only in the smallest towns, not located on the tracks, that the coaches continued to serve. A stage could meet passengers from the railroad in Stone Mountain and take them as far as Gainesville, not yet served by the railroad; or bring them in from Gainesville to the mountain — that "wonder of nature" that was the state's most famous landmark.

On the north side of Atlanta, Roswell threatened to languish despite its industries, while Marietta — sitting astride the Western and Atlantic Railroad — thrived until a spur connected Roswell with the railroads that ran to its south. A railroad bridge — the first across the Chattahoochee — connected all of

The oldest extant photograph of Atlanta shows the volunteer fire department lined up along the railroad tracks at their intersection with Central Avenue, c. 1857.
The Atlanta Historical Society, Inc.

Cobb County to Fulton County in 1856. Marietta could brag that it was connected via the Western and Atlantic Railroad to Milledgeville, Dalton, Augusta, Atlanta, Cumming and Canton. By the same token, residents in the middle and lower portions of Georgia had easier access via the W&A to the mountainous areas of the state and the many springs, creeks and waterfalls there. An engineer of the W&A reported in 1849: "The watering places along our line of road, and convenient to the same, are becoming very popular, and they may be expected to attract large crowds every summer, and thus contribute to swell the income of the road."

Equally important to the region as the increased wealth in established communities were the new towns, many of them planned by the railroad, that sprang up along the tracks. Acworth, Lithonia, Clarkston, Cumming and East Point (the eastern terminus for the Atlanta and West Point Railroad), for example, were all established in conjunction with the railroad, which accounts for their recognizable, linear layout. The main streets of these towns, if they did not parallel the railroad tracks, ran exactly perpendicular to them; usually the commercial buildings fronted on the tracks. Streets faced the railroads as did some houses, a phenomenon still visible in places like Clarkston and Acworth. Sometimes there was no street between the houses and the railroad, and the houses fronted directly onto the tracks. It would be hard to find such a house anymore in the Atlanta metro area, but such old houses can still be seen in some more rural parts of the state.

Sometimes there were no houses to speak of, only railroad service equipment, such as at East Point, which consisted of a large water tank, a pump and a pile of wood until the Civil War, after which the town began to take shape. In 1850 Acworth, a "village" along the W&A, had a population of 50 people. Jonesboro, settled in 1844 along the Macon & Western Railroad, attained a population of several hundred in just six short years; in 1850 it was already half the size of Lawrenceville, county seat for Gwinnett County and as yet a town without railroad connections.

The mill at Stone Mountain Park, though not in its original location, gives an authentic feeling of the old grist milling operations. Operative mills are extremely rare in all of North Georgia. *Photo by Riley Hayes*

Because of its multiple railroad connections, Atlanta became the primary market for the nearby counties, described by one commentator in 1850 as a place of "bustle and business." For awhile, the population of Atlanta had consisted largely of workers for the railroad, but by 1850 there was evidence of more permanent civilization — churches and families, a handful of cultural societies, two banks, two newspapers, several schools and a working municipal government. Exclusive of saloons, Atlanta had more than 50 stores; its several large hotels were each capable of rooming as many people as inhabited some of the outlying towns.

Large quantities of goods and produce passed through Atlanta daily, the annual amount of business having surpassed $500,000, a fortune in an age when a few dollars constituted a week's wages. Atlanta promoted wagon trade, encouraging nearby farmers and planters to bring their cotton, other cash crops and produce to Atlanta, and providing amenities for their stay — wagon yards, livery stables, saddleries, blacksmiths, grog shops, saloons and flop houses — and wholesale businesses proliferated on the lots near the tracks. More than 35,000 bales of cotton were bought and sold annually on Atlanta premises in the early 1850s, and more than $400,000 worth of dry goods sold. Goods from as far away as St. Louis came to Atlanta via rail, and as far away as England via ship to Savannah and rail from there. Atlanta boasted Northern manufactured goods, delicacies from New Orleans, and fine machinery from Cincinnati and Chicago.

The dozens of hardware stores, dry-goods shops, clothing, furniture, shoes and boots, produce, tobacco and tinware establishments lined the edges of Whitehall, Alabama, Decatur and Peachtree streets in the heart of Atlanta with the densest developments

The ancient Rex Mill that gave the town Rex its name could grind 60 bushels of grain a day. The mill remained active for more than a century until the late 1940s. *Photo by Riley Hayes*

lying on either side of the "Augusta" railroad, the Central of Georgia. Atlanta was well on its way to becoming "the" place to shop, even though the other county seats offered ample goods for the willing shopper. Marietta, Decatur, McDonough and Lawrenceville had their coterie of grocers, harness makers, carriage shops, dry-goods locales, fancy dressmakers, boot-makers, tobacconists and milliners.

Atlanta had superseded its neighboring towns more quickly than even the most positive predictions for its future. In fact not all the predictions were positive: it was destined to be "good for a tavern, a blacksmith shop, a grocery store, and nothing else," according to one of its early rail engineers, who must have had its slower growing neighbors in mind.

Yet Atlanta was a magnet, drawing to itself markets and industries. Even so, Georgia, especially in comparison with the Northeastern United States, developed manufacturing very slowly. The Atlanta region was not exceptional in this respect prior to the Civil War. At that time its local industries served only local markets; most of the industries consisted of mills or other agricultural processing plants of small size and scale. Sawmills, water-fed gristmills, planing mills, tanneries, distilleries and blacksmith shops were common enterprises throughout the region, but there were also brickworks, foundries, machine shops and pottery works.

Cobb County contained the typical assortment of local industries that were owner-operated service facilities, not large employers. Cobb County had 21 gristmills sprinkled throughout the county, along with 21 sawmills, a large tannery just outside Marietta, and an extensive distillery seven miles east of the county seat that pumped out 120 gallons of whisky a day. Typical of its industrial enclaves was Ruff's Mill in the Concord Covered Bridge district of Cobb County that comprised a miller's house, the gristmill, and a bridge to accommodate traffic to and from the complex. The mill and house were already in existence on the banks of the Nickajack Creek when Martin Ruff bought them in 1856, and his widow continued to run the mill after the Civil War, producing corn meal, flour and feed.

In most places in the region, capital was insufficient to create larger, more profit-driven factories, but a handful did exist. Cobb County, for example, built two paper mills along Sope's Creek in the 1850s that, along with other manufacturers in the county, kept 260 men and women employed. Cotton processing, usually funded through the investments of Northern capitalists, was the key to larger establishments. Between 1850 and 1860 textile mills developed in Georgia, most of them in the cities along the fall line where the rivers were navigable to the sea and where water power was the greatest because of the sudden elevations that occur at the fall line.

With cheap water-borne transportation and accessible waterpower, leading manufacturers located cotton mills in Columbus, Augusta and Macon with a secondary cluster of mills in Clarke County. The Atlanta region was not left out of this development even though it did not have the river transportation of the cities along the fall line. It had other transportation and enough waterpower. Two locations, one in Roswell (then part of Cobb County) and one in Campbell County at the town of Manchester on Sweetwater Creek, saw the creation of sizeable cotton processing plants. The Sweetwater factory was a large-scale plant capitalized at $50,000, with 6,000 spindles and 90 looms. In addition to the Sweetwater cotton mill, Campbell County also had 11 sawmills, 14 gristmills, two flourmills and four distilleries within its boundaries. A smaller mill was built in Carroll County — Bowen's factory near Carrollton — that had only 500 spindles. Carroll also had two stamp mills for gold ore plus an assortment of grist, saw and lumber mills, and two distilleries.

Roswell had by far the most well-developed cotton industries of all the towns of the Atlanta region before the Civil War. Roswell, named for its founder Roswell King, was established at the same time Atlanta was being staked out. King, a low-country planter, spied the area while on a trip to the U.S. Mint at Dahlonega for the Bank of Darien and decided its watercourses were sufficient to support industry. He, John Dunwody, James Bulloch and a handful of others established a summer colony that became a permanent settlement in the late 1830s.

"The Bricks" housed workers for the Roswell Mills. Still inhabited today, they are the region's oldest "apartment houses." *The Georgia Department of Archives and History*

The town of Roswell was incorporated in 1840, and the Roswell factory located on Vickery Creek was capitalized at $80,000 as a primary unit of the town. The main plant worked 3,500 spindles and 40 looms and occupied 150 operatives (mostly white) who worked 11-hour days. The mills produced cotton shirting, osnaburg and yarn. An unusual feature of the Roswell mill was the worker housing nearby, an element in many later mills but uncommon in the Atlanta region before the Civil War. Both "the Bricks" (the worker apartments) and the mill building still stand in Roswell.

Within the confines of the city of Atlanta, cotton processing was less important than other industries. Following closely on the heels of the early mills that processed grain and lumber, Atlanta had two planing mills, sash and blind factories, four tanneries and several shoe manufacturers. But then came the shops and metal-working factories that serviced the growing needs of the railroads in and around Atlanta. They were economically more significant and physically more sizeable than any of the other mills or small manufacturers in the local region.

Fully half of Atlanta's laborers were employed in some kind of railroad-related work — in the switching yards, railroad shops and yards, machine shops, foundries and smiths. In the 1850s there were four large machine shops in Atlanta, two owned by the railroads and two in private hands, that manufactured castings and "every variety of machinery on short notice." Of the early Atlanta metal processing and

Built just prior to the Civil War by a local railroad agent, the Warren House in Jonesboro (a private residence) was later used by both armies during the war.
Photo by Riley Hayes

manufacturing enterprises, the Atlanta Rolling Mill that specialized in re-pressing old railroad tracks (1,200 feet of them a day!) was the largest. It was also the largest in Georgia, and in the entire Southeast it was second in size only to the Tredegar Iron Works in Richmond, Virginia.

As Atlanta was expanding in size and increasing rapidly in population, the state responded to a recommendation made in the legislature to form a new county with Atlanta as its seat. Atlanta had completely overshadowed Decatur, which housed the DeKalb County government, and promoters of the city of Atlanta obviously felt that the newer, bigger city deserved higher standing, and even a county of its own. Two of the proponents of the bill to establish the new county were Dr. N.L. Angier and Col. John Collier, both DeKalb Countians with substantial interests in Atlanta. On December 20, 1853, the governor signed the act to

create Fulton County along with several others in the state — Catoosa, Pickens, Worth, Dougherty and Hart. Fulton County was created out of land from DeKalb County, namely the 14th and 17th districts, originally of Henry, then Fayette, then DeKalb County. The new county was named, not as many suspect for Robert Fulton, the inventor of the steamboat, but for Hamilton Fulton, the surveyor on the Western and Atlantic Railroad that brought Atlanta into being.

A few years later, in 1858, Clayton County was created from parts of Henry and Fayette, named for Judge Augustine Smith Clayton. Jonesboro, having also grown with the railroads, was made its county seat. At this time, county government was essential but limited. Each county had the right to tax and was responsible for its own elections, upkeep on county roads, administration of justice through inferior court proceedings, care for the poor and indigent, organization of local militia, and the provision of some education. Local cities and incorporated towns within the counties had similar responsibilities, including sanitation, policing, fire protection (still run on a voluntary basis), street upkeep, and care of the poor.

Having made themselves a county, the ambitious citizens of Atlanta now proposed to make themselves a capital. In 1853, even before Fulton County was established, Atlantans met to discuss the relocation of the state capital from Milledgeville. The move was supported by many in the legislature, provided a suitable new location could be found. Milledgeville was small and relatively inaccessible by rail. Macon and Atlanta were the two contenders to relocate the capital from Milledgeville, but there was little solid agreement as to where the new capital should go. Atlanta was pushing its rail connections; Macon, its location in the middle of the state. Neither city, for the time being, got anywhere in its bid.

Atlanta shared its growth with the other towns along the railroad, which also grew from their greater access to rail transportation. Marietta, for example, grew substantially in the 1850s. The town, though settled two decades earlier, was incorporated in 1852 with circular

The Concord Covered Bridge Historic District in Cobb County is the last surviving pre-Civil War mill complex in the Atlanta region. The bridge itself is one of only a handful left in the state.
Photo by Darlene Roth

city limits three-quarters of a mile in radius, a boundary that lasted only two years before it was expanded. Part county seat, part railroad center, part resort town and part gateway to the mountains, Marietta offered much to both residents and summer tourists. Marietta was an example to the rest of Cobb County that for the entire county to prosper, more railroads were needed to connect with the W&A.

Hopes to exploit mines in counties to the north of Cobb expanded the desires for railroads on other grounds, and thus, plans for the Marietta, Canton, and Ellijay Railroad were born. Other plans called for roads to run north to Dahlonega and west to the Alabama line. These roads were not constructed before the Civil War, and only the Marietta to Ellijay route survived to service the northeast Georgia quadrant.

Even this early, Atlanta was turning some of its closest neighboring towns into suburbs; sometimes it drained population from the nearby communities, for from the very beginning and for a long time, it was not unusual for businessmen to maintain offices in Atlanta and live elsewhere. They might speculate in Atlanta real estate, but they resided on farms or in small-town mansions in nearby counties.

This was particularly true of residents in Decatur, the "handsome, flourishing" town just six miles east of Atlanta, where citizens like Ammi Williams and Reuben Cone (after whom Williams and Cone streets in Atlanta were named) realized profit from their investments in Atlanta while they enjoyed the beautiful, smoke-free residential tranquility of Decatur. Perhaps the most vivid example of this is Samuel Mitchell, a resident of Pike County who was responsible for laying the first subdivision in downtown Atlanta. Mitchell owned property in Atlanta and donated part of it to the state to have the railroad depot constructed on its premises. Then he had the remainder of his land lot (Land Lot 77) surveyed for town lots and sold them at a tremendous profit. He, like many others since, did not have to live in Atlanta to profit from its bounty.

Many outlying metro-Atlanta towns, other than the county seats, had their origins in this period just before the Civil War. Not all were connected to the

Cotton was the primary cash crop for local farmers before the Civil War, but its post-war cultivation far exceeded pre-War production. Black slaves picked cotton on the plantations; everyone — black and white — picked cotton on the farms. *The Atlanta Historical Society, Inc.*

railroad. Some were established as post offices in the still settling sections of the counties. In DeKalb County, for example, there were thriving communities at Cross Keys (near Chamblee), Stone Mountain, Standing Peachtree, Rock Chapel (later Lithonia) and Panthersville District. The settlement at Roswell has already been described. Sandy Springs owes the bulk of its existence to the Spruill Family whose patriarch, Wilson Spruill, paid $80 for Land Lot 89 in then-DeKalb County in 1842. But the geographic center, focused in Land Lot 88, bounded by present-day Roswell, Abernathy, Mount Vernon and Brandon Mill roads, had been "purchased" a few years earlier by Lewis Wright from the original lottery winner, for a "jenny, a rifle, and a pair of boots." Wright family members lived on part of that land for generations.

Although Atlanta was attractive to residents looking for an alternative to farming as a way of life, most people in the region — indeed, most people in Georgia — farmed. They did not live in Atlanta or in any other town; they lived on farms or plantations, in small rural enclaves with colorful names like Kelleytown, Dutchtown, Locust Grove and White House (as in Henry County), and in crossroads communities in the midst of wooded settings that had no names at all. They made their living off the land where they lived in

A typical plain plantation style house from the region, the Tullie Smith house was moved out of the way of highway construction from its original location near North Druid Hills and I-85 to the grounds of the Atlanta History Center in 1965.
The Atlanta Historical Society, Inc.

self-sufficiency, raising enough crops for their own subsistence and prospering off what additional cash crops they could raise and get to market.

Farmers in the Atlanta region fit the state profile; for more than two-thirds of them, the farm rather than the plantation was their unit of occupation. By far the largest proportion of farms contained fewer than 500 acres; next in size contained between 500 and 1,000 acres, where another large group of landholders fell. Last were the plantations, which constituted the minority of land holdings in the state and in the Piedmont region where Atlanta was located.

The difference between a plantation and a farm was usually understood to be a difference in slave holding, not only a difference in the size of the farm. Those with 20 or more slaves were considered planters; those with fewer than 20, farmers. The poorest self-sufficient yeoman farmers, fully three-fifths of the farmers in the state, owned no slaves. Another segment of the white population worked as cultivators of a few hardscrabble acres, most of them in the northern sections of the state in the mountains. Many worked on farms but owned no property. The Atlanta region contained overwhelmingly large numbers of yeoman farmers, homesteaders and small-plantation owners. Most farmers produced enough food for themselves, their families and slaves. What was left over was sold. The primary cash crop was often cotton, but cash exchanges for crops were limited only by the industry of the farmers and included wool, tobacco, wheat, even milk and butter.

What was different in the Atlanta region from the rest of Georgia was the extent to which local politics were influenced by people who held occupations other than farming. Local economics and culture were not dominated by the planters the way they were in the areas around Savannah, Albany, Columbus and Macon, a difference between Atlanta and the rest of Georgia that set a course of distinctiveness that to this day has never disappeared.

Georgia was one of the leading cotton producers in the world before the Civil War, and cotton was grown throughout the state, especially in the middle region. But cotton cultivation in the mountains was slow to develop, so less was grown in the counties on the north side than in the counties on the south side of Atlanta. The best cotton lands lay along the bottomlands of the Chattahoochee and South rivers, and Utoy, Nancy and Peachtree creeks, where the land would bear 1,000 to 1,500 pounds of cotton per acre.

Small grains, sweet potatoes, tobacco, corn, wool and dairy products were also treated as cash crops, but in local market trading only. Probably more land was devoted to corn than any other single crop in this section of the state; next came crops to support self-sufficiency, and then, in what land was left, cotton or other cash crops. Crop statistics at the time reveal that cotton, corn, wheat, rye and oats were the most plentiful crops.

In Campbell County, cotton averaged a low 600 pounds per acre for an annual yield of 3,000 bags of cotton, alongside 18 bushels of corn, and 10 of wheat. Carroll County, where cotton culture had "but recently commenced," yielded 700 pounds per acre of cotton and plenty of fruits, apples, pears, plums, corn, wheat, oats, rye and barley. Land in DeKalb County along the creeks sold for $3-10 per acre for poor-quality soil and $20-25 per acre for top-quality soil. There, annual yields amounted to more than 1,200 pounds of cotton per acre, though the yields from the hilltop fields were far lower.

The amount to which Atlanta-region farming communities depended on slavery varied from county to county, depending on the size and productivity of the farms. If a line were drawn between the upper and lower Piedmont, that line would pass through the middle of Atlanta with the territory on the north side of the city falling into the upper Piedmont and the counties on the south into the lower Piedmont. The Piedmont was cotton country, and though a single physiographic region of the state, the upper and lower portions of the Piedmont did not share cotton prosperity in exactly the same proportions. Cotton came first to the lower Piedmont, where it flourished prior to the Civil War; cotton made its way only slowly to the hillier upper Piedmont.

The counties to the south, while not comparable to the old slave-holding areas along the Georgia coast, tended to have a higher rate of slave holding than the counties to the north. The percentages of enslaved people as a portion of the population ranged between 15 and 20 percent on the north side of Atlanta, between 25 and 30 percent on the south side. The difference was the land: to the south, rolling hills and open valleys offered much acreage to farm and large expanses of arable soil; to the north, deep ravines and tall hills kept cash crop farming of any considerable size to a minimum.

In the counties that constituted the old Cherokee Georgia, high-quality land was rare. In Cobb County, for example, less than 2,500 acres of its more than 400,000 acres were considered first-quality farmland. Little more than 100,000 of its acres were considered good enough quality to farm at all. The bottomlands along the Chattahoochee were highly prized and ultimately produced the most cotton. Cobb was not as dependent on cotton growing as other counties because there were no gins in the county until after the Civil War, but it still engaged in slaveholding. In 1850, out of a population of 13,842 people, 2,272 were slaves. This represents a little more than one slave per family in the county, not a high ration when compared to the rice- and cotton-growing counties in the lower Piedmont and the coast. The largest slave owner in Cobb County, Dr. Sydney Smith, owned 60 slaves; second to Smith was John Dunwody, who owned 26. There were only a half-dozen families in the county who owned more than 20 slaves. In DeKalb County there were 14,398 people in 1850, 2,994 of whom were enslaved. In Henry County to the south of Atlanta, 726 families owned a total of 4,969 slaves, among whom the owner of the largest number of slaves had 65.

Where there were large farms and plantations, there were slaves; where there were small farms and homesteads, there were fewer slaves; and in most instances none at all on the smallest farms. Despite the fact that the foreign slave trade had been outlawed before 1800, domestic trade in slaves was reintroduced in 1824, a practice Georgia participated in until the eve of the Civil War. Slaves continued to be imported illegally from Africa until the War as well, a fact not openly admitted in most Georgia history books. The city of Atlanta had two slave markets, both located in the heart of town next to the railroad tracks where the commerce in other sales items took place. There is no official record extant identifying the place of origin for the slaves who were sold in Atlanta.

The complexities of the slave economy were readily visible in Atlanta where the presence of railroad-related

The pre-Civil War Tullie Smith Farmhouse as it looks today on the grounds of the Atlanta History Center, restored with outbuildings to re-create a mid-19th century regional farm
Photo by Riley Hayes

businesses and industries pressed the populace for a larger class of skilled, nonagricultural workers than was readily available. The result was that nearby slave owners hired out their slaves for many local jobs. There were few immigrant workers to draw from, and many of the native-born white workers were available but often not skilled. Gangs of unskilled workers followed the railroads, the earliest of which contained a great many foreigners — Irish and Germans, some Chinese — who worked alongside slaves who were hired out to the railroads for some of the worst, backbreaking tasks. In most instances the slave owners received the wages "earned" by their slaves; and the low prices for which the slaves could be employed kept the wages of the other workers severely depressed.

As a retail center for all kinds of goods and wares, Atlanta was also a center for slave sales in this part of the state. This particular auction house was located on Whitehall Street (now Peachtree St. SW). *The Atlanta Historical Society, Inc.*

The problem did not disappear when the construction of the railroads was complete in the mid-1850s. Many of the foreign workers followed the railroad out of the state, leaving the maintenance of the railroads to low-skilled whites and enslaved blacks. Not many of the African-Americans in the Atlanta region were free, although the census for the city of Atlanta and each of the counties lists a handful of "free persons of color" who could act in any capacity they could muster. The majority of these free persons of color were women who hired themselves out as domestic labor, were restricted by the slave codes, required to have guardians, and who lived "free" but hardly at liberty.

Each of the local municipalities and county governments set its own restrictions upon the activities of the African-Americans, especially those who were hired out. Slaves who were visiting relatives, on business for their masters, or "working out" had to present a written permit (which presumably they themselves could not read) allowing them to pass. Local volunteer patrolmen checked passes and returned "stray" slaves to their masters. Other restrictions held, increasingly so in the 1850s. Slaves could not buy or sell liquor except with the consent of their owners, a law that extended to free persons of color, who had to have the permission of their guardian to traffic in spirits. Shop owners could not sell books, papers, pamphlets, writing paper, ink or stationery to slaves without the consent of their owners, nor could slaves receive these items as gifts without their owner's consent. In Marietta it was unlawful for a shopkeeper to sell goods to an African-American while the doors of his shop were closed. Blacks in Atlanta had to observe a curfew, and slaves could not walk with a cane or smoke in public.

Because of hiring practices and the many restrictions, African-Americans began to be associated with certain jobs and occupations such as driving wagons, domestic service and bricklaying. Despite the fact that some African-Americans in Georgia before the Civil War were among the most skilled laborers in the state, the black population as a whole was restricted in its economic opportunities, even after slavery was abolished by the war.

Fair competition for work between two people of different color for the same job simply did not exist. There were certain jobs that a "respectable white person" would not hold, no matter what. While this distinction did not apply to foreigners, few foreigners wanted to come where they could not compete effectively against the presence of such a cost-free laboring class. The result is that in Atlanta, a city with a strong industrial base where foreigners could have been expected to immigrate, the foreign population did not grow.

There were some foreign-born population groups — Irish and German, especially — but they were not numerous before, during or even after the Civil War. Small foreign-born populations tended to distinguish pre-Civil War Southern cities from all Northern cities, and Atlanta, even as one of the South's emergent cities, was no exception to this characteristic. A small group of German Jews settled in Atlanta, the first ones arriving in the 1840s, offering some innovation among the local retailers. And in the surrounding areas, there were sprinklings of foreign-born — again Irish and occasionally German-speaking families — among the farmers of the local Atlanta counties. The Lemons, Conkles, Ahls, Exums and Babbs of Dutchtown in Henry County constituted perhaps the only foreign "colony" in the Atlanta region, whose settlement near the Jonesboro Road represented the only non-English-speaking community known to exist in the region before the Civil War. Nonetheless, "foreigners" never constituted anything but 1 to 3 percent of the entire population in even the most densely populated places.

Cotton growing and trading, agriculture, manufacturing and commercial expansions all sustained the growing populace, a population that, except for its obvious racial differences, was fairly homogeneous in outlook, background, daily experience and education. Before the Civil War it was more the norm than the exception for Georgians to have little schooling. Despite numerous efforts on the part of the state government to establish free school programs in the counties that could support themselves, there were no public school systems, per se, anywhere in the state.

Schools in the Atlanta region were typical of what existed throughout Georgia; there were county academies, private schools, female seminaries and an occasional school for the poor. Most of the schools offered elementary education — the basics of reading, writing and "figuring" — and little else. They had a short school year because they could not be open during planting and harvesting seasons. The county academies were set up in the county seats; thus, Cobb Academy in Marietta served 149 students when it opened its first year in 1836. The Henry County Academy at McDonough, which had been established in 1827, educated female and male "scholars" of assorted ages from 6 to 21 years. By 1850 Cobb County had an increasing number of schools, both public and private — a select school for girls, a Female High School, a "tech" school for boys and the Georgia Military Institute in Marietta. Education was important in Cobb, where an estimated 500 of the 11,500 white citizens were illiterate, a fairly low percentage in the state. Cobb was representative of conditions in locales where there was some population density and industry.

Farmers were often reluctant to provide the private funds necessary to match state funding, so the older county academies largely disappeared before the war,

A view of the oldest and newest in Atlanta shows Oakland Cemetery against Atlanta's skyline. Oakland Cemetery contains sections for all Atlanta's pioneer citizens, Jew and Christian, black and white, rich and poor. *Photo by Riley Hayes*

A view from inside the tabernacle at Shingleroof Campground near McDonough, looking toward the family cabins — worshipers have gathered here every August for more than a century.
Photo by Riley Hayes

except in the most populous areas. Church-related schools were also common, such as Mt. Carmel Academy and Pleasant Grove Academy in Henry County. The only college was 60 miles away at Athens in Clarke County where the University of Georgia, one of the oldest universities in America, took root. The Methodists established Oxford College (now Emory at Oxford) in 1836 in Newton County, today the oldest school of any collegiate standing in the Atlanta region.

Sometimes the only education one received came at home. The family was the center of social and religious life, and families joined churches together and participated as groups in the large popular activities that the local counties and towns offered — agricultural fairs, political rallies, court and market days, militia musters, races and camp meetings.

The Southern Central Agricultural Society met in Stone Mountain in 1846 to sponsor the first state agricultural fair, the exhibits for which were comprised solely of "a jack and ginnet [sic] with their groom" (a pair of mated donkeys and their caretaker). The 1849 agricultural fair in Henry County boasted that "the presence of the ladies" added much "interest" to the fair, without whom the fair would have been little more than a stock show. The newspaper reported the names of the women who won the competitions in needlework, quilting, wax work and cloth-making, the only time in their lives that the women's names would appear publicly other than birth, death and marriage. By 1850 county fairs were common.

In summertime, religious revivals and camp meetings occupied the Protestant populations, especially the Methodists, who created a string of

Methodist campgrounds throughout the Southeast. Shingleroof near McDonough, founded in 1831, is perhaps the oldest continuously running campground in the Atlanta region. It got its name from its finished roof, one that set it apart from the brush arbors at Marietta and Sandy Spring. Then as now, camp meetings were held in August and lasted one week, a week when farmers would lay their crops by and whole families would "camp" in the wooden "tents" at the campground or in more primitive conditions. Each campground had to have ample water facilities, so each was located near a spring or clear creek. Some campgrounds, like Marietta, contained their own school buildings. The Methodists maintained campgrounds at Smyrna, Sandy Springs and Marietta. Most churches held camp meetings even if they did not have full-blown campgrounds complete with tabernacle, tents, eating commons, water supplies, wagon yards and other amenities.

The decade of the 1850s appeared to be a prosperous, promising one for the Atlanta region. Yet there were more than a few problems; there were not enough roads, and the ones that existed were usually in poor condition. Most routed through the countryside unpaved, narrow, muddy, rutted, rocky and dangerous. A "paved" road was one laid with gravel or wood planking. There were no bridges across the Chattahoochee, the largest river in the region, and few enough ferries. There were wooden bridges across the smaller rivers and creeks, which easily washed out in high water. While there were professionals in each of the towns — lawyers and medical men — there were no hospitals of any size, and cholera, infectious diarrhea, diphtheria and tuberculosis carried with them rampant fears of epidemics and death. Marietta prided itself on its nearby healing springs; Atlanta, on its high elevation and healthy, pure air. Yet both had occasional outbreaks of disease that haunted the locals. Worse, devastating fires that volunteer fire companies could not contain had already occurred in Decatur and Marietta.

And above it all, political disturbances in the nation over the issues of slavery, tariffs and state's rights became louder, meaner and more intrusive into all layers of society.

Chapter 3

If the region was but delicately held together by transportation systems in 1860, it was soon to be bonded in a shared experience. When war finally came to the interior of Georgia, it came with a vengeance. Atlanta, an important Confederate manufacturing and distribution center, was a primary target of Union offenses. As a result, the municipalities that were tied to Atlanta on the railroads were also vulnerable to attack. Although not everyone shared equally in the devastation of the war, everyone in the region shared its deprivation and tragedies.

The Civil War

At the end of the Civil War in 1865, it might have seemed to an outsider that war had been inevitable and that the local populace had been in easy agreement about seceding from the United States at the outset. Such was not the case, however, in the late months of 1860 between the time Abraham Lincoln (whose name did not even appear on the Georgia ballot) was elected to the U.S. Presidency in November and the time South Carolina seceded from the Union in January 1861.

The local preference for political moderation at the time is reflected in the fact that the great majority of Atlanta voters had not supported extremist candidates from any of the parties in the election. Atlanta already had something of a reputation as a "Yankee" stronghold, but Unionist sentiment was strong in the entire region, stronger than in other regions around the state. Many residents in the region had ties to the North, not just sentiments in favor of the idea of Union. A resident of Clayton County, for example, wrote to his brother in Wisconsin in haunting anticipation: "...I want to hear from you once more before our country is plunged into the horrors of a civil war... Can it be possible that our children are to be brought face to face in hostile armies, or that I may be compelled to draw the sword against my own dear brothers in battle? The Lord forbid that so horrible a thing should be permitted." Political preoccupations influenced everyone.

When the Georgia secession convention met in Milledgeville in January 1861, local area representatives divided their votes. Clayton County sent two representatives to the convention who split down the middle — one for, one against secession. Henry County sent three, two of whom voted against secession. All three Fulton County representatives voted to secede, but both DeKalb members voted against secession. (One of the DeKalb representatives, Dr. Peter Hoyle, then tried to add more weight to the county vote by casting a Unionist ballot

The depot and roundhouse for the Western and Atlantic Railroad in Atlanta was the primary target of Union forces and the primary defense point of the Confederate forces.
The Atlanta Historical Society, Inc.

for a member who had deceased just prior to the proceedings.) Gwinnett County sent three representatives who all voted against secession, but then submitted a resolution of support once the ordinance was passed. Their document enabled many who would have preferred a policy of cooperation with the United States to rally to the future defense of Georgia, in case of a "hostile invasion." The order to become "free, sovereign, and independent" of the United States was finally adopted by a vote of 209 to 89. George Smith of Stone Mountain, along with his 88 fellow Unionists, was forced to sign the ordinance under protest — a pledge that has been all too often characterized by subsequent historians as "consensus" on the issue of secession.

Unionist opinions still occasionally appeared in local newspapers, but with decreasing frequency after secession. In February a special convention in Montgomery, Alabama, created the Confederate States of America, and loyalists began to persecute nonloyalists in the press. Unionist sentiments ceased to have public expression altogether after the Confederates fired on the Union garrison at Fort Sumter on April 13, 1861, by which signal the formerly united states went to war with themselves.

All but a handful of the most diehard Unionists rallied to the defense of Georgia. The call went out from the state of Georgia for militia and volunteers, a call that received ready response from the local counties. Nearly 1,000 men volunteered from Henry County, mustering on the grounds of the Shingle Roof Campground. The Clayton Sharpshooters were the first company in the county to volunteer for service in the Army of Northern Virginia. The Kennesaw Dragoons, first to organize in Cobb County, had been practicing marches in the drilling yard at Kennesaw since the first of the year, and were eager to leave to fight with Gen. Robert E. Lee. The song "Dixie" (ironically, written by a Northerner for a minstrel show) became a rallying cry for the young men to arm and organize themselves as best they could.

Those who enlisted early went to fight the forces of U.S. Army Gen. Ulysses S. Grant on the eastern front; those who enlisted a little later went to fight on the western front and ended up defending their home territory against the forces of U.S. Army Gen. William Tecumseh Sherman. The excitement of the call, the parades and the spirit of patriotism were sobered at once by the losses, which were great, beginning with the Confederate victory at Manassas. That first year there were fatalities among the Roswell Guards and the Cobb Mountaineers; one DeKalb County company lost 28 of its men, and the Gate City Guards from Atlanta, devastated in Virginia, saw their remnants mustered out to other units. The young men in camps on the eastern front wrote home about their miserable conditions, the lack of equipment and supplies, the rampant diseases, the mud, the vermin, the loneliness and the fatigue. They cried for medical supplies, shoes, blankets and clothes. The Confederate army, though still winning encounters (or at least not losing them), could not keep up with the needs or the losses among its soldiers.

Despite the losses, the Atlanta region fared well enough during the early days of the war when it was far behind the lines of battle. Its farmlands lay in the interior, far away from the battlefields. Opportunities abounded in war-related industries, and local populations, especially among the railroad towns, swelled. The city of Atlanta developed from an overgrown small town of fewer than 10,000 people to a crowded, noisy city of more than 20,000 in the four years of the war, and all the counties in the region saw some population increase.

The natives and the newcomers began to experience privation and inflation in 1861 because blockades along the Atlantic seaports at Charleston and Savannah kept imported goods from reaching the interior. Yet, food was still plentiful, and blockade runners kept some supplies coming in, even if scarce, such as English furniture, guns and spirits. Atlanta continued to sell slaves, some of them illegally imported. Profiteering became a problem almost immediately, and several local governments sent appeals to the state to make it illegal. The state, however, was so dependent upon local industry — and the very profiteers themselves — to provide things never yet manufactured or processed in Georgia that it exercised a weak hand in curtailing the problem and never controlled inflation. Salt was a rarity at $18 a sack; sugar was scarce and expensive; molasses was simply priceless and not available. Butter was on hand for those who had cows, and yarn for those who had sheep.

Changes came in 1862 as war's toll became visible in arenas other than the marketplace. County roads, never very well finished, suffered from lack of maintenance as local resources and personnel were commandeered for

For the first two years of the war, people in this region felt quite safe and removed from action, but beginning in 1862 more serious attention was put toward building defenses. These trenches and picket lines were probably not built until early in 1864. *The Atlanta Historical Society, Inc.*

military use. Travel throughout the region, except on the railroads, became more difficult, time-consuming and dirty. Industries were converted for military use, even gristmills. The supply of ready volunteers exhausted itself in the first year of the war. The Confederacy issued its first conscription act in April 1862 for all men between the ages of 18 and 35, which was followed in July with a second order conscripting all men up to 45 years of age.

Jester's Mill survived the Battle of Jonesboro in 1864 but succumbed to later suburban development. Most regional businesses, mills and factories were commandeered for military production.
The Atlanta Historical Society, Inc.

By the end of 1862 almost all of the able-bodied men in the regional counties were in the military — some volunteered, but most had been drafted. Testimony after the war indicated that vigilantes raided and even murdered those who refused to go, although there were some who managed to avoid the draft or avert its effects. German immigrant Christian Kontz, drafted into service to fortify areas around Atlanta, stayed long enough to serve his term, then left Atlanta for Washington, D.C., where he kept a shoe shop until the end of the war. The Dailey family, whose mill in Henry County manufactured cloth for Confederate uniforms and yarn for Confederate army socks, managed to keep its boys at home, who, once conscripted, were detailed to the mill as managers of a "vital industry." Others sought employment in industries equally vital, for which the Atlanta rolling mill offers an interesting example. The owner, a Unionist who had failed to sell off his business before hostilities began and saw his business drafted into Confederate service, resolved his conflict of loyalties by hiring young Union sympathizers to keep them out of the Confederate army while they manufactured (undoubtedly with slow-downs and

Each year the Atlanta History Center hosts Civil War "encounters" with lectures, demonstrations and re-enactments that exhibit to the public the privations and experiences of the local citizenry and the soldiers of both armies before, during and after the Battles for Atlanta.
The Atlanta Historical Society, Inc.

delays) iron products for the same army. More than one Unionist family kept its boys hidden at home; more than one Confederate sympathizer, young and more afraid of war and the vigilantes than authority, simply headed for the hills to hide out. Others took advantage of the disruptions of war to become renegades and rebels in their own right, often for unspecified and usually unsavory causes. The hills of North Georgia were full of such desperate young men.

So chaotic were the conditions in and around Atlanta, the city itself came under military control in May 1862. The city was already one giant Confederate war machine — a hospital and military supply center, a transportation hub and a manufacturing center for war materiel. Now it was to be a military command post, and the army would subsume all civilian operations into its own purposes. Although geographically under the purview of Gen. Braxton Bragg, the military administration that evolved was actually independent of Bragg. Col. George Washington Lee, former saloon keeper and the commander in charge, exercised autocratic powers that extended into every walk of life, suspending civil liberties and even overtaking enterprises on the edge of the city, as he saw fit. If Lee thought a business or industry was needed by the military, he commandeered it; if he suspected citizens of disloyalty, he had them arrested.

There was much that was suspicious around Atlanta, even in some of the smaller towns. There was still a circle of Union sympathizers who were watched constantly, some of whom were business and industry leaders such as William Markham, owner of the Markham block on Peachtree Street near the railroad

station. Under martial law, visitors to the area had to carry passes approved by the military. These measures did little to keep the undesirables out. Riff-raff swarmed in, in the form of prostitutes, con-men, runaway slaves, deserters, draft evaders, refugees, desperados and scallywags of every sort who found their way to the crowds, the chaos and the railroads, creating more suspicious activity and disturbing what little peace was left.

The Kennesaw House still stands in Marietta, witness to Andrews Raid in which Union troops stole a locomotive out of Marietta, rode north toward Chattanooga, were captured and hanged. *Photo by Darlene Roth*

More importantly, the summer of 1862 brought to the region the first masses of sick and wounded Confederate soldiers, who arrived by the thousands — more than 3,000 of them. Their burdens taxed the resources of the region to the limit; all available hospitals in the city of Atlanta and the outlying towns were filled instantly. Homes became hospitals; churches became hospitals; schools were taken over to become hospitals. Newspapers ran the names of soldiers who had died, not only from battle, but also from the local hospitals. Soldier relief societies sprang up in every town and county, becoming commonplace midway through the war. Women, who had never organized themselves for any purpose outside their households, found themselves in groups — in knitting circles, in bands of nursing aids, in brigades of visitors — taking on public roles for the first time in order to care for the sick, the wounded and the displaced.

That summer of 1862 also brought scores of Yankees to the region as hundreds of Federal prisoners (some of whom were also sick and wounded) were shipped in and their presence complicated the arrangements for soldier relief. Scarcities in supplies kept Confederate army attendants from giving them more than scant care and often inadequate food and supplies. Relief for enemy soldiers was effectively no one's business, so no one much noticed when a handful of women, some of them silenced Union sympathizers, took it upon themselves in the company of their

Confederate sisters to offer the Federal prisoners more substantial care. The women did this at some risk and discomfort to themselves, for their efforts, officially, did give aid to the enemy. Yet they were never punished for their ministrations. Undoubtedly, had women been taken more seriously by the officers in charge at the time, these activities might have been more suspect than they were. As it was, even the newspapers commented on their humanitarianism.

Sacrifice among the populace became the order of the day, and some local residents, chiefly widows with small children, were soon in dire circumstances. Hardest hit were families on small farms who had no slaves and therefore no one to work the fields but the women and children. Even elderly people worked the fields. Occasionally farmer-soldiers addressed their family urgencies by deserting their duties and running home to put in a crop or reap a harvest. This departure from the army was not considered a type of desertion until much later in the war. Public funds for needy families were drying up and were, in fact, exhausted in DeKalb and Fulton counties and the city of Atlanta. Epidemics of dysentery, typhus and tuberculosis appeared with the wounded soldiers and the prisoners of war. The threat of small pox, until then unknown in Georgia, led officials from Clayton County to Roswell to order the isolation of all who were exposed, black or white. Citizens, especially ad hoc women's groups, sponsored fund-raisers — theatricals using local talent,

Map of the
Atlanta Campaign

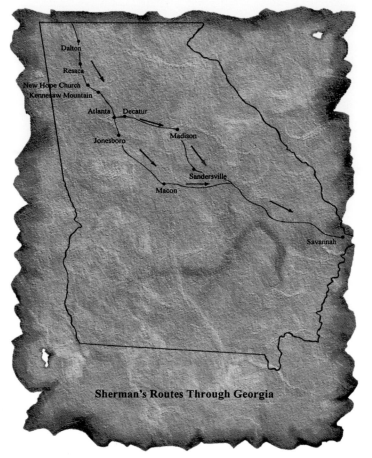

Sherman's Routes Through Georgia

them, urged self-imposed county limits on the distillation and other processing of grain. (In a twist of irony, it was a Union sympathizer and German immigrant, Christian Kontz, who set up a brewery in Atlanta to service these very needs and did so with the blessing of the military commandant.)

Something that should have made a difference in 1863 had no noticeable effect on the region. On June 1, 1863, U.S. President Abraham Lincoln issued the Emancipation Proclamation with the intent that slaves in the seceded states be freed. Georgia, like her sister Confederate states, ignored the proclamation, and the slave markets on Whitehall Street in Atlanta went on advertising sales of mechanics, coachmen, cooks, house servants and field hands as though nothing had transpired. The slaves themselves, who had heard about the edict and understood its meaning, were so constrained by the local black legal codes, military oversight and hostile authorities that lay between them and freedom, they could not easily depart. Black congregations worshiped in the presence of military authorities or police officers. Enslaved African-Americans on the streets after 9 p.m. were subject to arrest. The Underground Railroad was active in this region, giving enslaved people a means for escape, but its activities have not been documented well (if at all) in local histories.

A most shocking event occured in the early fall of 1863 — a battle on Georgia soil at Chickamauga in the northwest portion of the state. Chickamauga was the second-largest battle of the war, the largest in the western front, and it engaged 124,000 men. Bloody and terrible, the battle felled 34,000 men from both armies. Again, hundreds of wounded, sick and imprisoned came to the Atlanta region. This time Federal prisoners passed through the Atlanta region on their way to Andersonville, the shame of the Confederacy. Like its counterpart, Fort Delaware in the United States, Andersonville reflected the reality that the needs of the nation and its army outweighed the ability of the army to supply a POW camp adequately. Cholera, malnutrition and exposure killed two-thirds of the inmates at Andersonville. Such a

dances featuring homemade dresses, and fairs selling home-grown products — to raise money to support the troops in the field and to provide more sources of poor relief at home.

These undertakings constituted the normal passage of time and effort as the tide of Confederate victories continued through 1861, 1862 and 1863. The tide of war, however, turned at Gettysburg in July of 1863, from which time more stringencies emerged at home. To protect the interests of most of its citizens, the state of Georgia restricted cotton growing to three acres per farm. The Confederacy needed food more than it needed cotton, and in 1863, C.S.A. President Jefferson Davis was urging the Confederate citizenry to grow beans, corn, peas and other food crops. (There was little market for the cotton after England refused to support the Confederacy at war.)

The state entitled counties to manufacture alcoholic beverages for the relief of the citizenry in a last-ditch effort to build up its own coffers with a percentage of profits. This measure was soon carried to excess, however, and several local counties, DeKalb among camp was a low national priority in the army of the C.S.A., where standard uniforms for the troops were already a thing of the past and where morale was an increasing problem. "I am tired of this wicked war," wrote one Cobb County soldier to his sister at about this time, breathing the sighs of an entire regiment. For him as for his sister, Chickamauga was but a hint of what was to come.

From the outset of the war the Northern generals had identified Atlanta and its railroads as one of two primary objectives — Richmond, the Confederacy's capital, and Atlanta, its factory. Back in Tennessee after Chickamauga, Gen. Sherman sat on the edge of the factory — a land in the heart of the Confederacy with productive farmlands, bustling towns, and full stables and barns. In winter comfort, with the battlefields quiet, Sherman planned his greatest campaign yet — the Campaign for Atlanta. He intended to break the rail lines any way he could and bring the city to its knees. In pursuit of this objective, Sherman entertained battles all along the route of the Western and Atlantic Railroad from Chattanooga to Jonesboro. The campaign revealed vividly the talents and tactics of the two generals who waged war against each other over the W & A. Sherman flanked the movements of the Confederates in a series of attacks designed to skirt Southern entrenchments. Each time, from Dalton to Big Shanty (Kennesaw), Confederate troops under Gen. Joseph E. Johnston outmaneuvered Sherman's forces, drawing them farther into enemy territory and stretching Federal supply lines, the Southerners hoped, to the breaking point. The Confederates, even though heavily outnumbered and supplied, retrenched each time, saving resources and personnel as much as possible. The campaign — still one studied by contemporary students of war as possibly the first modern siege — was a battle of wits and courage, dangerous ploys and heavy losses of life.

Sherman began in May 1864 at Dalton, with fighting on the 9th of the month

through the 13th. Dalton was an important stop on the Western and Atlantic Railroad and was the headquarters of Gen. Johnston's Confederate forces in the summer of 1864. The Union troops pressed their way as far as Snake Gap Creek, from which Johnston, heavily entrenched but not pressed by the Federals, withdrew to Resaca. Thereafter ensued the battles at Resaca on May 14 and 15, Calhoun on May 16, Adairsville on May 17, and Cassville and Kingston on May 18-19. In the weeks of fighting, Sherman's army suffered heavy casualties, and it had been unable to break the Confederate defenses in any of the encounters.

When Sherman and his forces arrived at New Hope Church on May 25, he brought with him the sounds of battle, heard in the Atlanta region for the first time. This time the Confederate troops repulsed the Federals, but the toll of battle lay heavy on the minds of the local citizens. Those with kin in the army under Johnston heard reports of the slaughter from their sons, brothers, cousins and husbands at the front

Defenses such as this breastwork with cannons north of Atlanta surrounded the city of Atlanta and smaller towns as well.
The Atlanta Historical Society, Inc.

The quiet mountainsides mask the site of what was to be one of the bloodiest battles of the Civil War. Today the Kennesaw National Park protects the battleground where 4,000 fell in one afternoon.
The Atlanta Historical Society, Inc.

a few miles away. The Confederate soldiers reported seeing "hundreds and hundreds" of wounded, dead and dying on the fields of battle, more Yankees than Southerners. One Decatur soldier wrote to his family that though "they had been my enemies, my heart bled at the sickening scene." Locals began fortifying, arming and readying themselves, for war was now so near. All who were capable of bearing arms rallied to the defense of their homes, farms, towns and families.

Next came an even greater threat and an even more massive slaughter, the assault against Big Shanty (Kennesaw Mountain). Sherman attacked in two waves in an engagement that lasted nearly a month. The first wave hit June 8-9, the second between June 10 and July 2. After a number of successful flanking attacks, Sherman mounted a direct frontal attack on the Confederate troops entrenched on Kennesaw Mountain. In one day Sherman lost 3,000 men; however, his general, John Schofield, managed to circumvent Johnston's flank, opening up a wedge to the Chattahoochee River, so Johnston again retreated.

On July 7 Sherman reached the Chattahoochee River, forcing Johnston's troops to take cover in fortifications built by the corps of engineers who were assisted by slaves recruited from local plantations and farms. On July 9 Sherman started crossing the Chattahoochee. The populace in the Atlanta region knew how close Sherman was and so did President Jefferson Davis, who proclaimed July 10, 1864, a day of fasting and prayer. The Confederacy was running out of

bullets and men, spirit and time, so the threatened people of the Atlanta region went to their churches and prayed.

Gen. Johnston's future was as uncertain now as the Confederacy's. The retreat from Kennesaw to the banks of the Chattahoochee was to be Johnston's last; Jefferson Davis had him replaced, putting Gen. John Bell Hood in his position on July 18, 1864. Historians and Civil War buffs will argue to the end of the ages as to the wisdom of Davis' decision. One thing is clear: Knowing his new opponent's recklessness, Sherman had to change his own tactics, becoming even more aggressive in the process.

As Sherman's troops neared Atlanta, the city swelled with refugees from all the towns in northwest Georgia that had lain in the path of battle; their numbers included many from Tennessee. Then, suddenly, the city started to empty out, pouring its citizenry into the ranks of the refugees fleeing into the countryside and to points south. By the time Sherman reached New Hope, many residents in the region on the north side of Atlanta had already joined the ranks of the refugees en route to Macon or to destinations even farther south or more remote.

Confederate forces engorged the region; their military encampments sprang up, scattered everywhere over the landscape. On the outskirts of Atlanta, those locals still in residence could see the fires of the camps at night. Fear and the tense excitement of high drama dominated the emotions of those who waited. Some

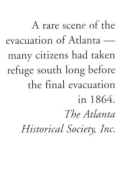

A rare scene of the evacuation of Atlanta — many citizens had taken refuge south long before the final evacuation in 1864.
The Atlanta Historical Society, Inc.

cursed, some prayed for rescue and many more desired release from the pain of war. According to one local diarist, there were three groups of people who looked forward for rescue from the "victors": Unionists, "those who love their Country and their Government with true loyalty of Soul; the poor who are suffering for the commonest comforts of life; and this nation of Negroes who have patiently waited through long years for their deliverance."

Sherman had a three-pronged attack in mind. Maj. Gen. George H. Thomas was to occupy Buckhead and the ridge between Nancy and Peachtree

creeks, holding the line at Peachtree Creek. Maj. Gen. John M. Schofield was to pass through Cross Keys to Peachtree Road, then move onto Decatur, holding the line at Decatur and breaking the railroad there. And Maj. Gen. James B. McPherson was to move toward Stone Mountain and destroy the railroad on the east. Sherman himself occupied the Samuel House home (now the Peachtree Golf Club), the House family having refugeed to Hall County.

The plan was to capture the city in two days; it took six weeks. The siege of Atlanta lasted from July 20 to August 25 and contained within it three major battles, a number of minor conflicts and countless skirmishes throughout the region until Gen. Hood evacuated Confederate troops from the region in early September 1864. None of the three major battles occurred inside the actual city limits of Atlanta. The July 20 Battle of Peachtree Creek, the result of the move toward Buckhead, occurred nearly six miles north of the center of Atlanta. It proved to be an inauspicious beginning for Gen. Hood, whose battle plan was complicated and poorly carried out. The fighting was very close and Confederate casualties were twice as high as Federal losses.

Sherman's Schofield got to Decatur and occupied it on July 19 with hand-to-hand combat occurring in the streets. On July 22 the Confederates took the city back, but it shortly passed back into the hands of the Union. Meanwhile, just west of Decatur the Battle of Atlanta waged, the result of McPherson's move toward Stone Mountain. Heavily contested, the largest and bloodiest battle of the Atlanta siege occurred on July 22 and took place on the hills in East Atlanta about a mile and a half from downtown Atlanta. After eight hours of continuous fighting, during which U.S.A. Gen. McPherson and C.S.A Gen. William Walker were both killed, the battle ended in favor of the Federal troops. There were 7,000 Confederate casualties and 2,000 Union ones.

The land east of Atlanta was full of Yankees. "We are cut off and in the enemy's lines," wrote Thomas Maguire in July 1864 in Rockbridge, where he lived 20 miles to the east of Atlanta. The next night he recorded the onslaught as the Union troops moved west toward Atlanta: "At midnight Yankees came here in force. Roused us up. The house was filled with them. They robbed us of nearly everything they could carry off. They broke open all trunks and drawers and carried away the keys."

On the outskirts of Atlanta, especially on the east side, skirmishing continued throughout the remainder of July and into August. On July 28 the Confederates suffered their third defeat in the campaign for Atlanta at Ezra Church. Then the siege took a new, more deadly form. Sherman had already instilled in his men the idea that they could attack "without demand," if fired upon from "the forts or buildings in Atlanta," in his orders to the troops in July. He also instructed them that "no consideration must be paid to the fact that [the buildings] are occupied by families," an instruction his men interpreted widely as permission to fire upon houses in the region, especially in Atlanta proper. Although the troops had been told to hold to cannon-fire range and await orders if they met no resistance; their actions were less restrained. When Hood's forces had been widely dispersed on the perimeter, Sherman's forces met virtually no resistance coming into Atlanta. Yet, on August 9, 1864, Sherman's troops began shelling the city. With church spires and tall chimneys as their targets, Sherman's guns aimed fire on a city full of civilians.

The Atlanta bombardment lasted until August 25, killed more civilians than soldiers, and wasted the property and lives of more Union sympathizers (the only residents willing to remain in town) than "rebels." A 10-year-old child named Carrie Berry kept a journal of the bombing, often taking refuge in the home of her uncle William Markham, whose house was at one point struck by the shells. When not in a cellar there or at home, she took cover in what was called a "bomb proof," a makeshift shelter dug in the ground and covered with logs and dirt. Some Atlanta bomb proofs were large enough to accommodate sleeping and cooking quarters for an entire family.

Even with the shelling, Atlanta did not succumb. Sherman had tried assaults from the west and north and a siege from the east, so the possibilities of attack from the south became both more urgent and more possible. The fighting had been going on around

As a child, Carrie Berry kept a moving diary of the bombardment and occupation of Atlanta during the Civil War. Her diary is one of the most poignant testimonies of what happened on a day-to-day basis to local citizens. *The Atlanta Historical Society, Inc.*

Atlanta for six weeks with little or no result for the Federal troops. Sherman's plan now was to attack the railroads to the south, the Macon and Western and the Atlanta and West Point. When he cut the railroad at Rough and Ready (Mountain View) and won a decisive victory at Jonesboro between August 31 and September 1, Sherman finally accomplished what he had set out to do.

Jonesboro was in and of itself important as a secondary rail center in proximity to Atlanta, and the fighting was intense. The battle occurred to the west of town, between the edge of Jonesboro and the Flint River, where the Confederates were repulsed, reunited and repulsed again, finally to withdraw to Lovejoy in defeat. The Union troops did not stop at winning the battle on the grounds west of town. Fighting ensued in the streets of Jonesboro, and damage to buildings from shelling and rifle fire was extensive. Ultimately, Jonesboro was burned, the first town in the region to suffer that fate. The commercial center was destroyed along with the courthouse and some residences.

The Battle of Jonesboro was the fourth and last major encounter in the Campaign for Atlanta and as a direct result of it, Atlanta finally fell. Gen. Hood, who had engaged the Yankees at Jonesboro, did not pursue them, but chose instead to turn north and east to try to cut off their supply line from the rear. Hood chased the tail of Sherman's troops all the way to Franklin, Tennessee, an inglorious venture at best when the remains of Georgia were about to be plundered.

When C.S.A. Gen. Hood evacuated Atlanta, he ordered his men to blow up the ammunition dumps and railroad cars on their way out of town. By September 2, 1864, the city was nearly empty. There were some Confederate stragglers, a goodly number of poor folks who could not afford to leave, and a circle of

Union sympathizers who had remained in the city throughout the hostilities, despite the persecution and insults they received at the hands of their Confederate neighbors. The mayor, James M. Calhoun, a cautious politician who had voted against secession and had grave doubts about the war, took a carefully selected party to surrender the city to Federal forces. Sherman was still in Jonesboro at the time, so the committee, composed of elite citizens, Union sympathizers and one free black man (Robert Webster) met Gen. William T. Ward on the outskirts of Atlanta on the Marietta Road. (Today a marker on Marietta Street locates the spot.)

Sherman entered Atlanta on September 5 and evacuated what was left of the citizenry in the city on September 7. The citizens, mostly women, children and house servants, and mostly Union sympathizers, were escorted in wagons to the edge of town. With her family ordered to leave, little Carrie Berry recorded in her diary, "Mama seems so troubled and she can't do any thing. Papa says he don't know where on earth to go." Residents in surrounding towns such as Decatur were not ordered to leave, but many left voluntarily. Sherman set up his headquarters, resupplied his troops and strengthened his position, remaining in Atlanta until mid-November.

Sherman's decision to march from Atlanta to the sea came with the heady victory at Atlanta, a victory that marks the defeat of the western front of the war. After leaving Atlanta it was only a matter of time, in the opinion of most, before the Confederacy fell. Only Richmond remained to be defeated, where Grant was having an even more difficult time than Sherman had had with Atlanta. The Fall of Atlanta gave President Abraham Lincoln the victory he needed to retain his leadership; many say that Atlanta's fall kept Lincoln in Washington. Had it not fallen, he might not have been re-elected, the war might have been halted by a treaty of peace, and

the United States might indeed be two nations today. Speculation aside, the Fall of Atlanta was a major turning point in the war, so significant that Sherman's remaining moves in Georgia seem to latter-day pundits to be more punishment than military strategy. There were no more military objectives in Atlanta — Savannah was already neutralized by the blockade, yet Sherman's intent was to defeat the will of the people, to "make," as he said it, "Georgia howl." His preference was to "march through Georgia, smashing things to the sea," a move that was sanctioned by U.S. Grant and rendered much of Georgia exactly as Sherman had hoped it would — "unfit for human habitation."

Before he marched to Savannah, though, Sherman left a burning altar to the gods of war — the city of Atlanta. His planning for Atlanta's destruction was detailed and definitive, to be carried out by at least three different segments of his staff. The depots, the round house, machine shops for the railroads, railroad support buildings, public buildings, commercial houses, blacksmiths, carriage and harness makers, military installations, and industries (such as the Winship Foundry and the Atlanta Gas Light Company, both operated, ironically, by Union sympathizers) were all scheduled for destruction. Sherman actually ordered some restraint in the destruction. First, the engineers

Federal troops occupied communities throughout the region; shown here is a federal encampment in Clayton County.
The Georgia Department of Archives and History

The railroads lay in ruins throughout the Atlanta region in 1864, as shown by these demolished lines in Clayton County. *The Georgia Department of Archives and History*

often taken, promises to respect human life and property not always kept. U.S. Brigadier John Geary led a foraging party from Decatur to Rockbridge and environs with a force of 2,000 men and 700 wagons to fill. After some skirmishing and some small loss of life, he obtained close to 10,000 bushels of corn, a herd of cattle, five loads of wheat and more. One of his victims was Rockbridge's Thomas Macguire, who had already been robbed in July and reported looting of horses and wagons, meal, flour, syrup and articles from his house in September. Macguire suffered even more in November. The night of November 16-17, Macguire slept in the woods to avoid troops in Sherman's left wing, and returned the next day to find "great destruction" to his property: "the gin house and screw were burned, stables and barn in ashes, fences burned and destruction visible all around. Carriage, wagons, corn, potatoes, horses, steers, sheep, chickens, geese, syrup and many other items carried away or destroyed." In Henry County, which was heavily ransacked, several small churches were dismantled for firewood and all the corn and gristmills were burned or otherwise destroyed.

were to knock the buildings down; only then were they to be torched. Soldiers set fire to the buildings before the engineers could get there, and many homes and businesses went up in flames on November 15, 1864, along with the military targets.

Sherman divided his army into two wings; he had nearly 65,000 men, including cavalry, cannon, ammunition and enough supplies for 40 days on the road. The two armies cut wide swaths across the eastern side of the Atlanta region. The right wing followed the railroad from White Hall (West End) via Jonesboro to McDonough, cutting diagonally across Henry County. Several skirmishes occurred en route, one at Rough and Ready and another at Stockbridge (with the so-called "orphan brigade," a group of Confederate volunteers from Kentucky (a slave state that did not secede and join the Confederacy). Confederate forces were driven to Lovejoy Station and from there to Griffin. At that point, Sherman's right wing moved on to Jackson and Liberty Church, a few miles from where the Indian treaty had been signed giving this land to the state of Georgia.

Sherman's left wing departed toward the east to Madison by way of Decatur and Covington, camping the first night on the road between Lithonia and Stone Mountain. Everywhere the troops went, the story was the same: possessions (especially food) stolen, valuables

Federal troops had been foraging through the Atlanta countryside since they entered the region. Directly after the Fall of Atlanta, Union foragers, the "scourge" of the countryside, were sent out from Atlanta into the farmlands, where, once successful, their parties were to return to Atlanta to resupply the headquarters. A Fayette County woman reported that on September 3, 1864, Federal troops took from her five mules, 2,000 pounds of bacon, 256 pounds of lard, 600 pounds of flour, six bushels of meal, 100 pounds of honey, 17 pounds of butter, 700 pounds of salt and six sides of leather. But farmers in the region were not only victimized by the Federals; Confederates, too, looted and vandalized the homes of the residents. Scattered, defeated and largely demoralized, the Confederate troops were even more desperate than their Northern counterparts. While locals would gladly give what they had to the soldiers, often they were given no choice by the military representatives of either side.

And so it was in Gwinnett County, which saw less actual battle action than most of the rest of the region. Overrun by Union troops even without major engagements, the county saw several small skirmishes. Young and old men organized into local home guard units — guerillas actually — who burned bridges, ambushed small units of soldiers, and otherwise confused and confounded the Federal troops. These rangers took the law in their own hands, protecting themselves and their home front as they saw fit, setting the foundation for the pattern of vigilantism that was so strong after the war. A DeKalb County citizen summed up the strong motivations these men had, these "thousands of men in the South who would rather an earthquake should swallow the whole country than yield to our oppressors. Men will retire to the mountains and live on acorns and

crawl on their bellies to shoot an invader wherever they see one." Indeed, they were doing just that.

Caught tragically in the middle were the African-Americans. As slaves, they were often offered "liberation" by the Union troops in exchange for assistance and information. If they gave the requisite assistance, the slaves were let go from their houses, but actually had few resources to escape. Not truly liberated and thus betrayed themselves, the slaves were then subject to punishment (or even murder) by the locals, especially the self-appointed "rangers." Often the Federal troops would save slave houses but burn down the "big" house, leading the slaves to believe that the land would soon be theirs, and instilling paranoia in the minds of the white owners. It was a cruel joke, perpetrated upon a people who were neither stupid nor helpless but caught in hellish circumstances.

Not free and no longer in servitude either, the African-Americans lived in a political and physical limbo. Scavenging food and necessaries was understandably common. Short on supplies themselves and already confident of final victory, the Union forces did

Mary Gay carried messages and goods across enemy lines, becoming one of several local heroines of the Civil War. Her house is preserved in Decatur as part of a complex of historic buildings.
Photo by Riley Hayes

not bother to take too many recruits from the masses of unarmed, untrained slaves in the Atlanta area, though they would take a few. African-Americans in the Atlanta region survived by their own cunning and courage, existing all too often at the shallow mercy of both sides — mistreated by the Federals, punished by the Confederates.

The fighting stopped, but the suffering continued among both blacks and whites. Those who returned from refuges took out their bitter frustrations on those who had stayed during Sherman's occupation. The Confederates took back control of the Atlanta region, re-establishing military rule in the city. Residents of the region were destitute. There was no money, as Confederate money was already rendered worthless. Businesses were barely operating; schools and churches held classes and services wherever they could. Schools met in churches, and churches in schools that were still standing, or in private homes. Food shortages in the cities and towns were so extensive, town residents began doing their own foraging in the countryside, adding civilian insult to military injury on the populace there. More than one fortune was made "overnight" by

opportunistic citizens who converted former cotton fields into food-growing acres. Grocers prospered. It was common for citizens to scavenge the battlefields for minnie balls in order to trade the metal pieces for food or cash. Carrie Berry recorded in her diary that she made regular trips through the streets to find nails to sell. Wood, too, was gathered in the fields. Horses were scarce and other animals, if not slaughtered for food, ran wild.

The end of the war came less than half a year later. Two dates are accepted to mark the conclusion of hostilities. Northerners accept the date April 9, 1865, the day Gen. Robert E. Lee surrendered to U.S. Grant at the courthouse in Appomattox, Virginia. However, those in the Atlanta region with more personal memories of the war date its end at April 26, 1865, the day Gen. Joseph E. Johnston, generally regarded locally as the "hero" of the Atlanta Campaign, surrendered the Army of Tennessee to Gen. William Sherman, generally regarded as the devil incarnate for having devised and carried out the Atlanta Campaign. (April 26 is the date that is universally commemorated in Southern states as Confederate Memorial Day, a state holiday in Georgia.)

Scenes of destruction such as this of the Ponder house just outside Atlanta were commonplace in areas where the shelling was heavy or battles had raged.
The Atlanta Historical Society, Inc.

Between the dates of the two surrenders, on April 14, 1865, President Lincoln was assassinated by an unemployed actor, John Wilkes Booth, who was aided and abetted by a group of conspirators from the South. The tragedy shocked the nation, but its repercussions resonated most strongly in the South, where, it appeared, the fighting was over but not the hostilities. Most in the Atlanta region did not love Mr. Lincoln, but they were just beginning to respect his moderate humanitarianism toward their region. The elimination of Lincoln from

the helm of government put the future of the South into the hands of men who were set upon a righteous, stringent reorganization of the former C.S.A. states, and who held racial issues as the cornerstone of their reorganization. Their priorities made the hardest problem to solve — what to do with the freedmen — the first problem to solve, to the consternation of Georgians and others throughout the South.

Slavery was over, but it was only illegal, not invisible. Many blacks simply signed on as tenant sharecroppers on the lands of their former owners and masters. Others hired themselves out, bit by bit getting enough money or trade goods to obtain horses, buggies, wagons, livestock and household goods. While some stayed in Georgia, many did not. Fayette County, which in the years before the war had the highest percentage of enslaved blacks in the Atlanta region, provides a good example of what happened. At the end of the war, there were only 300 African-Americans left in Fayette, who among them owned 1,182 acres of farmland. For the most part they were employed in the "old" occupations — farm labor, mechanics, smithing, masonry and domestic service. African-Americans founded Bethlehem Baptist Church in 1878, Flint Ridge, Mt. Olive, Edgefield Baptist and others in the 1870s. Freedmen's schools in Fayette lasted only a few years, and floundered after

Union support was withdrawn in 1870. When there were no longer black schools in Fayette County, the former slaves who could, traveled to Atlanta to get schooling, where the Freedmen and missionary schools had more support and viability.

Across the region, thousands of African-Americans left their owners, took new names, united with family members formerly enslaved on other plantations and headed out for a new future — in the North, in the cities in the South, in pockets of land granted by the U.S. government. Freedmen's Bureau programs, centered in Atlanta, were too few and too poorly funded to bring a whole black population to a truly autonomous status — fed, clothed, educated, sheltered, trained occupationally and protected from possible white reprisals. Still, liberated blacks left the regional countryside in droves, congregating in the cities, especially Atlanta, where they created all-black communities — until then an unprecedented phenomenon in Georgia — where the African-Americans created institutions of learning, church congregations and burial societies that in turn gave them support, succor and safety. Most of the black congregations throughout the metro region date from the years after the Civil War. Black populations in the rural sections of the Atlanta region dwindled while those in the cities swelled, and for the first time in its

Atlanta is surrounded by monuments to the Civil War including this marker and cemetery in Jonesboro.
Photo by Riley Hayes

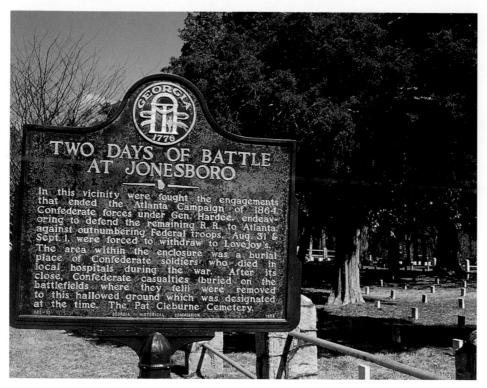

TWO DAYS OF BATTLE AT JONESBORO

In this vicinity were fought the engagements that ended the Atlanta Campaign of 1864. Confederate forces under Gen. Hardee, endeavoring to defend the remaining R. R. to Atlanta against outnumbering Federal troops, Aug. 31 & Sept. 1, were forced to withdraw to Lovejoy's. The area within the enclosure was a burial place of Confederate soldiers who died in local hospitals during the war. After its close, Confederate casualties (buried on the battlefields where they fell) were removed to this hallowed ground which was designated at the time. The Pat Cleburne Cemetery.

short history, Atlanta had a black population that constituted more than 10 percent of the total.

Yet right after the war, no one in Atlanta was completely free while the state of the state was in question. Georgia had ratified the 13th Amendment to the Constitution, which entitled Georgia to be readmitted into the Union, but because Georgia failed to ratify the 15th Amendment, giving the freed black men the right to vote, the state was not officially reunited with the United States. Instead, Georgia passed under military control again, and the Atlanta region was reoccupied by Union forces beginning June 27, 1865, just two months after the end of the war. Georgia was still "enemy" territory. The state's official status changed several more times in the ensuing years, and Georgia was readmitted to the Union for the last time in 1870 when it ratified the 15th Amendment — five years after the war ended. Altogether, Atlanta and its environs had been under military occupation of one kind or another for eight years and the continued military occupation left local residents embittered, even those who had been Union sympathizers.

Feelings between the former Confederates and the Unionists were still high on both sides. Those who had remained loyal to the United States could apply for redress of grievances for properties appropriated by

Federal troops or for other Union usage. Many former Union supporters in the area, wishing only to continue quietly with their lives, did not petition. Those who did were often subjected to excruciating scrutiny and the threat of exposure. Paranoia and suspicion, almost on the scale of prewar tensions, spread through the region. Unionists were exposed as enemies either to their neighbors or to their new authorities, damned for what they did or did not do. Not all who appealed were granted compensation, and not all who received compensation also received the blessings of their neighbors, business partners and fellow church members. With new Yankees flooding into the region — military men, government officials, speculators and settlers — many former Unionists, rendered personae non gratae by their fellow citizens, left. A few, such as the Atlanta banker Alfred Austell and real estate dealer Thomas Healey, had enough money and influence to overcome their erstwhile "Yankee" personal histories.

The region needed the energy and interests of all those who had stayed, who were so clearly committed to the future of this place. Its devastation was beyond imagining, and the territory affected was huge. The sweep of activities by both armies during the Campaign for Atlanta, either to protect it or to conquer it, took in land for miles. Atlanta — a small municipality with circular city limits set barely at a one-mile radius — had extended its "influence" as far south as McDonough, as far north as Kennesaw, as far east as Covington, and as far west as Dallas in the immediate metropolitan area. Like an eddy, Atlanta took the entire region down with it, along with the towns bordering the W&A all the way to Chattanooga and the lands in the wake of the 60-mile-wide tornado that constituted Sherman's March to the Sea from Atlanta to Savannah.

Chapter 4

If Atlanta was merely larger than its neighbors before the war, afterward it wholly diverged in character from them. If the region was perceived as rural, Atlanta was urban; if the region was white, Atlanta was black; if the region was a land of farmers, Atlanta was a city of tradesmen; if the region was poor, Atlanta was rich — all true, comparatively speaking. Atlanta and its environs were held together by a codependency of opposites. As the railroads recovered, so did the region. Yet, as uneven as the spread of progress seemed to be, it was felt and observed by all.

Before Century's End

In 1866, according to a special census, the city of Atlanta had not only regained its swollen wartime population, it had surpassed it. The population stood at 20,228, the second-highest concentration of people in the state after Savannah and slightly more than a fifth of the entire urban population of Georgia. In another two decades, Atlanta would overtake Savannah to become the largest city in the state and one of the three largest in the Southeast.

Between the end of the Civil War and the end of the 19th century, the state's population remained predominantly rural, but the urban population doubled as a percent of the whole, going from 7 percent to more than 15 percent. Atlanta did not account for all of the increase, but the city was growing at a much more rapid rate than the rest of the state, accounting for more and more of its urban growth. Georgia's small towns were also growing, especially those that were Atlanta's neighbors. But the postwar growth, when it came, was neither constant nor always remarkable.

The key to regional growth after the Civil War was the railroad, no doubt about it. Established by the 1868 constitution, the new state government eliminated direct subsidies to the railroads, but it created a more open, hands-off relationship with

investors, which was good for commerce and very good for the development of rail transportation. The state did begin to endorse rail bonds, which also helped. The Western & Atlantic was the first to recover; thus, the line that had brought Atlanta into being now brought it back to life. Though the state retained ownership, it now leased the W & A to private holders, creating a revenue stream for the state and a profitable enterprise for the new operators who benefited from the size and activity of the Atlanta markets.

Gradually, expanses of the track were relaid, the support buildings repaired, and passenger traffic resumed. In the two decades between 1873 and 1893, especially during the boom of the 1880s, railroad interests added roads to the prewar lines and connected main lines with branch lines to new, often industrial stops. All the lines increased their tonnage, speed and numbers; the spread of their support shops, yards and maintenance facilities; and the total number of their destinations in the northern half of the state.

The impact on the local Atlanta region was significant. The railroads created an intricate system of interdependencies between Atlanta and the outlying towns and stations, dubbed "Atlanta's tributaries" by the city's first historian, E.Y. Clarke, in 1879. Atlanta businessmen and real estate speculators invested not only in the new railroad lines but also in the land surrounding them. A good example of the impact

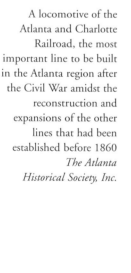

A locomotive of the Atlanta and Charlotte Railroad, the most important line to be built in the Atlanta region after the Civil War amidst the reconstruction and expansions of the other lines that had been established before 1860
The Atlanta Historical Society, Inc.

Atlantans could have on their neighbors comes from Stockbridge, incorporated in Henry County in 1882 in association with the railroad. An Old Stockbridge, an 1820s village that predated the railroad, was located one mile to the north. Two Atlanta businessmen, J.W. Grant and G.W. Adair, had purchased a tract of land to the south of the old town and offered it to the railroad at a more reasonable price than the citizens of the old town were willing to bear. The railroad accepted the offer, moved a mile south, and took the town with it.

The very heart of Atlanta, the Union Depot sat about two blocks below Five Points. The largest hotel in the state, the Kimball House is pictured on the left. The depot was moved in 1904 to a site presently occupied by the Richard Russell federal building. *The Georgia Department of Archives and History*

S.M. Inman, one of Atlanta's wealthiest and most pre-eminent cotton traders, built cotton warehouses in Hampton, south of Atlanta, creating an important market nucleus there in association with the railroad. In Fayette County, other of Inman's warehouses were so important to one locale that residents in the area ultimately named the town that grew up around them, Inman, after him.

The impact the roads had on the city of Atlanta was almost staggering; in a word, they defined the town. They set the direction of Atlanta's growth; they converged in the downtown, creating a steel triangle that served as a city icon for decades. The railroad terminal occupied the very center of town both geographically and symbolically. Railroads employed the most people in the city — indeed, in the state — in occupations other than agriculture. The railroads (and the real estate speculation that accompanied them) created Atlanta's first million-aires. And commercial development followed the tracks, radiating out from the terminal and out from Atlanta in virtually every direction.

By 1880 there were five lines coming into and out of Atlanta, the four that had existed before the war — the Western and Atlantic, the Macon and Western (now the Central), the Georgia Railroad and the Atlanta and West Point — and one new one, the Atlanta and Charlotte Air Line. Atlanta was the only city in the entire Southeastern region with connections to every other part of the South. In imitation of its greater, Northern model, Chicago, Atlanta adopted the nickname, "Gate City."

To get to the West from the Atlantic, or the North from the South, passengers and goods had to pass through Atlanta. "Atlanta must grow with her tributaries," said E. Y. Clarke, the city's first chronicler, as the area's "combined power and the prestige of success are continually extending trade into new and more remote sections." Atlanta enjoyed the competitive advantage in a territory 100 miles in radius. The rails were Atlanta's future, and by extension, the future of its immediate environs.

The railroad also reconfigured the outlying regions, creating new towns as it went, moving populations into new and old towns, creating villages out of antebellum station stops and towns out of prewar villages. Each of the counties bordering Atlanta shared in the growth — that is, to the extent that rail lines coursed through them.

Each line had its string of towns and stops, connecting each stop with Atlanta and also with all the other stops. The Western and Atlantic went through Bolton, Gilmore, Vinings, McEvoy, Smyrna, Marietta, Big Shanty (Kennesaw) and Acworth on its way to Chattanooga. Along the Atlanta and West Point were East Point (the eastern terminus of the line), Fairburn, Palmetto, Powell's and Newnan. The Central also went through East Point, then turned to go through Forest Park, Morrow, Jonesboro, Lovejoy, Hampton, Sunny Side and Griffin on its way to Macon. The Georgia Railway passed through Decatur, Stone Mountain, Lithonia, Conyers, Covington and Social Circle on its way to Augusta. Finally, the new line, the Atlanta and Charlotte, passed through Goodwins, Doraville, Norcross, Duluth, Suwanee, Buford, Flowery Branch and Gainesville.

Map of the railroads
at the turn of the
19th century

Railroads in Georgia - 1899

east of Atlanta, and as far out as Covington and Oxford. A second accommodation train ran between Marietta and Atlanta, and a third commuter train ran between Atlanta and Norcross, the "Air Line Belle," which brought workers and businessmen in from the northeast side of Atlanta and shoppers from as far away as Toccoa. While the pattern of commuting did extend to places like East Point, Oakland City and West End, it did not extend to the towns on the far south side of Atlanta to the same extent as those on the north and east. But then the counties to the south were not as well served by the railroads as DeKalb and Cobb. McDonough and Jonesboro were not as close to Atlanta as Decatur, but no farther than Marietta, yet they were not seen as the commuter locations that these other two cities were.

Nevertheless, towns in Clayton, Henry and Fayette counties felt the pull of Atlanta and experienced both the progressive growth of the railroads and a distinct loss to Atlanta from among their respective citizenries, as local professional and business talent sought out the greater, more profitable ventures to be had in the larger city — not just to work there, but also to relocate there.

County after county noticed the growth in population and enterprise that accompanied the railroads. The Atlanta and Charlotte Air Line made all the difference in Gwinnett, where Lawrenceville — nothing but an overgrown village — had for all this time been the only true "town" in the county. With the railroad, Lawrenceville grew, and to it were added Duluth, Suwanee and Buford, all of which were founded by the railroad and developed into small commercial centers. Buford was built on the same hilly spot where the railroad construction camp had been located. When the first train came through there in 1871 — the year the railroad line was completed — people came from miles around for the event, many of whom had never seen a locomotive before. Taking advantage of their

An hour's ride on the rails meant an easy commute from any of these places. Atlanta had workers from outlying areas and counted among its leading citizens residents of the nearby communities, especially Decatur and points due east, where some of Atlanta's first serious suburbanization took place. Decatur advertised its "unequalled" advantages as a suburban home for people who did business in Atlanta, as did its East Atlanta counterparts. Kirkwood, Edgewood and East Lake all stretched out on the line to Decatur, offering residents proximity to both Atlanta and the outlying countryside — the perfect suburban combination. "If you wish to live among good people, drink good water, have good health, and live a long time, come to East Atlanta and buy yourself a home," advertised the *DeKalb New Era* in 1897.

A commuter train, called the "Accommodation," ran twice daily to accommodate the people who lived collective innocence, one of the engineers cautioned the crowd, "you folks better lower your umbrellas or you'll scare this thing off the tracks." Ten years later, in 1881, a branch road was built making a second connection between Suwanee and Lawrenceville. In 1891 Lawrenceville was connected to yet another new set of towns, which included Carl, Auburn, Dacula and Lilburn.

In Cobb County the importance of the railroad is reflected in the fact that at the turn of the century, all the towns of any size with in the county were located along a railroad. Along the W&A were Acworth, Kennesaw, Marietta, Smyrna and Vinings; Powder Springs, Mableton and Austell were along lines now part of the CSX system. A new line built as the Marietta and North brought the mineral resources of north Georgia, chiefly marble and copper, to Marietta for further distribution and export. Begun in 1870, the line was completed to Jasper, lying in the foothills of the Appalachians, in 1883.

On the south side of Atlanta, the railroad did not reach Fayette County until the 1880s, when the Atlanta and Florida was built, connecting Kenwood, Fayetteville, Inman, Woolsey and Lowry to Atlanta. In Clayton County, Jonesboro was a well-developed rail center, connected by several lines to other destinations. Lovejoy, a stop on the railroad before the war, began to emerge as a town in the 1880s and was incorporated in 1891. McDonough, which had existed in a state of arrested development after being bypassed by the Macon and Western before the Civil War, came into its own prominence after 1882 when the Macon and Brunswick, a branch line, connected it to the Atlanta and Macon.

What the railroads connected, either politics or poverty or both often disconnected. Survival, not prosperity, was the region's primary objective for a full decade or more after the war, and even the resumption of railroad services suffered setbacks and delays under the influence of national policies

and Southern practices. In sequence there came first the difficult and confusing period of Reconstruction, next a decade of economic depression, then a decade of boom (finally!) followed by another decade of economic downturns. A people who were "crushed and sad" at the end of the war had all too many reasons to become embittered.

When the war ended, it was clear that no one knew what to do with the defeated Southern soldiers, the seceded states, nor, certainly, the newly freed slaves. The soldiers who returned to their farms and homes, if they owned their lands, were now land-poor and caught up in a system that kept the small and large landowners in poverty or on the edge of it. "This, then, is the Cotton Kingdom," wrote W.E.B. DuBois, the great black intellectual at Atlanta University in the last decade of the 19th century, "the shadow of a marvelous dream. And where is the King? Perhaps this is he, — the sweating ploughman, tilling his eighty acres with two lean mules, and fighting a hard battle with debt."

Atlanta's local counties were full of such farmers, who had much more in common with the rest of Georgia — a land where three-quarters of the people made their living as farmers — than they did with Atlanta. Cotton was still king, even though it cost twice as much to grow as it did before the war, and cotton prices were low for the remainder of the century. Still, cotton was easy to store, easy to ship, and in the Atlanta area relatively easy to sell. In the decades following the war, what began as extemporaneous convenience bred an intransigent system of tenancy and sharecropping

As evidence of the growth of the region, culture and recreation flourished at the Piedmont Chautauqua founded by Atlantan Henry Grady and others at Lithia Springs in Cobb County.
The Atlanta Historical Society, Inc.

throughout Georgia, no less in the Atlanta counties than elsewhere. Both former slaves and landless whites signed agreements by which they shared a portion of the as yet unproduced crop in exchange for their labor on the land. Landowners could in turn offer a lien on the crop in order to obtain seed, fertilizer, equipment, other necessary supplies and even more land from merchants, small bankers and other landowners.

The crop lien system entitled farmers to a source of short-term credit; however, high interest rates and bad crop years put most land-owning farmers into a perpetual cycle of indebtedness. Also indebted, sharecroppers were at least mobile; wherever they worked, they lived. If the laborers lived on the land they worked, they were tenants as well as sharecroppers. Tenancy tied laborers to the land but freed the landowners to live and work elsewhere. Thus it was that even in the smallest towns, many absentee landowning farmers lived and held mercantile interests.

Both railroads and streetcars passed through open country between Atlanta and the other regional towns. One of the electrified streetcar lines is shown here in 1895. *The Atlanta Historical Society, Inc.*

The plantation system was not dead after all; it simply persisted in a somewhat altered form and with greater dispersal of the resident parties. Agriculture remained a depressed industry; cotton ruled, and recovery in other economic areas was even slower than in agriculture. Diversification was difficult given the lack of capital in the region, the inadequacy of credit facilities and the strong footholds of traditional practices. During the 1890s, when national financial panics again brought economic constriction to the South, farmers in the Atlanta area were forced to turn to crops and

activities other than cotton growing — pecans, livestock, dairying, truck farming — with some success.

The population density of Atlanta enabled many local farmers to make a living truck farming. Their country produce, imported by wagon and train, brought fresh fruits, grains, vegetables, chickens, eggs, butter and dairy products into the city, not to mention also flowers, seeds and garden plants. Economies of scale dictated that the produce would retail at lower prices in Atlanta than in the neighboring small towns, which had less access and fewer customers. Yet Atlanta handled truck farming on such a large scale that truck farming was as important to Atlanta's economy as it was to the rural suburbs and outlying farms.

The foundations for some important 20th-century rural industries, such as nurseries and dairies in DeKalb County, and dairies, poultry and cattle in Cobb County, were laid in the decades of expansion after the Civil War and in the needs of the burgeoning Atlanta population.

Atlanta, described by one of its observers as a place "where the spirit of enterprise never sleeps," had nearly 200 commercial enterprises by 1880 and never experienced as severe an economic setback in the 1870s as did the people living off the land. Commerce did not require the same capital investments as railroads or manufacturing, so conditions in the towns, especially Atlanta, were conducive to quicker recovery and more economic security than on the land.

The national monetary crises of 1873 and 1874 did not cause an "absolute halt in its onward march" historian E. Y. Clarke reported in 1879, though the city did experience some slowdowns, chiefly in railroad expansions. Clarke described the chief functions of Atlanta as commercial and mechanical: commercial referring to the high levels of wholesaling, trading and retailing that took place in the city; and mechanical referring to railroads and the secondary businesses they spawned, such as machine shops, foundries and railroad supply houses.

The railroads also supported hospitality ventures — hostelries, livery stables, eateries and express services — setting an economic pattern in tourism that continues even today. These hospitality businesses located their facilities as close to the railroad tracks as they could afford to be. The Kimball House, the largest hotel in the state, sat directly across the street from the railroad terminal, along with banks and express offices, the post office, and assorted retail establishments. Atlanta's commercial center now constituted the largest downtown in all of Georgia.

After the war, Atlanta's wholesale markets were especially important to the city's growth. Wholesalers specialized in dry goods and produce, with $10 million worth of dry-goods exchanged by 1880 and a fruit market to rival the one in Savannah's seaport. Retailing was already the best in the state — for proprietors and customers. People came to Atlanta from 100 miles away to spend the day shopping. Among the dry-goods merchants, Morris Rich and his brother Emmanuel established what would become the largest local department store in the region, Rich's (still in existence but no longer locally owned). Whitehall Street, the heart of Atlanta's retail center, carried everything — hats, shoes, cigars, liquor, jewelry, furniture, tin stoves, even seeds and farming supplies.

Atlanta's growth in commerce and transportation was balanced by developments in manufacturing, which were supported by the Atlanta Manufacturing Association, founded in 1872, a precursor to the present-day Chamber of Commerce. Before the Civil War, Atlanta was not recognized as an important cotton market, but its extensive railroad system and its access to both raw and processed cotton allowed it market supremacy by 1880, when it was acknowledged as the third-largest receiving point for cotton in the South. There were more than 4,000 textile workers in mills within a 20-mile radius around Atlanta; by 1890 there were enough cotton processing facilities to rival what Columbus and Augusta were producing. Atlanta area

Blacks and whites picking cotton in DeKalb County in the early 1900s — cotton growing went through decades of boom and bust, mostly bust, between 1865 and 1900. *The Georgia Department of Archives and History*

mills could already handle 150,000 bales of cotton a year, up from 17,000 just after the war, but by the end of the century, Atlanta area mills more than doubled their production.

Exposition Cotton Mills, established in 1879 on the northern edge of Atlanta, and Fulton Bag and Cotton Mill, founded in 1881 on the eastern edge of town, were the largest in the region. Cabbagetown, the mill village associated with Fulton Bag, contained 3,000 residents. Mill owners like the Elsas family of Fulton Bag often recruited laborers directly from the outlying counties. Because mill village residents came straight from the country, they introduced a rural element to Atlanta, offering yet a different kind of connection between the city and the countryside.

In terms of Atlanta manufacturing enterprises, however, none was more successful or destined to be more "Atlantan" than Coca-Cola, which was invented by Dr. John Pemberton in 1886 as a headache remedy and went into commercial production under marketing wizard Asa Candler in 1892 as a soft drink. Atlanta also had furniture manufacturers, cigar makers, distilleries, breweries, hardware manufacturers and distributors, carriage makers, coal dealers and mule traders. Atlanta's mule market was, in fact, the largest in the state.

By 1890, Atlanta's population — 65,553 people — was three times the size it had been during the Civil War. Its size and economic status stood in sharp contrast with most of the rest of Georgia, including its own neighboring counties. The edges of Atlanta were soft, and the lines where the city ended and county jurisdictions began changed several times in the late 19th century, contributing to a confusion of identities and authorities that continues today.

In the 1880s and 1890s, as a response to the ancillary suburban growth around its edges, Atlanta began "eating up" its neighbors. It annexed land, increasing the city limits in 1873 and again in 1889, until its borders extended one and three-quarter miles in every direction. Extending its limits was to become a recurrent Atlanta practice, and the city would continue to grow through annexation — like most American cities — making frequent increases in its territory in the 20th century, sometimes at the request of its suburbs, sometimes not.

Among Atlanta's neighboring towns, Decatur and Marietta were the next largest in size in the growing metropolitan area, and yet the populations of the counties in which they are located, DeKalb and Cobb, in no way equaled that of the city of Atlanta. Cobb had a population in 1890 of 22,286 people, and DeKalb recorded 17,189 people in the same census year. In truth, no other metropolitan area town or county came even close to Atlanta in population density and commercial productivity.

DeKalb County, the closest geographically to Atlanta, continued to be defined as a predominantly agricultural county. At the end of the 19th century, the county was still ranked among the top producers of cotton in the state. DeKalb enjoyed some economic diversity with the presence of granite quarries, especially

near Stone Mountain and Arabia Mountain, which began commercial operation in the 1880s. Stone Mountain granite was needed initially for postwar rebuilding, but the granite was of such a fine quality, it ended up in notable public structures from Georgia to Washington, D.C., Cuba to the Panama Canal. Elsewhere among DeKalb industries, grist milling remained important, and truck farming and dairying increased in importance as the century wore on. Vegetable farms and strawberry fields lay on land near the present site of Emory University, and Cheeks flour mill and cotton gin, one of the largest and longest-lived operations in the county, was located at what is now a main intersection in Dunwoody (Mt. Vernon and Chamblee-Dunwoody roads).

Doraville, the antebellum community founded upon two old churches, Prospect Methodist (1826) and Prosperity Presbyterian (1836), incorporated in 1871 as a town on the Atlanta and Charlotte Air Line. Doraville retained its rural flavor despite its connection to the railroad, and at the end of the century was a typical area village — with its two churches, a handful of stores, a gin and a mill, a post office and other conveniences.

Chamblee was similar; it had antebellum roots in the Nancy Creek Baptist Church, founded in 1824, but it remained a wide-spread, loosely identified community stretching from the Samuel House plantation (Peachtree Golf Club) on Peachtree Road to the intersection of the Charlotte Air Line railroad with the buck line from Toccoa. Elsewhere in DeKalb, farms dotted the roadside along the highway from Decatur out to Lawrenceville. By 1900 DeKalb County still had more cows than the city of Decatur had people.

Cobb County, too, remained predominantly rural. Not unaffected by trends toward urbanization and industrialization, Cobb nonetheless resisted significant changes in these directions. By 1890, Marietta, its largest city, had a population of 4,000 people, barely half the size Atlanta had been before the war, and slightly larger than Atlanta's largest mill village. Cobb's increases in population were smaller overall than DeKalb's, even though in the Atlanta

In high contrast to its rural neighbors, downtown Atlanta in 1882 already featured all modern conveniences — horse-drawn trolleys, street lamps, power poles for telegraph and electricity for the office buildings along Whitehall Street. *The Atlanta Historical Society, Inc.*

region its population in pure numbers was the next highest after Fulton County, which contained Atlanta. Cobb had not been a cotton county before the Civil War, but it made up for that after the war. The county relied on corn and cotton — corn for consumption (human and animal) and cotton for cash — but the very low cotton prices through the last decades of the 19th century kept Cobb County from enjoying very great economic prosperity.

The Fulton Bag and Cotton Mill and a portion of Cabbagetown (lower right) as they appeared about 1950; the oldest section of the mills was built in 1879. *The Atlanta Historical Society, Inc.*

While the amount of cultivated land doubled, individual farm size, never large to begin with, remained small; in fact, by the end of the century, Cobb County's average farm size had decreased from 112 acres to just 72 acres. More than half of Cobb's farms were operated by tenants, most of whom were black. Yet Cobb was beginning to lose its black population — much of it to Atlanta — a trend that increased in the early decades of the 20th century. Absentee ownership increased, and owners, instead of having to work the land, could focus on improving its productivity through other means — through improved farming methods or new agriculture-based industry.

The Cobb County Agricultural Association, formed in 1870, sponsored county fairs and exhibits. With the assistance of the newly created Georgia Department of Agriculture founded a few years later, it taught new scientific procedures for farming such as terracing, optimal fertilizer usage, crop rotation and soil testing.

The Farmers Alliance, an offshoot of the Populist movement in the 1890s, was active in Cobb County but, even in this agriculture-bound county, it did not dominate the local politics. Industrialization in Cobb County continued to resemble prewar models. Cobb had active saw, grist, and flour mills to which were added, slowly over time, a paper mill, cotton mills,

woolen goods factories and a leatherworks. The cotton mills outside Roswell were particularly important to the county, though industrialization at this time did not promise the salvation of the county in the way its residents might have hoped.

The Atlanta region was in transition, moving from an agrarian to an industrial economy, and Atlanta sat at the center of the transition not only economically, but also politically. Atlanta's role as the dominant economic center in the state came about partially through its new role as the political center, since the state capital relocated there in 1868.

"Foreign" rule had determined that Atlanta was the right location for the government center, but the functions of government had no permanent quarters until the citizens of the state passed a referendum in 1877, endorsing a new state constitution and making Atlanta the permanent capital. The legislature mandated that a new statehouse be created, but it took another decade to accomplish. The capitol — which serves the state today, faced with Georgia marble and crowned with Georgia gold — went under construction in 1884 and was completed in 1889.

Politics in Georgia between the end of the Civil War and the end of the century were, in a word, chaotic. There were so many changes that had to be put in place after the war, so many differences of opinion about the right course to take, and so much allegiance to the idea of the Old South and what it stood for — not slavery, but its agrarianism, devotion to colonial-era principles, its cause for independence, and loyalties to home, family, country — that resistance to change grew as mightily as the attempts (by the federal government in particular) to turn the state around.

Atlanta, struck with epidemics of typhus, diphtheria and tuberculosis following the war, with its dirt and its overcrowding, its criminal element, its "slavery" to money and its "race-mixing," was hardly seen by many in the region as the epitome of what the future might hold. Those who clung to the idea that the farmer was still "lord" of the land wanted no part of what Atlanta stood for. They might let political functions reside in Atlanta, but political power, never. Though the political positioning aligned itself along city-county oppositions, the pivot point was always race — what to do about the African-Americans.

races. He believed, like that of many in leadership positions, that white supremacy was a fact of life; it did not need to be cruel in its manifestations, but it needed to be upheld. Racial equity at the time did not mean equality, nor anything near equality. White Georgians as a group were unprepared for the degree to which the question of black citizenship would determine their own political status, not just during the years of Reconstruction, but for decades — indeed a whole century — into the future.

Originally, President Andrew Johnson's program for reunification after the Civil War had been a relatively compassionate and straightforward one: if the confederate states annuled the acts of secession, repudiated the war debts and eliminated slavery, they could be readmitted to the Union. The Georgia convention did as it was asked, almost unanimously, but while it was still in session the U.S. Congress (without representation from Georgia or the other Southern states) decided that Reconstruction was not a Presidential matter, it was a Congressional matter, and more would be required of the states seeking repatriation.

The quarry at Stone Mountain, a thriving post-Civil War industry, furnished building materials for communities in the Atlanta region and for national buildings in Washington, D.C.
Riley Hayes

Georgia and her sister states had not only to eliminate slavery but also to protect equal rights under the law and enable the freedmen to vote. Because it failed to provide for Negro suffrage in 1865, Georgia became occupied territory again, and Atlanta, as the headquarters for the Third Military District encompassing Alabama and Florida, was now placed under military rule for the third time in its short history.

Typical of the mainstream view in his approach and understanding was Alexander Stephens, formerly vice president of the Confederacy and now active in Georgia politics after the war. His racial beliefs were not the most radical nor the most enlightened, yet he understood, in his words, that "the relation of the black to the white race, ...was a question now of vastly more importance than when the Old Constitution was formed." In Stephens' mind, some form of "proper subordination" of the blacks to the whites was necessary because it suited the contemporary worldview of the

Because of its association with the activities of the Radical Reconstruction authorities, Atlanta, sometimes of its own accord and sometimes unwittingly, became more and more identified with the outsider notions of what were wise and proper political measures. Atlanta's notoriety in the proceedings of what became known as Radical Reconstruction was less the product of its political leadership than its "guilt" by association.

The constitutional convention of 1867 began meeting in Atlanta in December and had the new constitution finished by March of 1868. That constitution,

This scene of market day in Marietta occurred all over the region in the primary market towns, where the wagons met the railroads to ship cotton to local or distant manufacturing centers. *The Georgia Department of Archives and History*

more liberal that any subsequent documents, was destined to last only a decade, but its legacy was greater than that. The constitution guaranteed Negro suffrage, mandated a free public school system for all children in the state (black and white), granted property rights to married women for the first time in the state's history, and insured debt relief for debts contracted before the end of the war.

In 1868, following an election in which both black and white men voted, the Legislature opened its sessions in temporary quarters at the Atlanta opera house with 29 blacks seated among the 172 members of the house, and three blacks among the senators. The black legislators — some of whom were distinguished educators and religious leaders — had limited impact, as the white legislators had all but the lightest-skinned African-Americans expelled from office after only two months. Then, the whites

encouraged the remaining blacks to vote Democratic in the proceedings or to not vote at all. Such "tinkering" with the new national system kept Georgia under military rule for several more years.

In a state where the preponderance of the vote was agriculturally rooted and becoming annually more Democratic (which was then seen as the conservative party) in its leanings, Atlanta remained identified with Radical Republicanism, urban ideas, big money interests, liberal leanings, elites, scalawags, carpet-bagging merchants and black politicians. Even the Independent movement that sought to be an alternative voice to both Democratic conservatism and Republican radicalism, had its Atlanta connections.

The election of William Felton from north Georgia to the Legislature spearheaded the Independent movement. Felton's outspoken, feminist and opinionated wife, Rebecca Latimer Felton (a native of DeKalb County), kept a running dialogue in the Atlanta newspapers with her letters to the editor. A kind of political gadfly, "Becky" Felton poked her literary finger at both Republicans and Democrats in the service of her husband's and her own pet issues — elimination of the convict lease system (which offered a "free" pool of labor to railroads, public works and other industries), education for poor whites and votes for white women.

The first black college founded in Atlanta, Atlanta University (fd. 1867) — now part of Clark-Atlanta University — provided a bastion of education and enlightenment for African-Americans during Reconstruction and Jim Crow segregation. This campus now belongs to Morris Brown College. *The Atlanta Historical Society, Inc.*

Republicanism waned during the 1870s when the Democratic Party assumed primacy in Georgia's political leadership, adjusting the public values toward rural laissez-faire ideals and away from private (especially railroad) interests. The constitution of 1878 reduced the authority of the state government, especially in the executive and judicial branches. More importantly for the Atlanta region, it also increased the authority of the rural, lightly populated counties in the state by making representation to the legislature equal across the board. Each county could elect two representatives to the legislature, except the most populous counties, which could elect three representatives.

Inside the Negro Building at the 1895 Cotton States Exposition, where a half-century of "progress since Emancipation" was exhibited to the public — this was the first time African-Americans had such a showcase before the nation.
The Atlanta Historical Society, Inc.

Thus, power remained in the hands of the rural counties and out of the hands of the cities, especially the most populous one, Atlanta. The county unit rule, aimed at "correcting" carpet bag rule and curbing big government, actually did little to support the needs of a forward-looking state by thus crippling its own capital city. This constitution, as reactive as it was, served the state until 1945; but was barely out of the envelope it came in before it was burdened with amendments to make it a more viable, effective and modern set of laws. Republican rule had embittered the state; the new Democratic rule merely disempowered it. Yet, except for a bump in their hegemony caused by Populists in the 1890s, the Democrats were to remain in power for more than a century, espousing the one-party system, freedom from government regulation, and white supremacy — the last, most vehemently of all.

In the 1890s Georgia hardened its racial stance. The state and local governments made unofficial segregation official by enacting a series of laws that regulated what African-Americans could and could not do, own or control. All the Southern states passed such black codes, and in 1896, the U.S. Supreme Court ruled that "separate but equal" was a constitutional measure of equality acceptable throughout the nation.

In Georgia the black codes successfully segregated the railway cars, all public accommodations and industrial facilities, and maintained separate systems of education and health care. As the nation was accepting "separate but equal," Georgia was beginning to legislate "separate and equal as practicable," legitimating inadequacies in every public service available to black people. Local governments, including Atlanta, passed their own versions of black codes where everything was segregated except the trolleys.

At the time Atlanta had the largest black population in the immediate region, the highest percentage of blacks in any local population and the greatest number of employed blacks — most of them female domestic servants who, though still house servants, were employed under different circumstances than in slavery times. Always complex and often illogical, black codes created physical distance between the races that had been intimately associated before the war. Distance bred ignorance, isolation, prejudice and victimization.

Ironically, some of the reactionism was caused by the Populists, who started out appealing to the black voters on the basis of common interests, i.e., economic problems stemming from low cotton prices and widespread indebtedness. The Populist creed was embodied by its chief spokesman, Tom Watson, who was elected to Congress in 1890 on a platform friendly to the farmers, small landowners, and mill workers, and unfriendly to the "big money" parties.

Watson spoke out against the economic ills of the South, including its growing dependence on industry, on banks, and on modern urban evils, but when accused of threatening white supremacy, Watson backtracked on his stand with black voters. In fact, he did a complete turnaround and began trying to convince poor whites that the black man was their enemy. Watson was to end his career as one of the most virulent race baiters in Georgia history, yet he had started out with more progressive, color-blind, agrarian ideas as his focus.

If Tom Watson was the spokesman for agricultural interests, Henry Grady was the spokesman for industrial interests. Grady, a popular orator and the editor of the *Atlanta Constitution*, is usually credited with coining the term "New South," which, if he did not actually invent, he made popular throughout the country. "There was a South of slavery and secession — that South is dead," Grady would declaim to his rapt audiences, and "there is a South of union and freedom — that South, thank God, is living, breathing, growing every hour."

Some of the tenets of Grady's New South were inextricably identified with Atlanta — harmony between the North and South (did not Atlanta receive a lot of Northern money?), diversification in economic interests (meaning the promotion of industry as well as agriculture) and economic autonomy for the South. "We have sowed towns and cities in the place of theories, and put business above politics," Grady espoused, as much to encourage the continuance of Northern investment as to illuminate Southern progress.

Grady was not only a spokesman for progress in his home state and city, but he also followed through personally, putting his private money where his New South orator's mouth was, supporting every progressive measure in Atlanta, from education and hospitals to the creation of grand expositions and a Southern baseball league. He also supported prohibition and the racial status quo.

Grady was no advocate of racial equality, though he spoke strongly for some kind of equity in education and public transport. "We have found out," he liked to say, "that... the free Negro counts more than he did as a slave. We have planted the schoolhouse on the hilltop and made it free to white and black." Grady provided vision and intellectual leadership at a time when both were needed in the Atlanta region. Too liberal for some, too conservative for others, his devotion to Atlanta was cut short by his premature death at the age of 39. Grady was joined at the *Constitution* by two other extraordinary talents — the best journalists in the state really — both of whom blended gentle humor, sagacity and urbanity with down-home concerns.

Joel Chandler Harris, the illegitimate son of a wandering Irishman, who came to Atlanta from northeast Georgia, was the first of these; Bill Arp, originally from Gwinnett County (whose real name was Charles Henry Smith), the second. Arp's editorials — satires, really — were stories from the countryside (where he preferred to live) and were often given in the form of letters to the editor. His stories were as pungent and picturesque as they were wise, poking fun at everyone and everything. Arp somehow managed to straddle the fence between urban and rural and maintain a striking popularity with readers from both environments. He was good at straddling: "I'm a good Union man, " he wrote, "but I'll bet on Dixie as long as I've got a dollar."

Harris' contributions to the newspaper more often involved straight reporting than satire — though he tried his hand at that too — but his writings for the newspaper have not survived into posterity with the reverence and acclaim that his Uncle Remus stories have. In his spare time, Joel Chandler Harris created the character of Uncle Remus, in part to evoke and celebrate the spirit of the Old South as he understood

Raising the statue to New South spokesman Henry Grady — the statue still stands on Marietta Street in downtown Atlanta, though it was moved west a block in preparation for the 1996 Olympics. *The Atlanta Historical Society, Inc.*

it to have been. In the process, though from a patronizing and sentimental position of perpetuating stereotypes about the "faithful" black slave, Harris managed to preserve an entire collection of traditional African folklore — sayings, beliefs, stories, legends and archetypal figures.

As the state's pre-eminent news source, the *Constitution,* which had been anti-Radical during Reconstruction, was nevertheless identified with big money, big business and industrial interests. Widely distributed throughout the state, "covering Dixie like the dew," as its motto declared, the *Constitution* usually ended up on the opposite side of the political spectrum from the 200-plus local county papers that carried county gossip, news and issues to their readers.

Each local county in metro Atlanta had at least one such newspaper, none of which was serious competition for the *Constitution,* but all of which tested its popularity in the outlying districts. Beginning in 1883, the *Constitution* received its first serious competition from the *Atlanta Journal,* founded in that year. With a tendency toward popularization, and a capacity to scoop the news, the *Journal* quickly caught on with readers in the Atlanta region.

Despite what seemed like a proliferation of newspapers, the state still had a literacy problem. In the 1870s the counties comprising the Atlanta region leapt into the education business, but all of the county and city public school systems, as mandated by the 1868 constitution, were inadequate for the needs of their school populations. Atlanta already had a number of private schools, but built eight grammar schools and two public high schools in 1871.

The grammar schools served both blacks and whites, but high schools served whites only and were separated by gender into a boys high school and a girls high school. At first less than one-third of Atlanta children could attend school — 2,800 of 9,400 school-aged children — because there were not enough seats. Tiny Clayton County, with fewer than 7,000 residents, built two schools in response to the free school act. More populous Gwinnett established 36 schools, two of them for blacks.

Even with this many schools, only half of the school-aged children were accommodated, and the county estimated that 17 more schools were needed, most of them for black children. The school term varied — county to county, often school to school — but it lasted on average about three months. The curriculum varied too, but focused on the basics — spelling, reading, penmanship, arithmetic, English, history and geography. It was not uncommon for the counties to have private schools that offered not only longer, but also frequently

This postcard depicts the Wren's Nest, home of journalist-folklorist Joel Chandler Harris, which is operated today as a house museum. Harris, like his colleagues Henry Grady and Bill Arp at the *Atlanta Constitution,* spoke for the region, never just the city. *The Atlanta Historical Society, Inc.*

more substantial, fare. In Gwinnett, at least, the private-school term extended for six months, twice as long as the public-school term.

The increase in educational opportunities in the Atlanta region was probably the most progressive advance made in the region after the Civil War, especially in the 1880s when Atlanta became a center for public and private higher education. Within one decade Atlanta became home to a half-dozen colleges and universities. Not the first, but probably the most important in terms of public subsidy, was Georgia Tech, established first as a branch of the Athens-based University of Georgia.

Until 1888, when the Georgia Institute of Technology officially opened as an independent school, there had been no real engineering and technical education available in Georgia, only agricultural and mechanical studies at certain A & M schools scattered around the state. Some say that the state pursued the establishment of Georgia Tech in Atlanta because it was an established center for black education and housed Atlanta University, where some mechanical and technological education was already made available to African-Americans. (AU was also open to whites, but few attended except the children of the white faculty members.)

Atlanta University had been founded in 1867 as a freedmen's school and began offering college-level training in 1872. It was joined by Morehouse College, founded in Augusta, which moved to Atlanta in 1879; and Clark College (now Clark-Atlanta University) also founded in 1879. The Atlanta Baptist Female Seminary was founded by two New England missionaries in 1881, located near the other black schools, and was later renamed Spelman College in honor of the mother of its most famous white donor, John D. Rockefeller. In Decatur, the Decatur Female Seminary opened in 1889 to offer the first collegiate education to white women in the region,

Lawrenceville, as it appeared at the turn of the last century, was representative of many of the smaller outlying towns. Notice the unpaved streets. *The Georgia Department of Archives and History*

and its name was changed to Agnes Scott College to honor the mother of its biggest donor, Col. George Scott, who owned fertilizer plants and textile mills in the Decatur suburbs.

There were colleges, public and private grammar schools and a sprinkling of high schools, but there were as yet no kindergartens in Atlanta, nor in the entire state, except for a few parlor schools that operated completely privately. However, following national trends, an energetic local kindergarten movement, with parallel organizations serving both black and white communities, undertook to lobby the state Legislature each term, beginning in the early 1890s, and never gave up.

The establishment of Georgia Institute of Technology in 1888 anchored Atlanta as a center for higher education. The competition between "Tech" and the University in Athens has reigned for more than 100 years. *The Atlanta Historical Society, Inc.*

It took nearly a century: kindergartens were not added to the Georgia curriculum until the early 1980s. But emerging from the Atlanta regional kindergarten movement was another organization, the national PTA (Parent-Teacher Association), founded in 1897, whose two founders were Selena Sloan Butler, a graduate of Spelman College, and Alice McLellan Birney, a native of Marietta.

The Cotton States and International Exposition of 1895 was the region's most glittering moment of glory until the Centennial Olympics a century later. *The Atlanta Historical Society, Inc.*

There were other signs of progress than those in education. Black communities, experiencing the push of segregation and the pull of want, did not wait for the state or local governments to meet their needs. On their own, and often with meager resources, they established churches, schools and health care facilities. Some of the oldest black churches in the region that have been significant community-builders in their own right date from this period after the war, such as Atlanta's Big Bethel AME and Friendship Baptist (whose congregation has roots that predate the war), Thankful Baptist in Decatur, Mt. Carmel in Doraville and St. Paul AME in Lithonia. The AME Church, too, is responsible for the creation of Morris Brown College, which joined the other black schools in Atlanta to help form what was to become the largest collection of historically black colleges in the country.

Black welfare, industrial development, education for all — these spelled progress after the war, progress that was put on public view in Atlanta in the last two decades of the 19th century. In 1881, 1887 and 1895 Atlanta held three major expositions, each designed to showcase the region — its products, progress and industries. They combined entertainment with education, displaying Atlanta's and Georgia's potential toward modern evolution with demonstrations of new technologies (telephones and electricity) and displays of newly manufactured goods and services.

In keeping with traditional county agricultural fairs, the exhibitions also awarded prizes in almost every category from painted china to prime heifers. The resources of the South (not just Georgia or individual counties) were celebrated, as were the abilities of the local populace to live in harmony with their neighbors.

The expositions were not only the strongest expression of the New South creed, they were also the largest nonmilitary public events the Atlanta region had ever seen. The last of these great shows, the 1895 Cotton States and International Exposition, was by far the most ambitious. With a midway full of dancing gypsies and moving picture shows, a main concourse filled with buildings for agriculture and manufacturing, displays from every Southern state, many Northern states and a few foreign countries, and a Woman's Building modeled after the Woman's Building at the Chicago Exposition two years earlier, the fair also managed to feature something that was altogether new and unique — a Negro Building dedicated to the progress the African-Americans had made since the end of the Civil War. When Booker T. Washington, the most famous black educator of his day, came to dedicate the building, thousands heard him promote racial accommodation, a tacit acceptance of the policies of segregation. His speech, which has come to be called the Atlanta Compromise, was music to the ears of the assembled whites who believed that racial harmony had at last been achieved. To the assembled blacks, it bespoke a more cautious optimism, one that, for all its fervor, could not have predicted the disturbance to progress that was about to come to Atlanta.

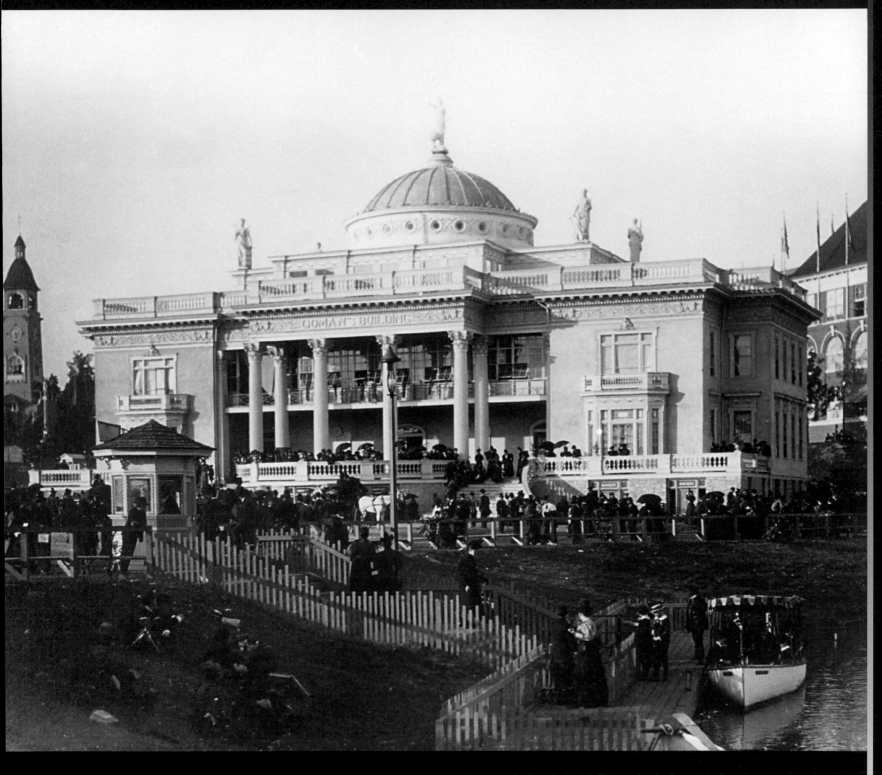

ONE OF THE MOST POPULAR ATTRACTIONS AT THE 1895 EXPO, THE
WOMAN'S BUILDING OFFERED SPECIAL EXHIBITS MADE BY WOMEN
FROM ALL OVER THE COUNTRY, A MODEL KITCHEN, A KINDERGARTEN
AND A SERIES OF DAILY LECTURES AND DEMONSTRATIONS.
THE ATLANTA HISTORICAL SOCIETY, INC.

Chapter 5

THE GROWTH THAT MARKED THE END OF THE 1800s ACCELERATED DURING THE EARLY 1900s; NOTHING IN THE ATLANTA REGION WAS LEFT UNTOUCHED BY THE CHANGES THAT ENSUED, AFFECTING RACE RELATIONS, TRANSPORTATION, THE PHYSICAL SHAPE OF ATLANTA AS A CITY, THE LOCAL ECONOMY AND THE COTTON KINGDOM ITSELF, WHICH HAD SUSTAINED EVERYTHING IN THE SOUTH FOR A CENTURY. THE REGION'S DIRECTIONS FOR THE FUTURE WERE SET IN THE DECADES BEFORE WORLD WAR II, AT WHICH TIME SOME OF ITS MOST NOTABLE — AND SOME REGRETTABLE — HISTORICAL EVENTS ALSO OCCURRED.

Before the Second War

Booker T. Washington's speech at the Cotton States and International Exposition gave the appearance of sanctioning racial segregation, by which the separation of the races became fully legalized and white supremacy the official national practice. The Southern states experimented with an American version of apartheid, within which African-Americans suffered second-class citizenship, which, when it came to voting, was tantamount to no citizenship at all. Blacks could not vote in white primaries at all and could vote in general elections only under the most constrained and restricted of circumstances. There were property standards and literacy tests required of black voters not required of white ones; and the poll tax, universally adopted in the rural counties but only intermittently enforced, precluded the very poorest ones from registering.

Life under Jim Crow meant that public facilities were racially segregated (except, often, for house servants). Erecting duplicate facilities — such as parks — taxed municipal budgets, and many towns did not create anything approaching equity; some did not bother with public amenities at all, especially parks. *The Georgia Department of Archives and History*

There were no black judges or jurors in any of the region's courts, and no black policemen in any of the towns. Everything was segregated — the schools, courthouses, city halls, even the public cemeteries. In the smaller towns, racial etiquette tended to be a bit more relaxed than in a large town like Atlanta where most encounters happened between strangers.

In Atlanta as in other towns, restaurants and hotels were completely segregated, meaning there was no black admittance at all except for the service employees, who were admitted in the rear or side entrances. A few dining places allowed blacks to eat at specified times apart from whites or in the kitchen, and there were black-only eating places

along specified streets in Atlanta — Auburn Avenue, Decatur Street and Mitchell Street.

Public facilities such as the railroad depots contained separate waiting rooms and rest rooms for blacks and whites — the black rooms designed to be inferior in every way to the white rooms. Railroad cars themselves were segregated, with special cars attached to the end of the trains for African-Americans; or, if they chose, black people could sit in the integrated smoking cars. Blacks' eating and sleeping spaces were curtained off from the whites' sections in the cars, but most African-Americans adopted the practice of bringing their own food and sleeping in their seats if they had long train rides.

Atlanta's trolleys were supposed to be segregated, but Atlanta blacks waged a successful boycott against the trolley company in the early 1900s, so the streetcars were effectively the only integrated facilities in the region. Still, they offered their own experience of indignity since blacks had to sit to the rear or give up their seats to whites if the cars were crowded.

The first movie theaters were segregated by section or in their entirety; Atlanta had one all-black movie house, constructed in 1908. Those theaters that did admit blacks forced them to enter by a side door and sit in the most remote seats. The new Atlanta public library that opened in 1902 did not admit blacks, and there were no other black libraries in the region outside of the book collections in the schools. Segregation existed even in the smallest towns in the region. Decatur had its black enclaves, one notably large one focused in the area around Atlanta Avenue. Even outlying Fayette County had its United Benevolent Association, which founded the only school in Fayetteville for African-Americans and owned the hall where the black masonic lodge began meeting in 1911.

African-Americans existed in the white world in service positions, or lived in a world apart. In this all-black environment it evolved quite naturally that

African-Americans would build their own businesses to serve themselves. In the absence of public support, they founded their own charities, schools, welfare agencies, entertainment locales, and as seen earlier, their own churches that tended to foster much of this community development. The majority of blacks continued to serve the white world in skilled and semiskilled occupations in fields familiar to them from antebellum days — domestic service, building trades and transportation — but now greater numbers of them were becoming specialized laborers — railroad porters and postal carriers — and more importantly, professionals such as doctors, lawyers and business entrepreneurs serving a black population.

In the course of "obeying the law," Atlanta, like her sister towns and cities throughout the South, was becoming two cities. The barriers between the two heightened, for without an official forum for exchange, without a shared sense of human dignity across racial lines, suspicions increased and race relations worsened.

Amidst undercurrents of resistance and tension, violent acts and outbursts were not uncommon on the part of either white or black citizens, nor was lynching unknown in the Atlanta region, though the local history books are silent on the

subject. The worst racial incident occurred in 1906 when Atlanta reached the nadir of race relations; ironically the same year Atlanta hosted the annual convention of the recently formed National Negro Business League (founded by Booker T. Washington and others, including leading black businessman Alonzo Herndon of Atlanta).

On September 22, a riot broke out in which perhaps as many as 10,000 whites indiscriminately attacked black people on downtown streets, chasing after them on the streetcars and invading their neighborhoods after dark. The riot occurred after a particularly vicious year of political campaigning in which both candidates for governor called for further disfranchisement of Georgia's black citizens. The newly elected governor Hoke Smith, progressive and controversial, had been especially strong in his comments. Just prior to the riot, his former newspaper, the Atlanta Journal, and the other Atlanta newspapers published a series of articles alleging black rapes of white women and calling for justice. White people were incensed and black people were terrified.

The riot lasted from Saturday to Tuesday, and the state militia had to be called in to restore order. Scores were killed; hundreds were injured (the exact numbers will probably never be

Racial segregation at railroad stations, no matter how small, was the rule in the first half of the 20th century. *Vivian Price*

Atlanta received negative national press coverage after the Race Riot of 1906, in which scores were injured and dozens killed. This photograph appeared in *Harper's Weekly*. The riot was the nadir of regional race relations.
The Atlanta Historical Society, Inc.

A new mercantile establishment in Duluth at the turn of the 20th century — simple brick buildings like this one marked the commercial expansions in towns throughout the region in the early 1900s.
The Georgia Department of Archives and History

As a result of the riot, Atlanta lost some black population; at least, the size of the black community grew much more slowly than it had for half a century. As a percentage of the whole, the black population stayed between 33 and 38 percent until well after World War II. After the 1906 riot, Atlanta black businessmen and residents tended to draw even more tightly to themselves, and a new nucleus of Atlanta's black community grew up along Auburn Avenue, soon to be the very center of black entertainment, culture, business and religion, and renown far beyond Atlanta's borders.

In 1900 Atlanta's black population numbered 35,727 out of a total of 89,872 people, four times the total number of people who had inhabited the city in 1870. In 10 years the total population nearly doubled, rising to 154,839 persons in 1910, the largest and fastest increase since the days of the Civil War. In 10 more years, by 1920, Atlanta had 25 percent of the state's

known). The riot put a black mark on Atlanta's progressivism that stained it for decades to come, and it badly tarnished Atlanta's image as the city earned national and international criticism.

There were many repercussions from the riot. The city of Atlanta built a municipal auditorium and armory (complete in 1909) as future protection, because no assembly area in the city had been large enough for the militia to use when it came to quell the riot. The riot persuaded the city fathers to instigate yet more racial restrictions and tighter control of public drinking, since the riot started on Decatur Street in one of the "divey" parts of town. The riot was the straw on the back of Georgia's resistance to prohibition, and in 1907 the Legislature re-enacted a statewide ban on the sale and manufacture of liquor, an act that only affected the major urban areas, i.e., Atlanta, since most of the rural counties were already dry.

urban population and ranked 38th among the most heavily populated cities in the country.

At no time during the decades before World War II did the city of Atlanta lose total population or face anything but rapid and excessive growth. Municipal services were taxed to the limit and beyond; it seemed that as quickly as the city made improvements, more were needed. Atlanta's pro-business stance kept taxes low, enterprise high and commerce growing, but municipal services at a minimum. For instance, police and fire services, though now professionalized and no longer volunteer, focused on the commercial downtown and intown neighborhoods only. People who lived outside the central wards were underserved. Sanitation services were improved when the city installed a large incinerator to replace the refuse dumps that had been in use since the 1880s, but sewers were still unknown in areas of town outside the business district.

Schools were grossly inadequate; one estimate suggests no more than half the city's children were enrolled in school, and overcrowding was endemic to the system in both black and white facilities. Black schools in number and offerings lagged behind white schools, for until World War II Atlanta was spending three times the money on white schools it spent on black schools. When Georgia finally passed a compulsory attendance regulation in 1920, all schools got a boon in state support and attendance. But when the Depression hit, money for schools everywhere evaporated again. In addition to education, Atlanta had problems with streets, street maintenance and water supply as well.

In the early 1900s, part of Atlanta's physical growth came about through annexation. In 1903 Atlanta added Piedmont Park and the area immediately surrounding it to the city, and in 1910 it annexed territories to the south. Among the south-side communities, Oakland City was added to Atlanta at the request of the residents there, who voted overwhelmingly to join Atlanta, thinking they would get better city services from the larger metropolis than their small enclave could otherwise supply. (Ironically, many years later the old commercial section of Oakland City and several historic residential blocks were demolished by MARTA construction.)

Most of the small towns in the Atlanta region were having their own growing pains, expanding city limits, building new commercial structures, and adding municipal services. Decatur, imitating its larger neighbor to the west, annexed territory that had come to be called "Greater Decatur" — the developed subdivisions south of the railroad tracks and undeveloped land north of the downtown. Fayetteville was large enough to incorporate as a city in 1902, having been town size for decades, and it increased its city limits in 1911. Marietta initiated a bond referendum in 1908 to provide the town with modern

sewers and water lines; with the issue passed, the new services were installed by 1910, but the streets in the main square were still unpaved. Jonesboro installed an electric power plant in 1904 to provide lights in the business district and nearby residences. When Jonesboro sold the municipal power company to the Georgia Power Company a few years later, the city used the money to build its first sewage disposal system and to expand the capacities of its water lines and communal wells. Fayetteville, not to be outdone, installed lamps in its central district — six gas lamps to be exact — to illuminate the blocks occupied by the school, the courthouse and the primary business houses.

Fayetteville also gained its first bank, a sign of the times reflecting prosperity that existed between 1900 and 1920, when cotton prices were high. Fayetteville was still a typical small country town in these early decades of the 20th century, where most of the town's business affairs were controlled by a handful of local families, in this case the Blalocks and the Redwines, who also had extensive land holdings in several of the southern counties as well as businesses in Jonesboro. Active in Georgia politics and with business interests in Atlanta, the Blalocks dominated local affairs.

The Blalocks built the Bank of Fayetteville just after the turn of the century; then a few years later, in 1906, the Redwines incorporated the Farmers and Merchants Bank. Rivalry between the two families over the economic and political future of the two counties and their central cities — Fayetteville and

The neighborhoods around Fort MacPherson, established in the 1880s at its present location, were annexed to Atlanta in 1910.
The Atlanta Historical Society, Inc.

Jonesboro — continued for half a century, sometimes impeding progress, sometimes speeding it on. The addition of a railroad, the Atlanta, Birmingham, and Atlantic to the western part of Fayette County in 1907 introduced a new economic element in Fayette County and did its part to speed up progress along its lines. Tyrone, Brooks and Woolsey had all incorporated by 1912, more testimony to the growth of the small towns in the region resulting from a combination of the railroad and fortunate harvests.

Nearby Jonesboro, which had a reputation for being something of a tough town, performed a cultural turnaround at the turn of the 20th century by closing its bars and saloons. Jonesboro was years ahead of its sister towns in the region, who did not adopt prohibition until Georgia adopted statewide prohibition in 1907, more than a decade before National Prohibition took effect in 1919. The town definitely quieted down. In the early 1900s Jonesboro was prospering, too, and

Despite growth, many small towns still had unpaved streets, as this picture of downtown Roswell indicates. It is easy to see why the advent of the automobile brought a demand for better roads.
The Georgia Department of Archives and History

joined the ranks of the Atlanta commuter towns when it gained a "Dummy" run to the city. Five times a day, Jonesboro citizens could take the train to Atlanta, to work or to shop, and return. Since Jonesboro had no roundhouse, the locomotive drove backward into Atlanta and forward into Jonesboro, where it parked in the center of town. Regular service was congenial, and frequent travelers enjoyed the acquaintanceship of the train crews. So close were passengers to crew, according to one local historian, a single lapse in ticket possession by a regular customer was likely to be overlooked until the next trip. It was not at all uncommon for people to shop in Atlanta once a week or even more often,

indicating the level of dependence the people in the smaller towns, like Jonesboro, had upon the larger city.

Population growth in the region's towns came from natural increase, from continuing in-migration from the rural sections as both blacks and whites relocated from the country to the cities, and, in the city of Atlanta especially, from a trickle of foreign immigration, the largest group of which were Jews from different nations.

The local foreign-born population had stayed at about 3 percent of the total for several decades, fed at first by Irish, Germans and Jews before, during and after the Civil War, then fed in the 1890s by Germans, Russians and East Europeans, and fed now at the turn of the century by Mediterranean immigrants and Sephardic Jews coming from Turkey and Greece. The Atlanta Jewish community was augmented by isolated Jewish families who settled in the outlying region, worked in towns and villages across the region but worshiped in Atlanta. The Jewish population in the region doubled between 1900 and 1910, and in the interim became both a more sophisticated and complex community, with varying levels of orthodoxy observed and different degrees of assimilation accepted among the several sects.

In 1902 the Jews had at least three synagogues to serve the various sects, and in 1904 the old-line German Jews created the Standard Club, the Jewish equivalent of the prestigious Piedmont Driving Club that had been established two decades earlier for the Protestant elite. Anti-Semitism had not been an especially oppressive problem for the Jews, as long as they remained hardworking, unobtrusive and quiet. Many Atlanta area subdivisions had codes barring both blacks and Jews from owning property, but a number of Jewish real estate developers could counter that kind of exclusion with their own property sales.

With the arrival of the conservative Sephardics and the Old World Jews from East Europe who seemed less assimilable than the Jews who had been in the area for several generations, the highly assimilated German Jews determined to set themselves apart from their

Jewish counterparts, a withdrawal that worked only until the entire Jewish population was indicted by association with one of Atlanta's most controversial and dishonorable events. In 1914 a member of the Jewish community, Leo Frank, was accused of a particularly ugly crime, the murder of Mary Phagan, an employee at a pencil factory where he served as the superintendent.

His trial took place amidst the most vitriolic anti-Semitism Atlanta had yet seen. Frank was convicted on the testimony of a black man (the first time in Georgia history) and circumstantial evidence. Gov. Slaton, at his own political peril, commuted Frank's guilty verdict (from death to life in prison) and had Frank removed to the state penitentiary 75 miles away at Milledgeville. In 1915, however, a group of well-organized vigilantes had Frank removed from his cell, took him to Marietta, where Mary Phagan had lived, and lynched him at Frey's Gin near her old neighborhood. Frank's brutal demise left the Jewish community intimidated for the first time in Atlanta history, and many Jews left. Jews across the nation, convinced of Frank's innocence, were concerned enough to reinvigorate the Anti-Defamation League of B'nai B'rith.

In a wholly different act of post-lynching assertiveness, a group of area citizens met in secret in Atlanta, burned a cross atop Stone Mountain and revived the Ku Klux Klan. Prior to this time the Klan had always been identified with the countryside, but now it expanded into the city. Headquartered in Atlanta, the new Klan had active members across the country. Locally, there were active members of the Klan from throughout the region, none more visible than the mayor of Atlanta, and none more active than the members of the Venable family, who owned the property on which Stone Mountain stood and the granite quarries associated with it.

In the same year that Leo Frank was lynched, members of the United Daughters of the Confederacy (UDC), under the inspiration of Mrs. C. Helen Plane, conceived of a plan for a monumental carving on the side of the mountain to rival Mount Rushmore in the

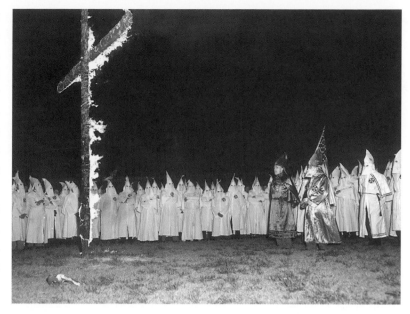

The Ku Klux Klan, revived after the 1913 murder trial of Leo Frank, made its headquarters in Atlanta for many decades. Many public officials belonged openly to the Klan in the 1920s, but later (as when this photo was taken), membership reverted to clandestine status. *The Atlanta Historical Society, Inc.*

Dakotas. The UDC hired the same carver, Gutzon Borglum, to carve Stone Mountain and shared with him their ideas for a carving a records archive in the mountain, an amphitheater on the grounds next to the carving, and a resort to draw Americans from all over the country. There were delays and Borglum did not begin carving until 1923. Borglum, whose views were either too supportive of the KKK or not supportive enough, did not last and was replaced by Augustus Lukeman, who also was unable to complete the carving. It took more than 50 years before the monumental undertaking was declared done; the work suffered postponements from changing plans and priorities, controversies over ownership, the Depression (the WPA was not supportive of the monument), and World War II. The state of Georgia purchased the land in 1952 for the park that now exists at the mountain, and the carving was completed in 1972.

When Gutzon Borglum started work on his carving, Stone Mountain was more accessible to the region's citizenry than it ever had been before. Since the 1840s, Georgians could travel to the state's most popular attraction by horse, wagon and railroad, but now in the 1920s it was accessible by trolley direct from the center of Atlanta. Atlanta had had some kind of streetcar service at its disposal since the years immediately following the Civil War, when horse-drawn passenger wagons kept regular routes and schedules between the Atlanta business center and the residential neighborhoods. In the 1880s certain close-in suburbs, such as West End and Inman Park, were connected by trolley lines to Atlanta a decade or more before they were annexed to the city. Joel Hurt, the creative developer of Inman Park, who planned not only subdivision, but also a skyscraper connected to it by rail, electrified his car line, thereby creating one of the first electric streetcar lines in the country.

There were 16 different trolley lines founded in and around Atlanta between 1866 and 1889, which mushroomed to three dozen by the turn of the century. In 1902, in what some have described as the Second Battle of Atlanta, the many different lines merged into just two, and H.Y. Atkinson of the Georgia Power and Electric Company managed to consolidate them under his control, defeating Joel Hurt, his primary competitor, in the process. By then, a spider web of streetcar lines connected destinations in the Atlanta region within a six-mile radius of downtown, competing successfully with the commuter railroad trains.

The village of Stone Mountain got a boost from the mountain-carving activities between 1912 and 1928. The creation of today's attraction waited for state initiatives after World War II. The carving was finally completed in 1972.
DeKalb Historical Society

Atlantans had frequent, quick and cheap connections to Decatur, East Lake, West View cemetery (further west on the West End), Piedmont Park (where the 1895 Exposition had been held), Lakewood Park (where the agricultural fairs were held), Fort McPherson in South Atlanta, the soldiers home southeast of the city, and Brookwood (a new garden suburb to the north). By 1920 the region hosted the largest inter-urban street railway system in the Southeast, with the longest stretch of tracks going to Marietta, and the second longest to Stone Mountain.

Also connected were Oglethorpe University, Camp Gordon (the federal army camp set up in World War I

near Chamblee), Inman Yards (the largest railroad yards in the region), Hapeville and College Park to the south of the city and Emory University in the northeast (which had relocated to Atlanta from Oxford, Georgia, in 1916). By 1920 Atlanta region streetcars were carrying more than 50 million passenger trips a year. The trolley lines provided access between the working-class subdivisions and the industrial areas as well as the downtown commercial sections; the primary textile mills were connected to the routes, as were the railroad shops and yards at Mechanicsville and Pittsburgh in south Atlanta. Decatur had three trolley lines that came into town including the Decatur "Main," which followed a new street, Ponce de Leon, straight into heart of the town. Nearly half of Decatur's older residences date from the first three decades of the 20th century, a direct testimony to the town's commuter advantages as a regional community.

The trolley lines invited residential and commercial development wherever the tracks led. Stops along the trolley lines, like stops along the old railroad lines, evolved into postal stations, subdivided communities, sometimes full towns. Thus, on the Marietta inter-urban line, notable residential improvements appeared among the stretches of woods and fields, including Fair Oaks, Mozley, Smyrna, Gilmore and Oakdale. Transportation ease provided one strong incentive for development, but other growth factors were at work throughout the region as well. Marietta and Cobb County, for example, benefited not only from the trolley traffic but also from the fact that the Georgia Power Company, which owned the trolley lines, chose the southern portion of Cobb County to locate the power installations that were to produce the electricity to run the trolleys.

In 1904 the first large-scale hydroelectric power plant in the Atlanta region was built at Morgan Falls on the Chattahoochee River, and expansions to the plant extended into the 1920s. Cobb became a veritable center of electric power production in 1930, when Plant Atkinson, a coal-generated power station was added to what was already in place. Plant Atkinson was to provide electrical energy for much of the Atlanta region and parts of north Georgia. The damming of creeks to create Lake Allatoona, the first project by the Army Corps of Engineers in the Atlanta region, demonstrated yet more potential for electrical energy in the region. It also promised greater flood control and improved water supply for the surrounding area.

Flood control was a welcome relief to some of the county's farmers, but the availability of electrical current far exceeded any local demand for it at this time either in Cobb County, or in the fast-growing city of Atlanta. The distribution systems were simply not well developed enough yet, and customers were few, especially in the region's rural sections, where there were still no electrical connections at all. Local residents, unused to the idea of introducing electricity into their homes, which seemed dangerous, were slow to benefit from electrification.

Most of the electrical power that was available went into the central cities — Marietta and Atlanta. Outlying areas had to wait. With new hydroelectric water impoundments that could be also utilized for recreation purposes, however, Cobb Countians experienced a resurgence in what had been a boon to the county before the Civil War — tourism. New lakeside resort environments, with endless shorelines and inland beaches to exploit, joined the county's mineral springs — Blue Springs, Lithia Springs and Powder Springs among others — in enticing vacationers, visitors, summer transplants and weekend escapees to settle in for awhile.

Not all the growth in the region outside Atlanta proper came from the development of trains, trolley lines or hydroelectric projects. War again spurred growth in the Atlanta area, just as it had in the Civil War, especially in the communities on the north side of the region. Chamblee had been a typical, small

Map of trolley routes in the Atlanta region

"Greater Atlanta" Trolley Lines

agricultural community miles from Atlanta with a blacksmith shop next to the train depot, a dry goods store, and little else when World War I brought an overnight increase in its population and physical facilities. There the U.S. Army established a large cantonment called Camp Gordon, in the midst of corn and cotton fields, where at the rate of eight buildings a day, more than 2,000 acres were transformed into barracks. In a few months the camp had 150 buildings and a direct connection to downtown Atlanta via the Peachtree Street streetcar line that had been extended past Oglethorpe University to the army camp. The wartime population of the camp, with 30,000 recruits, was many times greater than the population of the town ever had been (or would be for decades).

The effects on Chamblee were instant and significant; in a few months the one store-village grew into a budding town with 40 stores, movie theaters and hotels. The tract for the camp had been selected in June of 1917, the buildings were constructed that summer and the camp opened up in August 1917, staying busy throughout the war and processing more than 150,000 soldiers. (The same location served military purposes in World War II as a navy hospital and now is the site of the Peachtree DeKalb airport.) Chamblee's experience elicited the most spectacular growth during World War I, but there was more. Cobb County benefited from Chamblee's expansion during the war, since a large artillery camp was built there near Blackjack Mountain to serve the soldiers in training at Camp Gordon. The Cobb County camp covered nearly 500,000 acres of woodlands and fallow fields.

Between the beginning of the century in 1900 and the entrance of the United States into World War I in 1917, the entire Atlanta region experienced a prosperous boom. Cotton prices were high, cotton markets were good and the national economy was healthy. The region, especially its agricultural parts, benefited from the "high cotton" years in one respect certainly: the higher the price of cotton, the more cotton farmers planted. Farmers in the region produced more than cotton, of course, but the average farm produced fewer bushels of corn, oats and wheat than it did bales of cotton.

In the first decade of the 20th century, the value of the average Georgia farm doubled even as the average size shrank from just over 100 acres to just under 100 acres. In 1909 cotton production in the state of Georgia reached an all time high — 2 million bales — second only to Texas in quantity. Farms were becoming more efficient, utilizing machines to do the work formerly done by field hands, even though not every farmer owned every one of the new machines. It was common for farmers in the same family or community to share a single thresher, moving the thresher from one farm to another and the work crew with it. The historian for Fayette County reports that "Threshing Day," the day the machine arrived, was a big day on the farm when the women got up early to cook for the crew, and all hands and family members turned out to help.

The cotton boom overrode all other farm successes, though there were others. Those farmers near the railroad lines that took advantage of their access to Atlanta could prosper with truck farming, as did many in Cobb, DeKalb and Clayton counties especially. Among the truck-farm products produced before World War I were cow peas, peanuts, Irish potatoes, sweet potatoes, honey, milk, butter, cheese, poultry and eggs. Sometimes the counties had specialties, such as dairy products in DeKalb and sweet potatoes

The metropolitan region was held together in the early 20th century by a network of trolleys with some of the longest streetcar lines in the Southeast. Local bus service still follows many of the old trolley routes.
The Atlanta Historical Society, Inc.

in Clayton. There were 33 dairies in Chamblee alone, and DeKalb County produced more milk than any other Georgia county, enjoying a reputation as one of the largest dairy producers in the entire South.

The rural counties were not notably rich at this time, though the farm residents' needs were met. Those who were wealthy usually had interests in addition to farming, such as merchandising, cotton brokering, small-town banking, or occasionally, even moonshining. State officials pushed for increasing diversification, fearing that over-dependency on cotton made Georgia farmers vulnerable to declines in the world cotton market. Officials also feared the arrival of a small insect, the boll weevil, making its way from Mexico into Texas and gradually across the Southern states. Before it arrived in Georgia, World War I put an end to the best cotton markets the South had yet seen.

The war reduced overseas shipments of cotton, and so England, the South's largest cotton buyer, began to turn to other growing areas, to India especially. The embargo on cotton during the war lowered cotton prices and presaged a disaster in cotton growing for the local farmers and farmers throughout the state. The boll weevil arrived in Georgia in 1913 but did not do its worst damage until 1919 and 1920, wiping out several years of cotton production. In a few years, between 1918 and 1922, Georgia's cotton production dropped from an annual level of 2 million bales to less than half that — 725,000 bales. In 1925 agricultural woes increased as the

(Both photos) The cantonment at Camp Gordon outside Chamblee went up almost "overnight" and turned the village of Chamblee into a budding town. Military activities from Camp Gordon stretched into the woods and fields of Cobb County.
DeKalb Historical Society

The Atlanta Historical Society, Inc.

driest year on record parched crops and burned fields. Thousands left the country for the city, many simply abandoning their lands. Many blacks left Georgia altogether, bypassing its cities, including Atlanta, for an unknown future in the industrial markets of the North and Northeast. In five years, the farm population of Georgia dropped by more than 300,000 people.

Merchants in the small towns suffered as their customers disappeared and their small local banks went bankrupt. The rural sections of the Atlanta region emptied out, and Atlanta, the city, grew at their expense. All the local counties except Fulton lost population in the 1920s, while the city of Atlanta experienced another momentous increase in the number of people who called it home.

Scottdale Mills in DeKalb County was the last of the local textile mills to be established in the Atlanta region. Scottdale village was both industrial and rural in its character; the mill closed in 1970 but the village remains.
DeKalb Historical Society

Between 1920 and 1930 another 70,000 people were added to the residents inside the city limits, and as many more in the closest suburban subdivisions. However, Atlanta was also undermined by the catastrophe on the farms, as it was unprepared for the in-migration of so many hungry, poor, often illiterate, industrially untrained people. Rich's department store tried to help keep the farmers on their land, trapped as they were by poverty, by purchasing hundreds of bales of cotton from them, warehousing them for sale at some more propitious time. Still the rural in-migrants came; there were not enough jobs for them. Atlanta was recovering from its own ills, among them the global flu epidemic of 1918, which killed thousands of people, and one year earlier, the worst fire the city had ever experienced, even more costly than the burning of Atlanta during the Civil War.

The Great Fire of 1917, as it has come to be called, began on a hot May day and destroyed more than 50 square blocks of city property, about 4,000 homes and other buildings, and displaced 10,000 people. Perhaps no single incident speaks louder of the inadequacies of Atlanta's municipal services than this incident, which required fire equipment from communities in the surrounding counties, from south Georgia, Alabama and Tennessee to bring it under control. Even with this additional assistance, the fire burned out of control for four days. True to its sense of philanthropy,

Rich's department store extended credit to the victims and donated some extra stock for their relief.

The fire reshaped 50 blocks of the city near the downtown, which itself had been transformed from the appearance it had at the beginning of the century. The first alteration came when the railroad station moved away from the old center of town out to the "outskirts" on the edge of downtown. In 1903 the railroad companies joined forces to build a new terminal, large in size and worthy of Atlanta's voluminous rail traffic. At the height of railroad traffic in the 1920s, Terminal Station served more than 300 trains a day with 10,000 passengers on board, some who stopped, many who passed through on their way to other locations. It was possible to get a train from Atlanta to anywhere in the United States.

The terminal was a few blocks from the old downtown, and a jitney or trolley ride from the new downtown. Commercial development in the early 20th century "jumped" across the old railroad tracks. The center of retailing followed, moving from its original location at the intersection of Whitehall and Alabama Street to Five Points, and from there, it began expanding north following the Peachtree Street corridor to the city limits at Brookwood Station, the first suburban railroad station in Atlanta, built in 1917.

The look of the downtown changed enormously as skyscrapers loomed on the horizon. Atlanta built its first skyscraper in 1897, the "flatiron" building, built before the flatiron building in New York, but made notable by sharing the nickname. After the flatiron building came the Candler Building, the Grant building, the Healey Building, the William-Oliver and many others, most of them demolished in the wake of even larger constructions in the late century. By 1940 Atlanta had more commercial office space than any other city its size, bringing Charles Palmer, a local developer and friend of Franklin Roosevelt, to declare that "office buildings were to Atlanta what furniture was to Grand Rapids or automobiles to Detroit."

A new city arose, a white city — white, from the marble and granite stone used in the buildings, taller and more elegant in its way, and different from the red-colored, low-rise brick commercial district that preceded it. It was white, too, in another way, since downtown Atlanta had become two downtowns; one for white people, centered at Five Points and stretching north along Peachtree Street, and one for black people, centered on Auburn Avenue and stretching east from Peachtree Street. There on Auburn Avenue were churches, office towers, real estate businesses, insurance companies, funeral parlors, restaurants, hotels, banks, newspaper offices, drugstores and theaters — an entire commercial district of its own — attached to what was then the most elite residential neighborhood in black Atlanta.

Atlanta was actually overbuilt for the period. It had offices but not businesses to fill them, laborers but not jobs enough to occupy them. Prompted by the influx of new jobless residents, the loss of developmental monies to the postwar Florida Land Boom, and the threatened exodus of Georgia talent to the North, the Atlanta business community undertook a large-scale promotional campaign called "Forward Atlanta," aimed at getting jobs and bringing new business to the region. Forward Atlanta lasted four years in two separate campaigns and stressed the region's transportation connections and its abilities to distribute goods and services throughout the Southeast.

Through advertising and direct appeals, the Chamber of Commerce asked every national business it could one question, "can you get along without an Atlanta branch?" The businesses responded. Nabisco, Sears-Roebuck, Southern Railway, and General Motors along with more than 700 other corporations built Atlanta branch offices or new independent facilities. Nearly 20,000 jobs were created by them, worth nearly $35 million in the regional payroll. Local counties piggy-backed promotional efforts on to the Forward Atlanta thrust: "If you wish to engage in farming, come to Gwinnett," invited one bit of publicity, "Atlanta stands at our front door and will buy every product of the farm. If you wish to establish a new industry, come to Gwinnett. Competent and intelligent labor is plentiful. If you wish to build a new home, come to Gwinnett. We are a friendly people."

Friendly, yes, and increasingly mobile, for nothing had greater impact on the region, the shape of its flagship city, and the relationship of the many regional parts to the whole than the automobile. The first automobiles made their appearance in the region before 1905; in 1909 Atlanta hosted an automobile show at the newly opened armory, and both newspapers sponsored automobile rallies and races. Asa Candler, the Coca-Cola mogul, built a racetrack south of the city where the wealthy could race their four-wheeled, horseless carriages. (Often, not they themselves, but their chauffeurs did the actual racing.)

Because of the relative prosperity in the region at the time, automobiles sold well, spawning an increase

Still the worst disaster in Atlanta history, the 1917 fire burned 50 blocks of Atlanta residences and displaced nearly 4,000 people. Fire-code restrictions changed throughout the region as a result of this fire. *The Georgia Department of Archives and History*

in automobile-related businesses and a widespread interest in more roads, better roads and safer roads. The local gas station made its appearance, as did dealerships, repair shops and driving schools. There were even local automobile manufacturers such as Hanson, White Star and John Smith; and the Ford Motor Company built a factory in Hapeville in 1915, assuring a good market regionally for the Model-T. The streets were crowded with a mix of vehicles — wagons with horses and mules, electric trolleys, bicycles, private automobiles, motorized and horse-drawn jitneys, and horse-drawn police and fire wagons. (Fire and police services were not fully motorized until after World War I.)

In 1916 there were approximately 6,000 cars registered in Fulton County, and the same year the state highway commission began to seek federal support for highway construction. By the mid-1920s there were more than 45,000 cars in Atlanta and the city was now connected by highways to the other major cities in Georgia — Savannah by way of Macon, and Brunswick by way of Savannah. In 1929 the Dixie Highway opened and ran from the Great Lakes to the Florida Keys, through Atlanta and through Marietta, Smyrna, Jonesboro and towns in between, roughly following the W & A line from the Tennessee border to Atlanta and the Central of Georgia line from Atlanta to Macon. (Remnants of the old highway today can be traced along

state Route 3 and U.S. Highway 41, but have largely been surpassed by the interstate system and I-75.)

The rural areas in the region had to wait for paved roads and highways except for what local initiatives could accomplish. It was 1934 before Fayette County had its first paved roads, the route from Fayetteville to Jonesboro, joined four years later by Highway 54 from Fayetteville to Newnan. Then, there were no more roads paved in Fayette County until after World War II. The first paving project in Gwinnett County covered the road from Lawrenceville to the DeKalb County line in the 1930s, but no more than 100 of the 1,500 miles of road in the county were paved before the war. It was a little better for Cobb and Clayton counties, which lay on the path of the Dixie Highway. Cobb saw the opening of Bankhead Highway in 1924, the year after the Dixie was officially opened. Cobb had 1,500 miles of public roads, but only a few of them were paved — a section of the Dixie between Smyrna and the Chattahoochee River, the principal streets in Marietta and not much else.

The presence of so many automobiles and motorized wagons in downtown Atlanta created many accidents between cars and trolleys, cars and trains, cars and people, cars and horses, and cars and other cars. The problem that had existed in downtown Atlanta since its inception, namely, the pollution and danger of the trains coming through, was exacerbated by the number of cars. The City Council finally acted, adopting an idea that surfaced in 1909, called the Bleckley Plan, to cover the railroad tracks and raise other vehicular traffic above the grade level of the trains. The consequence of their decisions produced one of Atlanta's most notable features, the 16 blocks of viaducts that now create Underground Atlanta and a number of lower-level parking decks in the old downtown. Original Alabama Street and old Whitehall (Peachtree Street SW) disappeared under

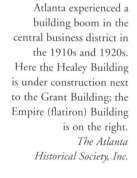

Atlanta experienced a building boom in the central business district in the 1910s and 1920s. Here the Healey Building is under construction next to the Grant Building; the Empire (flatiron) Building is on the right.
The Atlanta Historical Society, Inc.

new streets, and addresses had to be changed to distinguish between the accessible upper stories from the now hidden, below-ground original first stories.

Confirming Atlanta's many changes, its centrality to the Southeast, and its growing importance as a regional city within the United States was the development of the municipal airport. Candler Field was purchased by the city in 1929; it had formerly been a race track where the rich and playful raced their automobiles.

Then Alderman William B. Hartsfield encouraged lease of racetrack for use as airport; the city paid for some improvements including a weather station and a post office. For awhile the racecars and the airplanes shared the space; the center of the field was used for stunt flying, and the tracks by the cars. In 1928 the federal airmail route to New York was given to Atlanta over Birmingham, initiating the beginning of Atlanta's runaway development over the steel city, which hitherto had run neck-and-neck with development in Atlanta. Pitcairn Aviation opened the mail run, a predecessor to Eastern Airlines, which ran a successful New York to Atlanta passenger shuttle for decades, until Eastern went bankrupt and the New York shuttle was acquired by Atlanta-based Delta Air Lines, which had located to Atlanta in 1941.

Atlanta's pro-business stance tended to keep taxes low and services minimal in the city. Throughout the region, not just in the city of Atlanta, paved streets and working sewers were a rarity. When the nation began to suffer the effects of the economic Depression of the 1930s, the region came to a standstill. Georgia and its sister Southern states had already been depressed for more than a decade when the stock market fell in 1929.

The results locally were horrendous: building projects were abandoned or (at best) postponed; local banks went into bankruptcy in all the local towns, not just in Atlanta; private charities were overwhelmed

with the needs that none of the municipal and county governments could meet. It was not unknown for the homeless to die in the streets. Local businesses failed, and many never revived. There were no more skyscrapers built in downtown Atlanta until the 1950s. Even among local entertainments, which are usually more resistant to recession, the Atlanta (white) baseball team, the Crackers, went into receivership, and the Fox Theater closed for a season. Local libraries stayed open only with staff members subsidized by the federal government. The public library in Lawrenceville opened in 1936 with one staff member supplied by the city and one supplied by the federal government. Others were not so lucky. Typical was the Margaret Mitchell Library in Fayetteville, which was built in the 1920s but closed entirely during the Depression, though the building was preserved by the New Deal's Works Progress Administration.

The drop in production in the countryside had ironic repercussions in transportation. Even as the WPA was building roads and paving highways, the Interstate Commerce Commission was approving the elimination of railroad tracks in the region because of reduced traffic and trucking on the rails, caused in part by the increase in automobile and motorized traffic and trucking. Local Campbell County, with unpeopled

The arrival of the automobile changed the face of the Atlanta region as it did every other metropolitan area in America, perhaps a bit more slowly than some but no less dramatically. Here the Aycock family of Atlanta poses in front of the First Christian Church in their White Steamer in 1909.
The Atlanta Historical Society, Inc.

farms, no major industries, and without railroads, was so "pore and needy" by its own assessment, that it could not maintain a county government and petitioned to become part of Fulton County; in 1932 the two merged.

When Franklin Delano Roosevelt was elected to the presidency of the United States, he breathed fire and hope into the South. A part-time resident of Georgia, whose Warm Springs spa helped not only his polio condition but also that of hundreds of others, Roosevelt knew firsthand what hardships the South was experiencing, and called what he saw the nation's "number one" problem. His New Deal programs for rural electrification, soil conservation and loans for farm purchase came directly from his familiarity with the problems in rural Georgia.

The Electric Membership Corporation brought power to rural areas in the outlying region, though it could not stop the exodus from the land. The Farm Security Administration could make farm improvements possible, and the Agricultural Adjustment Administration could subsidize food crops and soil building measures, but no agency could increase the

trade in cotton. New Deal agencies ran county health departments, something new for those counties (like Gwinnett) that had no hospitals. Nor were cities left out of the efforts to support local welfare. Atlanta gained sewers, roads, parks, library expansions, work on the airport, hospitals and more.

In Atlanta Roosevelt personally dedicated Techwood Homes, the first federally funded housing project in the United States, and oversaw the model farms at Pine Mountain Valley near his home at Warm Springs, which introduced new techniques for raising chickens and cattle and whole new crops to the region, such as grapes. The New Deal was tailor-made for Georgia, and the whole state gained much from it.

In the midst of the New Deal programs, National Prohibition was repealed in 1933, leaving the states to deal with the question of alcohol as they chose. Alone in the region, Atlanta commercial interests had opposed Prohibition as not being good for business, and now the city could act. Bootleg whiskey was a regular accompaniment brought to Georgia Tech football games, and Atlanta had one of the highest arrest rates for drunkenness of any major city in the United States,

The Atlanta skyline of the late 1920s shows the red brick buildings of the old central city and the new marble and granite skyscrapers of the early 20th century. This view and the downtown remained relatively unchanged until the mid-1950s.
Riley Hayes

and it was common knowledge that the police were involved in profiteering with the moonshiners and bootleggers. Prohibition had not worked except to give the city a bad name. Atlanta passed a law to allow beer even before the state adopted its new local option policy in 1934. The state's foot-dragging had the effect of perpetuating bootlegging in the many counties that remained dry. Corn whiskey continued to be manufactured in the region in dry counties. What was good for the moral sensibility, it seemed, was also good for the local pocketbooks. During the Depression at least one Atlanta regional dry county, Fayette, sustained its depressed economy largely through the production and distribution of moonshine.

A c. 1940 view of the airport, originally called Candler Field and purchased by the city of Atlanta in 1929 — over the years the airport has crowded the neighboring cities of Hapeville, College Park and East Point. *The Atlanta Historical Society, Inc.*

By the end of the 1930s, Atlanta had gained its place in the world as an important regional city, known for housing branch offices of national businesses and hosting national conventions for both black people and white organizations. In 1939 the world Baptist Congress convened in Atlanta, whose crowds were so

The first federally funded housing project in the United States, Techwood Homes was located near Georgia Tech and matched during the 1930s by University Homes — Techwood for whites, University Homes for blacks. Techwood was demolished for the Olympics. *The Atlanta Historical Society, Inc.*

large, the meetings had to be held in Ponce de Leon ballpark where the Crackers usually played.

Nothing, however, put Atlanta on the map so brilliantly as did *Gone With the Wind*, Margaret Mitchell's "little" novel about the Old South. The book became a runaway best seller, making its author retreat for the rest of her life from the notoriety and public acclaim. When the movie version appeared, almost twice as long as other movies of its generation, the American public went nuts, and David O. Selznick had the biggest hit of all time on his hands. The movie previewed in Atlanta, appropriately enough, and the event was the brightest, most celebrated of the 20th century with the possible exception of the 1996 Centennial Olympics.

Atlanta in 1940, prior to World War II, was a city of more than 302,000 people with a well-developed metropolitan district surrounding it that contained an additional 200,000 residents. The important satellites lay in Fulton, DeKalb, Clayton and Cobb counties, which had the best transportation connections to the capital city. The city lacked the density of Northern cities because there were no natural obstacles to its growth — no mountains, rivers, seacoasts or canyons to hold it back, only the surrounding countryside. Surrounded by wooded tracts and arable fields, the city had a decidedly country look to it and a rural cast to its citizenry, so many of whom had been born in the country and newly arrived. The "flavor" of Atlanta was obvious from the fact that in many of its neighborhoods, regardless of income level, residents grew large vegetable gardens and kept chickens and cows. (Even the governor, who lived in fashionable Ansley Park, kept a cow and menagerie of other farm animals.)

The Atlanta city limits were small compared to the developed district surrounding it. Six miles from the center, Buckhead, which began as a weekend retreat community, was beginning to be settled by the wealthy whites, who were pushed out of the downtown Atlanta area by the expanding commercialism and pulled into Buckhead's wooded subdivisions by their attractiveness, the availability of trolley routes nearby, the easy automobile access and the distance from the dirt and crowds of the city.

ATLANTA NOVELIST MARGARET MITCHELL WROTE A "LITTLE BOOK" ABOUT THE OLD SOUTH, WHICH BECAME THE BIGGEST MOTION PICTURE OF THE MID-20TH CENTURY. ITS PREMIERE STILL STANDS AS ATLANTA'S BIGGEST SOCIAL EVENT — EVER.
THE ATLANTA HISTORICAL SOCIETY, INC.

Chapter 6

If the story of the Atlanta region for its first century was a story of the region keeping up with the city, the story of the last 50 years has brought the reverse; the city today keeps up with a growing region. Since World War II the Atlanta region has become a seamless union of suburban counties — tied together by an extensive highway system — that have far more in common with each other now than ever before. Atlanta's success in promoting itself has brought the entire region with it into the spotlight, especially in 1996 as the world watched Atlanta host its most spectacular event to date — the Centennial Olympic Games.

Before the Millennium

When the United States entered an already raging European war by undertaking battles across both oceans, the city of Atlanta was a sleepy, overgrown, Southern country town with an undisputed reputation as the South's premier distribution center and the home of Scarlett O'Hara. The Atlanta region constituted a close nucleus focused on Fulton, DeKalb and Cobb counties all connected by an extensive trolley system that bound Marietta, Stone Mountain and Decatur to the central business district of Atlanta. Beyond that, Atlanta was within commuter distance of Jonesboro, Lawrenceville, East Point and other points within a 20- to 30-mile radius. The regional territories, even the city, were marked by low-density developments, where small town centers sprinkled themselves across an endless sea of woodlands, abandoned fields and active farms. Each of the central metropolitan counties was still largely rural. The cities and small towns occupied very little actual geographic space, but their expanding transportation and communication networks spelled changes in the air. There were plenty of cars at this point, for example, but the region had not yet become auto-dependent in the way it was after the war. The first indication that the region's lifelong dependence on rails was about to subside emanated from the replacement of the electric street railways with "trackless" trolleys. These electric buses covered the same routes as the trolleys and used the same power sources, but rolled through towns on wheels instead of tracks. The conversion began in 1937, but was not completed until 1949 when the last regular trolley ran, well after the war, when the change was barely noticeable among the myriad other projects of the post-war bustle.

Most historians of Atlanta agree that what the New Deal did not accomplish for Atlanta (for the South as a whole) World War II did — in the way of modernizing, revitalizing and nationalizing the economic base. The citizens in the region suffered the same losses and deprivations that Americans across the country felt from the war, to be sure, but their community leapt forward with the changes in infrastructure that the war provided in a way that was admired by other Southern cities and even envied by some.

The first thing the war did was to provide greatly increased material capability in the form of military facilities and factories carrying out defense contracts. Among the bases, Fort McPherson, which had dwindled in activity since World War I, became the largest processor of soldiers as an important army induction and training center. The army established an enormous new supply base and General Depot in Conley, Georgia, at what is now Fort Gillem, which opened just before the bombing of Pearl Harbor. The federal coffers funded expansion of the rail yards in Clayton County and the Atlanta municipal airport in Hapeville, under the umbrella of supporting strategic resources. Meanwhile, the Navy revived the old World War I Camp Gordon site in Chamblee into a flight training station, spending $3 million on hangars and runways. Lawson Veterans Hospital took over a portion of land on the same grounds, which at its peak had a population of 10,000 people, including patients, staff and some German POWs. The most important installation, however, from the standpoint of its value for regional employment, was the Bell Aircraft plant in Cobb County. In 1940 Cobb had a population of 37,000; it also had some

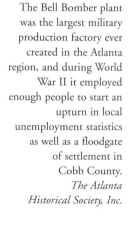

The Bell Bomber plant was the largest military production factory ever created in the Atlanta region, and during World War II it employed enough people to start an upturn in local unemployment statistics as well as a floodgate of settlement in Cobb County. *The Atlanta Historical Society, Inc.*

forward-thinking politicians and a connection with Gen. Lucius Clay, who proposed the Atlanta region as the appropriate spot for a major military installation. In 1941 Cobb County purchased 600 acres for a regional airport, but military use took precedence over the local use during the war and the property was turned over to the federal government. The Army Corps of Engineers built Rickenbacker Field on the premises. The army moved its airfield, which had been located for more than a decade at the Atlanta municipal airport, to this site in Cobb County, later to become Dobbins Air Force Base. On another part of the acreage, Bell Aircraft leased space for a factory. There, near Marietta, a municipality with barely 10,000 residents, some 30,000 workers cooperated to build B-29s for the Army air corps, beginning in 1943. In two short years the plant produced 700 bombers. The Bell Bomber plant offered the first viable nonfarm, large-scale, year-round employment in Cobb County and at the same time functioned as the largest wartime employer in the Atlanta region. Service on the Atlanta-Marietta interurban trolley line quadrupled during the war. The expansions at Bell, Fort McPherson and elsewhere netted an immediate 50,000 increase in the regional population, 29,000 of them in the city of Atlanta alone, forcing a housing crisis of huge proportions.

The impacts of the war were not limited to physical changes. As a transportation and supply center, Atlanta carried the same high value as a potential target, or so the locals believed, that it had during the Civil War. In addition to living with an elevated sense of paranoia, residents met situations that challenged them during the course of their daily lives — rationing, gas and food shortages, housing shortages, blackout drills, entertainment curfews, and scrap, rubber, metal and bond drives. The most impressive bond drive in Atlanta occurred on the heels of the sinking of the USS Atlanta at Guadalcanal in 1942, barely a few months after the

ship had been christened in 1941, with Margaret Mitchell doing the honors. Intentionally scrapped by the Navy so the ship would not come into Japanese hands, its loss became a rallying cry for Atlanta patriotism. Challenged by local businessmen and symbolically spearheaded by the authoress herself, the people of the Atlanta region and their compatriots throughout Georgia rose to the occasion in an outpouring of loyalty and national pride. Challenged to raise $35 million, the

Margaret Mitchell christened the first *USS Atlanta* to go to sea during World War II, which was scuttled at Guadalcanal. She also christened its replacement ship, a gift to the United States from the people of Georgia, in 1944. *The Atlanta Historical Society, Inc.*

citizenry raised $165 million, enough for the federal government to build more than two ships to replace the one lost. When the next USS Atlanta was christened in 1944, Margaret Mitchell again raised the ribboned champagne bottle against the hull. The size of the gift to the war effort was impressive enough, but the fact that the money was raised in little over four months suggests the powerful feelings underlying the campaign.

The Atlanta region was exposed to a multitude of new wartime influences, many positive, some not. Retail trade increased, which had languished during the 1930s, but venereal disease, hitherto politely hidden, reached epidemic proportions, directly attributable to the increased, open military presence in the region. The state of Georgia received more servicemen for training than any other state in the union save Texas. Atlanta's share of the numbers was considerable, since

Highway map
in 2000

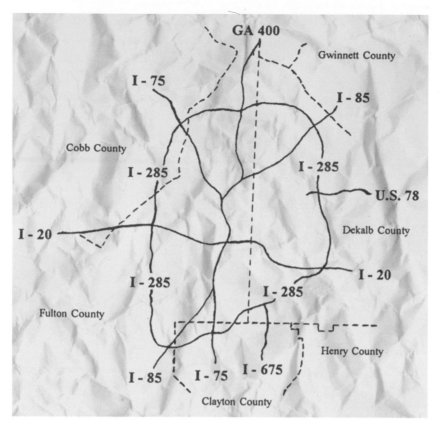

the railroads that brought them to other locations in Georgia came through Atlanta. Young men, black and white, coming into Atlanta from all over the country, opened up the city to new ideas and different traditions. The armed forces were still segregated at this time, which, in Atlanta, meant several things. White men were mustered at Fort McPherson; blacks continued on to Fort Benning. Both sides of town were active recruiting young men from other counties in Georgia for military service, acclimating the recruits to their new roles and entertaining soldiers on leave who appeared by the thousands in the railroad stations. USO workers at Terminal Station in Atlanta met incoming soldiers in the segregated lobbies and directed them to the facilities in town, the Butler Street Y, various canteens around town, the hotels on Auburn Avenue and on Peachtree Street, cafeterias, boarding houses, private homes, cafes and special (always segregated) dances — a scene repeated in the railroad stations and USO clubs throughout the region. Georgia Tech and Emory offered special courses on their campuses for the (white) soldiers in order to keep their enrollments up, for the civilian populations at the local colleges (especially the all-male ones) suffered from the same

lack of manpower the local industries did. The region was full of women who volunteered to keep the USOs going, the Red Cross supplied, victory gardens planted, services maintained, delivery trucks running and factories operating.

People from all over the region, the state and some from out of state worked in the metropolitan war industries, among them thousands of women employed in large number for the first time since the flowering of the textile industry. Women worked in the factories, both on the line and also in supervisory positions; hundreds of government jobs were filled by women while the men went to war, and the ranks of local corporations swelled with white women workers in higher positions than clerks and secretaries. Black women had access to better-paying jobs as well; many left domestic service for whatever was available to them. Sometimes what was available was only a different form of service. It was not at all uncommon for the wartime road crews, landscape maintenance workers and sidewalk cleaners in the region's cities and towns to consist entirely of black women. Local restaurants employed women as waitresses, some for the first time, and it was the women, black and white, who kept family businesses going while husbands and fathers did their service.

Much of the military, commercial and industrial infrastructure put into place during the war remained afterwards to support economic growth. The Bell Bomber plant, for instance, was taken over by the Lockheed Aircraft Corporation in 1951 during the Korean War, and continued as an important regional employer through the 1980s. (The plant went on to build B-47s, C-130 transports and the massive but controversial C-5A.) As a direct result of the war, the Atlanta region had increased rail and air transportation networks, underused industrial plants, federal funds that continued to pour into the region, and the groundwork for improvements in highways, utilities, public health care, education and government services.

Economic progress in the urban, industrialized areas was shared by the rural sectors. During the war the federal government had put restrictions on farmers, offering to bank cotton lands for subsidies, encouraging cultivation of food crops instead. By 1950 cotton was all but dead as a cash crop in the region; in Cobb County, for example, only 165 farms were still growing it. Other crops were becoming more prominent and productive. During the war, local farmers also suffered a shortage of field hands, but they managed to bring in their crops by hiring students and civilian field workers "imported" from the cities. Farmers also began to use more machinery. Agribusiness was aborning after the war as the numbers of farms decreased, the size of farms began to increase, and mechanization became more common. Georgia farmers, who had been reluctant recruits to tractors before the war, flocked to them afterwards. The war also hastened the decline of tenancy, which had peaked in 1920. By 1950, less than half the farms in the state were run by tenants, far fewer than half in the Atlanta region. Rural electrification, rural roads, soil conservation, agricultural diversification and market expansion for agricultural products all received impetus from the war.

At the end of the decade of the 1940s, while it could not be said that all of the farmers were better off, it was certainly true that agriculture was in a stronger state than it had been since the early 1900s. Farm efficiency was improving as fewer people were producing more; about one-quarter of the population now made its living from farming, down from a century earlier when everyone made a living from the land. The whole of Georgia was starting to become less rural in the character of its population, a profound change demanding new political stances as well as new economic patterns.

At first, it seemed that the old sociopolitical systems would simply become more entrenched as people tried to return to normalcy after the war. Yet the war severely tested segregation as a rational social system. Black veterans came home with a spiritual wound cut by the deep dichotomy between the promises of democracy, for which they had just fought, and the prejudiced political practices of the South, where many of them returned to live. The Atlantans came home to a place where Negro votes constituted but 4 percent of the electorate in 1945 — 3,000 men and women — and where buses, restaurants, public facilities and department stores each practiced their special form of segregation. The black press continued its rhetoric from the war years — African-Americans had to fight on two fronts, one abroad, one at home. Winning the war abroad now made winning the war at home more important. Among blacks at this time, enfranchisement more than segregation was the issue. If blacks had more votes, they had more voice; if they had more voice, they had a greater chance to gain political and economic equity.

They took courage from several important recent events, among them the elimination of the poll tax in Georgia in 1944, and the ruling by the United States Supreme Court that the white primary was unconstitutional. The exclusionary primary was struck down in Texas in 1945 and in Georgia in 1946, whereupon it became illegal everywhere. Meanwhile, local associations — the NAACP, the Atlanta Urban League, the YMCA, and special citizens' committees such as the Atlanta Civic and Political League — combined under the auspices of the All-Citizens Registration Committee to conduct extensive, well-organized voter registration drives among the African-Americans in

The road system that today defines Atlanta began in 1945 with a transportation report recommending a perimeter highway and connecting spokes of a wheel design. World War II had slowed local development, but the 1950s and 1960s made up for the delays.
The Atlanta Historical Society, Inc.

Atlanta. To the 3,000 were added 18,000, and in a few short months, black voters rewrote Atlanta political history.

In a 1946 special election to replace Robert Ramspeck in the U.S. Congress, a field of 19 candidates faced each other. One of them, a white woman, was the only candidate to meet with black voters (even the two most likely winners had refused to sit down with them). The night before the election — after the newspapers were delivered and the last radio broad-casts had aired — the word went out through the black community across fences and over telephone wires, "vote for the woman, vote for the woman." The next day Helen Douglas Mankin was elected to Congress on the strength of the black vote. The election caught the stunned attention of all the local white politicians, and Helen Mankin years later continued her pioneering efforts by assisting the successful attack on the county unit system. In 1949 African-Americans formed the Atlanta Negro Voters League, which became the source for black political power under all the subsequent Atlanta mayors from William Hartsfield in the late 1940s to Ivan Allen Jr. in the early 1960s. The leaders of the voters league filled Hartsfield's "Kitchen Cabinet" during the strenuous political transitions between 1945 and 1960, when integration became the strongest and toughest focus of their attention, and they advised Ivan Allen, Jr., through the tense moments of the 1960s when violence threatened.

In 1944 the Southern Regional Council, an interracial consortium headquartered in Atlanta and successor to the Commission on Interracial Cooperation that had been the only interracial forum in the South for more than 20 years, took a moderate stand on segregation in the schools, one of the first breaks in the wall of Southern silence about it. Mindful that their deliberations had impact throughout the South — not just in Atlanta and its environs — the council members came just short of endorsing integration (it would be another seven years before they did so) and opted for a broad-based program of education, research publica-tions and behind-the-scenes negotiations to promote moderation. Their commitment to moderation and justice reflected the general sentiment of most of the people in the Atlanta region, who tended to be prag-matic if not enlightened, fairminded, if often ignorant of the true state of deprivation among the region's black citizens. Not all of the people were pragmatic, enlightened, fairminded or even ignorant about the black situation. Some espoused racial separation as necessary, desirable and important — at any cost.

Atlanta was not only the "capital" of interracial cooperation in 1946, it was still the capital of a race-divided Georgia. The free-for-all that emanated from the gubernatorial election that year witnessed the last gasp of one of the state's most colorful figures — the charismatic, controversial, powerful, red-suspendered, down-home, Georgia lovin' white supremacist and race-baiter, Eugene Talmadge. Talmadge was elected by a majority of the county unit votes, though in the same electoral count, James V. Carmichael of Marietta, a racial moderate, won the popular vote. (Carmichael had carried the Atlanta region.) Talmadge died before he could be inaugurated as governor, however, and in the popular refer-endum that ensued, his son and heir, Herman Talmadge, won. Talmadge, the son, carried on his father's tradition of conservatism (without the red suspenders), appealing best to small towns, rural areas and working-class urban

From the 1940s through the 1960s, local organizations spearheaded voter registrations and "get out the vote" drives among the region's black citizens, especially in the city of Atlanta itself. *The Atlanta Historical Society, Inc. Photo by Boyd Lewis*

neighborhoods. At the end of the decade of the 1940s the Atlanta region was symbolically divided in its political sentiments by Gov. Herman Talmadge on the one hand, a lawyer-farmer turned politician who believed in segregation and lived only part of the year in Atlanta, and Mayor William Hartsfield, a lawyer, technology buff and aviator manqué who was an Atlanta native and believed in whatever was good for Atlanta.

Reorganized after World War II, the Atlanta symphony orchestra and chorus achieved national and international acclaim under the direction of Robert Shaw. *The Atlanta Historical Society, Inc.*

If 1946 was the year that kicked off the movement toward the great modern divide between those who would ultimately defend segregation and those who would give it up in the name of something else (pragmatism or justice), it was also the year that another critical problem in the Atlanta region was addressed. Voters that year approved both a new traffic plan (to be introduced in Atlanta, but with regional consequences) and a $16 million package to support the assemblage of its rights-of-way. The Lockner Report, issued in 1945 at the end of the war, called for the creation of a north-south limited-access highway through Atlanta, more elevated roads over the railroad tracks, a plaza over the tracks downtown, a central parking lot over the railroad tracks (today the Decks near Philips Arena), and a circular road ringing the central business district. It was 10 years before the federal highway program rendered local funding "redundant," so the plan moved ahead on its own.

In 1949 construction began on what today is the primary artery between the south side of the Atlanta region and its north side — the downtown connector — that hub in the Atlanta highway wheel in which I-285 is now the ring and all the interstates the spokes. All of Lockner's important recommendations found their way to fruition in the decades that followed, some in larger or lesser forms that Lockner had proposed. I-285, the business "ring," is clearly larger than intended, and the plaza over the tracks in downtown is clearly smaller. (Only half of it was ever built, and in the last

renovations to Underground Atlanta, in fact, the plaza disappeared altogether.)

Much that was to serve Atlanta well in the late 20th century came out of the years immediately following World War II. WSB, Atlanta's first television station, went on the air in 1948. The Atlanta Symphony, founded during the war as a children's orchestra, and reorganized just after the war as an adult orchestra, became part of the national syndicate in 1948. In a clear response to the demand for housing after the war, Rich's department store opened up its Store for Homes across the street from its flagship "Store for People" on Forsyth Street downtown. Rich's, television, the symphony — all of them had regional significance, but nothing spoke more articulately of the real changes in the region than Mayor Hartsfield's Plan of Improvement for the City of Atlanta, proposed in 1949, enacted in 1951 and put into effect in 1952.

It was already clear to Hartsfield when he first took office after the war that the Atlanta region was growing and that much of the important growth was happening outside Atlanta's city limits. The Bell plant in Marietta was just the most striking example of the kind of residential and industrial growth that occurred as a result of the war. The war had brought the same kind of growth to the rest of the South that it brought to the Atlanta region, so the regional distribution center that Atlanta had become grew into a greater role. As the South grew, Atlanta became more important economically. And as Atlanta grew, the region grew. When the South was pressed into war service, it also became

Decatur skyline as it was taking shape in the 1960s — after a short period of stasis, Decatur is again booming.
DeKalb Historical Society

exposed to non-Southern people and influences. According to many reports on the period, much of the immediate post-war growth came about as the result of the influx of both people and money from outside the South. As Mayor Hartsfield humorously, but bitingly, expressed it, "we roll out the red carpet for any damn Yankee who comes here with two strong hands and some money." The appeal that Atlanta had to these newcomers was its greatest asset — its suburban character — by which residents could buy relatively large housing lots at reasonable, even low, prices.

Suburban development in the 1940s was strongest along the pathways of the well-developed transit systems of the late 19th century — north toward Marietta, east toward Decatur and northeast toward Chamblee and Doraville. Cobb County's population nearly tripled in the decade of the 1940s, standing at 114,000 people. Even the counties south of Atlanta grew during the war decade, especially Clayton, whose small 1940 population of 11,000 doubled by 1950.

Doraville's story illustrates the patterns. In 1947 the town of Doraville reincorporated as the city of Doraville, a reflection of its aspirations as much as its growth. During the war DeKalb County issued bonds to build a new water plant near Doraville, a county-owned system that was unique in the state of Georgia.

Completed in 1942, the system was the main attraction for relocating businesses, especially General Motors, which located in Doraville in 1944. The big 30-inch water main in DeKalb gushed prosperity for the county and accounted for $75 million in industrial development in north DeKalb. Plantation Pipeline constructed a facility in 1942, bringing oil through the region to safeguard its wartime overland passage from the ports of New Orleans to the shipbuilders in North Carolina, and spurring the development of tank farms in this small town outside Atlanta. Shell Oil, Standard Oil, and American Oil all maintained tank farms in Doraville for the kerosene, gas and oil used by the planes, trucks and trains of the region.

Almost as soon as General Motors occupied its facility in Doraville, it started to plan expansions, prompting the city to undertake a zoning plan in 1946. GM, it discovered, owned one-fourth of the city premises, which prompted the city to begin asserting itself toward the industrial giant that was now swallowing up its lands. The town saw its first suburban subdivisions (one black, several white) grow up as a result of the GM plant, and saw the dusty trail that was old Peachtree Road paved and renamed Peachtree Industrial between the DeKalb County line and the GM plant in 1947. Doraville installed street lights, instituted a street numbering system to assist postal deliveries that were doubling every year, annexed some territory outside the city limits in 1949, and in the same year collected city taxes for the first time. As if crowned for its building mania, in 1949 Doraville was pronounced to be the fastest-growing city in the fastest-growing county in the United States.

Neighboring Chamblee also benefitted from the growth. Peachtree Industrial was paved with employment riches as U.S. Envelope, Westinghouse Lamp, General Electric, John Deere, American Hospital, Allis Chalmers, Sieberling Rubber and many more local and national companies built facilities on the northeast side of the region. Chamblee, like Doraville, saw black and white subdivisions developing around its perimeter, demonstrating so much growth that Chamblee's territorial growth bumped up against Doraville's and precipitated a series of boundary disputes between the two communities — signs of serious growing pains indeed!

It should be noted that at this time the Atlanta region was on the cutting edge of manufacturing development in the entire state of Georgia. Approximately one-quarter of all growth in manufacturing in the state after the war was accounted for by the developments in Cobb, Fulton and DeKalb counties. The leading industries in the Atlanta region fell within the category of transportation — planes, trains and cars, and the materials that supported them — and reiterated the historical importance of transportation to the original development of the region. These same industries — with high capital and high wages — dominated state statistics for several decades, tipping the balance toward manufacturing and away from agriculture as the most dominant statewide source of income. So important was this Chamblee-Doraville industrial expansion to the fortunes of downtown Atlanta that telephone dialing between Atlanta and the Chamblee area became toll-free in 1950, presaging the establishment of the largest geographic toll-free calling area in the United States, a hallmark of today's Atlanta region.

The Ford manufacturing plant was symbolic not only of the size of post-war installations but also of their placement in ever more suburban locations. *The Atlanta Historical Society, Inc.*

Of all the growth that was transpiring, however, nothing tempted Mayor Hartsfield more than Buckhead. Buckhead was the plum because it housed the highest per-capita family income sectors in the entire state and contained the homes of Atlanta's business leaders. Educated white elite seemed to be essential to the continued prosperity of the region. The wealthy whites had been moving north toward Buckhead from the 1910s when summer estates and weekend retreats dotted the rolling terrain around what was then a rural post office and crossroads village. With trolley extensions and then the automobile, white middle-class workers also found homes in the area. The new neighborhoods all seemed to tack themselves to the prestige of at least one Peachtree name, either a subdivision — Peachtree Hills or Peachtree Gardens — or a principal street — Peachtree Hills Avenue or Peachtree Battle. This gave rise to another quality that continues to mark the region today — the proliferation of thoroughfares named Peachtree. The churches of the white elite had already followed their congregations to the Northside, signifying both the size and the permanence of the out-migration from the city. St. Philip's Episcopal relocated to Buckhead in 1933, following the hundreds of families who had built large estates in the 1910s and 1920s. Second Ponce de Leon Baptist Church, the result of a 1933 merger of Atlanta's Second Baptist and Ponce de Leon Baptist, followed its respective congregations to Buckhead in 1939. The Catholics, Presbyterians and Methodists all followed suit.

What Hartsfield's glimmering eyes saw when he looked at Buckhead was a stronger tax base for the city and a political balance to the increasing black political power. The Plan of Improvement was intended to widen Atlanta margins in several directions, but its primary target was Buckhead. When the Plan took effect it did indeed annex Buckhead to the city along with all the land between Buckhead and the old city limits. The annexation also added 100,000 people to the Atlanta electorate and tax rolls, and tripled the city's territory — from a paltry 37 square miles to an impressive 118 square miles. The Plan of Improvement was a local hallmark in two different ways: it was the largest and most valuable addition of property to the city of Atlanta, and it was the last territorial annexation Atlanta was able to mount successfully in the 20th century. The next time Atlanta viewed its northern neighbors as potential citizens, this time in Sandy Springs, the residents there voted "no, no, a thousand times no" in a local referendum in 1971, and again killed the idea in the popular press in the 1980s (in response to proposals to annex all of Fulton County).

Map of Atlanta annexations

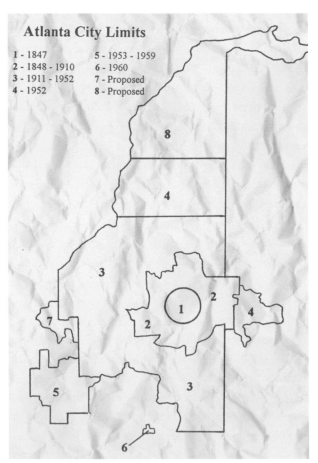

Atlanta City Limits

1 - 1847
2 - 1848 - 1910
3 - 1911 - 1952
4 - 1952

5 - 1953 - 1959
6 - 1960
7 - Proposed
8 - Proposed

Growth on the north side was matched by growth on the south side chiefly around the airport, where the acreage that constituted the airport and its immediate support facilities had also been annexed to the city. Chevrolet built a manufacturing plant in nearby Hapeville, of the same general size and proportions as the General Motors plant in Doraville, but its impact on the surrounding neighborhood was dwarfed by the expansions of the airport. Service through the airport doubled during the war years, reaching a peak point in 1942 when the most take-offs and landings on a single day were recorded.

Delta Air Lines, founded in Macon, Georgia, but headquartered for more than a decade in Monroe, Louisiana, moved its general offices to Atlanta in 1941, in anticipation of the passenger growth Atlanta expected to see as much as for the aviation support the federal government gave all airlines during the war. The hangars and maintenance facilities around the airport filled with activities for flight training — the only flight schools in the state were located there — and with private flying alongside the commercial offerings of Southern, Eastern and Delta airlines. By the mid-1950s the airport was groaning under its load of 2 million passengers a year, all of them flying out of an uncomfortable, unattractive and oversized Quonset hut that served as the terminal. Hartsfield undertook ambitious plans for a jet-age airport, which his successor, Ivan Allen Jr., successfully accomplished in 1962 at a cost of $21 million. As the airport was expanding, so were its airlines, especially Delta, which gained a transcontinental route that enabled it to fly nonstop to cities in California. Hartsfield's state-of-the-art airport added ancillary concourses, rotunda gates and a second runway shortly after it was constructed, but in 20 years, it was entirely outmoded.

The airport of today, a $500 million project that has still not stopped growing, required the efforts of 16 airlines, five federal agencies (Transportation, Agriculture, Aviation, Immigration, and Customs), two state agencies (Transportation and Agriculture), three municipalities, two counties and the local fire marshal. The sharing of authority and bureaucratic coordination it took to create Atlanta's modern airport, now the busiest in the country, was a signal to the region's future.

From the time of the Plan of Improvement on, Atlanta's growth has been far more metropolitan than municipal in character and far more attuned to national — even international — aspirations than regional ones. The 1950s brought suburban residential growth and industrial growth around the perimeters of the city of Atlanta, but very little happened to build up the central business district. Only one skyscraper, the Fulton National Bank Building on Marietta Street, rose up in 1954 as a sign that the city was indeed modernizing. It was almost as if Atlanta were reverting to type — a sleepy Southern town — while its outskirts pursued the American Dream on their own terms.

The calm surface was misleading, however, as changes stirred beneath. For one thing, the U.S. Supreme Court startled a complacent South with its ruling that "separate but equal" public accommodations were inherently unequal under the law and therefore unconstitutional. Since the court's verdict dealt directly with a board of education (albeit in Topeka, Kansas), every school system in the South held its breath to await the outcome. In Georgia, a raging Marvin Griffin, the sitting governor, threatened simply to close all the state's schools rather than succumb to some unknown and federally dictated mandate. Both the state Legislature and the alliance of county governments supported his stance, and they watched as elsewhere in the South — in Little Rock, Arkansas, and New Orleans, Louisiana — attempts to integrate the schools had led to civil disturbances and massive resistance, which led to violence.

Locally, the population was divided. Pro-integration forces were strongest in the inner city where the black leadership was the strongest, but even among black Atlantans there was some fear of what integration might mean. Pro-segregation forces seemed to hold the winning hand for awhile, but in the city of Atlanta, business leaders, many citizens who wished to avoid violence, ministers and organizations such as the League of Women Voters joined in support of the now-former segregationist Mayor Hartsfield, who was able to exercise caution and progress at the same time. His success led him to proclaim Atlanta the city "too busy to hate," a slogan that kept a positive vision alive if it did not describe any actuality.

Hartsfield Airport was reconstructed in 1962 to accommodate jet airplanes. That airport, obsolete in 20 years despite its modernity, was replaced by the present facility in 1984.
The Atlanta Historical Society, Inc.

Through Hartsfield's commitment to moderation, through the behind-the-scenes habits of Atlanta dealings (often directed by Robert Woodruff, the brains behind Coca-Cola), through the vigilance of the now-integrated police department, which exercised extensive surveillance of the KKK and other white supremacy groups, and through the grace of the citizenry (black and white), nine black students peaceably registered at Atlanta's white high schools on August 9, 1961. Their quiet, uneventful integration led President John F. Kennedy to make an example of Atlanta before the nation in a widely televised speech, a compliment that was not lost on the city's leadership, or indeed on the outlying communities, who took note and followed the example.

Most local counties adopted a voluntary approach to integration at first, but few students (black or white) volunteered to integrate the schools of the opposite race. When voluntary integration was determined insufficient by the U.S. Department of Justice, then school busing became the rule in the towns and cities as well as the unincorporated sections of the counties. It cannot be said that integration occurred without incident, or without some additional rearrangement of the population between the cities and the suburbs. The integration of the schools through busing required an exhausting and expensive approach that, while it integrated the schools, accomplished its mission at the cost

Greetings from Lake Allatoona! This lake is a little further out and a little older than the larger and more heavily used Lake Lanier, which was merely the largest of the Army Corps of Engineers projects that have changed the face of stream and river beds through the region. *The Atlanta Historical Society, Inc.*

of that familiar community anchor, the neighborhood school. It could not and did not alter the more intransigent problem — that de facto residential segregation not only persisted but increased over the decades of the 1950s and 1960s. White flight to the suburbs north and west of Atlanta and middle-class black flight to the new suburbs south and west of the city created an entirely new checkerboard of racial residence.

As residents flocked to the suburbs, retail enterprises followed them out of town. The establishment of Lenox Square in 1959 in the Buckhead area, eight miles from downtown, signaled the shift of the retail center from the original central business district in Atlanta to the outskirts. The 1950s brought a number of other turning points for the region, ones that declared Atlanta a prime focus of the growing "Sunbelt" expansions. When Buford Dam opened up, creating Lake Lanier and guaranteeing Atlanta a water supply for decades to come, it was Mayor Hartsfield from the city of Atlanta who presided at the ceremonies, not the local officials, because it was Atlanta much more than the rural counties around the lake that needed the water, the flood control systems and the access to recreation that the lake promised. And by lifting Atlanta's quality of life several notches, Lake Lanier

immediately became the Army Corps of Engineers' most heavily used lake project in the nation.

As for another Sunbelt characteristic, air conditioning changed both the patterns of business and the habits of community socializing, as the front porch gave way to the television set in front of the air conditioner. Atlanta actually housed the first office building in the Southeast to use air conditioning, back in the 1920s, and air-conditioning systems were commonplace in commercial and industrial settings, but by the 1950s houses were also beginning to be built with air conditioning. As the local populace cooled off, Georgia Power Company announced that its peak load was shifting from the winter to the summer months. Air conditioning more than any other single factor created the Sunbelt phenomenon.

The most telling measurement of all, metropolitan Atlanta reached the "magic" number in terms of population: in October 1959 Atlanta contained 1 million persons. The new enumeration now included Gwinnett County as part of the census area, along with Fulton, DeKalb, Clayton and Cobb. The city itself counted for approximately one-third of the total. *Newsweek* magazine declared on the occasion that Atlanta was the "nerve center of the New South." Atlanta had leapt ahead of Birmingham, Alabama, with which it had retained a neck-and-neck race for the leading spot in Southern statistics. Atlanta was even edging out New Orleans, which had been the South's largest city throughout most of its history.

The Atlanta of the early 1960s was poised to take the next step in municipal reputation, to achieve national city status. At the time, it was famous as the home of Coca-Cola and Georgia Tech football; it had the reputation of being a graceful Southern town, where the magnolias were plentiful and the livin' was easy. When Ivan Allen Jr. was elected to the mayoralty of Atlanta in 1961, he began to pursue a course that put Atlanta on the national map, a place it had not been since the Civil War. Allen picked a handful of lofty aims; chief among them was the acquisition of a major sports team. And so, in one of the most amazing moments in Atlanta history, Allen created a sports stadium for a team that the city did not have, on land it did not own and with money the city did not have, either. It was the first true expression of "build it, and they will come." In three short years, between 1965 and 1968, Atlanta acquired the Braves baseball team from Milwaukee; the Falcons football team, an expansion team during the war between the National Football League and the then-new American Football League; and finally, the Hawks basketball team, who played their games at Georgia Tech until their new home, the highly innovative Omni sports arena, was built in 1975.

Following in his father's footsteps of a generation earlier, Mayor Allen fostered a second "Forward Atlanta" campaign, this time aimed at the Fortune 500. By the time the campaign was finished, 440 of the Fortune 500 had operations in Atlanta, and eight of them were headquartered there. Allen supported new investments in the downtown; he oversaw large urban renewal projects (which cleared out slums but failed to rebuild some black communities); most of all he preached nonresistance to integration and himself became a soft-spoken convert to Civil Rights. Allen was the only Southern mayor to speak to Congress for the federal Civil Rights Act of 1964. Allen was elegant and gutsy — he calmed the potential race riots down in Atlanta by getting on the streets himself and confronting citizens face to face. He utilized all of Hartsfield's behind-the-scenes tactics, he confronted issues and people head-on, and he listened. He stood ready to support a proposal to honor Dr. Martin Luther King Jr. with an interracial dinner when King won the Nobel Peace Prize (the only Georgian to do so), and his action inspired other whites to accept invitations. The Nobel dinner was the first public occasion where blacks and whites in Georgia sat at the dinner table together. When Dr. King was assassinated, it was Mayor Allen who saw to it that Mrs. King and her family had the transportation and municipal support they needed throughout the funeral proceedings that followed.

Like dominoes, the obstacles to progressive social and political evolution for the region were beginning to fall — the white primary, the county unit system, the prohibitions against African-Americans in political office and women (of any race) on juries. Atlanta was becoming cosmopolitan, and it showed. By the end of the 1960s, Atlanta was a player on the national field — in corporate

A young Maynard Jackson presiding over the City Council, prefatory to being elected Atlanta's first black mayor
The Atlanta Historical Society, Inc. Photo by Boyd Lewis

Magic reigned at the opening ceremonies for the Centennial Olympic Games held in Atlanta in 1996. The mood was global but the dance and music themes were as down-home Southern as they could be. *The Atlanta Historical Society, Inc.*

business, in political visibility, in leadership in national movements and, of course, in sports. Atlanta's moderation during the worst of the times was based more in pragmatic concerns for the effects that resisting change would have on business than it was in a commitment to justice, but justice got a foot in the door nonetheless.

The decade of the 1960s has often been called "Atlanta's Decade," for it led the way for the state and grew faster than the state. Largely because of Atlanta metropolitan growth the state experienced a positive net gain in population for the first decade in many. The 1970 census showed the extent of changes in Georgia: the state had become an urban state, and Atlanta had a black majority inside the city limits. Some 60,000 whites had moved out, and 70,000 African-Americans had moved in. The black vote had put Ivan Allen Jr. in office. A transitional candidate between the old and new power structures, Jewish Sam Massell, won Atlanta's mayoral election in 1971 with Maynard Jackson at his side as vice-mayor. Jackson went on to become the first African-American to hold the position of mayor in Atlanta, and since then the position has remained a black post.

In 1970 the Atlanta region contained one-third of the population of the state and earned nearly half of its income. The counties around Atlanta were growing so fast, their budgets could not keep up. Cobb County, the fastest growing at the time, already had a population approaching 300,000 people, 10 times the size of the county just 30 years earlier. Infrastructure questions — utilities, sanitation, water, roads, court rooms and jails — pressed the counties to raise taxes, establish independent planning commissions and complain mightily about Atlanta's insatiable appetites for expansion. Capacities were exceeded in Fulton and Cobb, and also in Gwinnett and Clayton. Fayette and Henry were only beginning to feel the sprawl. Without adequate water delivery systems, these counties did not receive the industrial development Clayton and south Fulton saw, so did not experience much growth until the residential subdivisions started spreading out that far a decade later. Retail followed, then commerce and education, which shows up today in two suburban colleges that are now bursting at the seams — Kennesaw State University and Clayton State in Morrow. In addition to their educational roles, these schools have contributed to the suburbanization of culture in the region, especially Clayton with its acoustically exquisite Spivey Hall. The 1970s saw the completion of the expressway system binding the region together, and the start-up of the rapid rail system under MARTA, which now connects the airport directly to the edge cities on the perimeter.

The 1980s were a period of continued growth for the region, but also a period of testing. The counties, met with greater populations to support, were not the only ones with infrastructure issues. Atlanta faced the encumbrances from decades of deferred maintenance. Sewers, water distribution and supply, landfill access, bridge and viaduct safety, and street sanitation and upkeep — all seemed to demand immediate attention. The downtown, altered almost beyond recognition with construction for the rapid rail system, the World Congress Center and new high-rises in the 1960s and 1970s, was in danger of losing its essence. Its very survival was in question. It was a time when the differences between the city and its suburbs became more pronounced, with Democrats inside the ring and Republicans outside, a discrepancy that continues and was most pointedly symbolized recently by the presence of Democrat John Lewis and Republican Newt Gingrich in the U.S. House of Representatives.

If the 1980s were a time when Atlanta seemed to be falling apart, the decade of the 1990s began to stitch it back together. Nothing stands out in the decade more than the 1996 Centennial Olympic Games as a measure of what the Atlanta region could do. From the moment the announcement was made in 1990, six years before the games, to the moment the last Olympic visitor returned home, Atlanta — city, region and representatives from around the state — experienced a kind of Olympic mania, a combination of

euphoria and high anxiety. It is a tribute to the habits of the place that when Atlanta lawyer Billy Payne birthed the idea of hosting the Olympics, many of the

The Olympic sculpture at Five Points symbolizes the region's most historic intersection — Marietta Street (from Cobb County) meets Peachtree Street (from Gwinnett County south and from Fulton County north), Decatur Street (from DeKalb County) and Edgewood Avenue (from Atlanta's first planned suburb, Inman Park). *H. Randal Roark*

Atlantans around him thought it was impossible to achieve, but no one thought it was a bad idea. Typical. "Think big, think possible; think Atlanta" really ought to have been the operative slogan.

There were only three missteps in what now seems like a morass of fallibility in the Olympic movement. Atlanta had Izzy as its mascot, which, however clever, was not endearing to anyone over the age of eight. Atlanta experienced the worst Olympic tragedy since the shootings in Munich, when a bomb exploded in Olympic Park. A woman from south Georgia was killed and scores wounded. Though the bomb failed to kill the Olympic spirit in the city, it kept Juan Antonio Samaranch from declaring these games "the best ever" at the end of the ceremonies. The third problem was the press. The Atlanta Committee for the Olympic Games made a budgetary decision: it would go all out for accommodations for the athletes (and it did), but it would sacrifice some of the comfort of the press. ACOG could not afford comfortable accommodations for both. Unfortunately, the press rose to the occasion by condemning lodging, transportation, communications, Atlanta professionalism, Atlanta "greed" and the city itself before the entire world. Yet anyone who was actually present at the games knows that the word on the street was just the opposite. The people who came and the people who served loved the games, and the region has never had such an outpouring of human warmth and connection. Nothing in the past was equal to the excitement, the size, nor the splendor of it — not at the end of the Second World War, at the 1895 Exposition, nor at the end of the Civil War!

One touch to the games, entirely voluntary and representative of the spirit of the whole, came from the Georgia Quilt Project, which on its own, undertook to make lap quilts, 400 of them, for each of the teams and national Olympic committees, as a gesture of Georgia hospitality. In a ceremony full of meaning and beauty, the quilts and the quilters were presented to their respective countries, and today the quilts reside in every corner of the globe. The quilt project inspired the look of the games, and leaves in green, gold and purple found their way to banners, programs, flags and uniforms. The gift-quilt gesture has become something of an Olympic tradition, as both Salt Lake City and Japan have imitated it.

As a symbol of the largest nonmilitary gathering in the world and a tribute to Georgia's agrarian roots, the Olympic quilt could easily embody the changes that had happened in a single generation. The state of Georgia itself had gone from being a rural state to an urban one. In the 1990 census, 4 million of the state's 7 million residents were tallied as urban dwellers, and of those, 3 million lived in the Atlanta region. Atlanta is, in fact, a point of reference for half the population of the state, since half of it lives within an hour's drive of the region. Like an amoeba, the Atlanta Standard Metropolitan Area now spreads into 18 counties (Fulton, DeKalb, Cobb, Clayton and Gwinnett; Bartow, Cherokee, Coweta, Fayette, Forsyth, Hall, Henry, Newton, Paulding, Rockdale, Spalding and Walton). Among them all, Fayette to the south and Forsyth to the north are the fastest growing. The physical city holds less than 15 percent of the total population of the region; the state, courtesy of Atlanta area (and other municipal) suburbs, is now growing at a much faster rate than is the city of Atlanta per se.

Most Atlantans, if they even consider themselves Atlantans (which the suburbanites do not unless they are out of town or watching a Braves game), live and work outside the perimeter. Many residents of the region do not know the old city or the new downtown. Like their predecessors of old, who took the train into town from Jonesboro or Kennesaw to shop in Atlanta for the day, residents in the region treat the city of Atlanta as an "excursion," but one whose rewards are often fraught with the frustration of traffic jams and crowds. There are many "downtowns" to Atlanta now, with "edge" cities dotting the perimeter from the airport on the south to the "golden crescent" on the north perimeter between I-75 and I-85. The center does not dominate commerce or transportation as it once did. In fact it has become more a symbolic, ceremonial place, with live entertainment and sports venues, where the parades still march, the Peachtree Road Race is still run, and other major public ceremonies and celebrations take place. The city, especially the very center of it, still holds the spiritual core to the region, a role which is growing and whispers to those who will hear, "come to Atlanta, where success happens, where dreams can come true. Look at Atlanta and see what she has done."

ANYWHERE, GREATER ATLANTA
PHOTO BY DARLENE ROTH

Partners in Atlanta

Peachtree Doors and Windows, Inc.

Founded more than 40 years ago in Atlanta, Peachtree Doors and Windows, Inc. has grown from a small patio door manufacturer catering to a select group of builders and remodelers into one of the nation's leading manufacturers of premium doors and windows. From its humble beginnings with four employees working out of the basement of a local bakery, Peachtree has become the third most recognized brand name in the U.S. door and window industry.

Peachtree founder James (Jimmy) Hewell, a 1958 graduate of Georgia Tech, realized early on that innovative new products that specifically address customer needs were the keys to success for his emerging company. Shortly after the company's founding in 1959, Hewell, his brother Rae and a small cadre of dedicated employees earned the respect of the industry by designing a universal frame for patio doors that allowed a panel to slide from either the left or the right side, an industry first.

"We were the first to design a patio door with a sliding panel on the outside for a tighter seal and easier operation," said Andy Culbertson, senior director for new product development. "Peachtree has also been a pioneer in developing energy-efficient windows and doors. We developed an insulated patio door long before it became an industry standard."

Throughout its existence, Peachtree has been a driving force in the industry. In the 1960s, the company pioneered the use of tempered glass, now a building code requirement. Until 1966, Peachtree's product line consisted entirely of aluminum products. Since then, the company has expanded to include steel and fiberglass entry door systems, fiberglass and steel patio doors, aluminum-clad wood windows and composite windows with aluminum-clad frames.

In 1992 Peachtree introduced its Insulated Patio Door line, which raised the bar on standards for energy efficiency, ease of operation, safety and security. Today, the company holds more patents than any other company in the marketplace. The company thrives on the same philosophy on which it was founded — continual improvement of existing products along with innovative new product development. And, as standards in building codes become more stringent, Peachtree is well positioned because it already adheres to standards far above the current minimum. For example, Peachtree doors and windows, with the low-e^2 glass option, have met the ENERGY STAR® guidelines for energy efficiency. ENERGY STAR-labeled windows and doors are 40 percent more efficient than products required

Peachtree doors and windows add beauty to any style of home.

Brochures from the 60s and 70s illustrate original products from Peachtree.

under the most common national building codes.

Peachtree Doors and Windows operates under a customer-focused manufacturing process allowing the company to concentrate on customer service, quality and on-time delivery. "By increasing efficiency through streamlined, less complex manufacturing, we've positioned ourselves for dramatic growth, building a better and more profitable business for our employees, customers and suppliers," said Robert C.L. MacDonald, president of Peachtree.

Through its Voice of the Customer (VOC) program, Peachtree employees listen — and respond — to customer needs. "Today's customers are very knowledgeable about building products," said George A. Tremblay, vice president of sales. "They want more for their money, added value, low maintenance, energy efficiency and beauty. When customers ask for doors that open more easily, lock more securely or are easier to clean, then those requests become the design criteria for new products. Once new designs are created, our design engineers go back to customers with prototypes to ensure their specific needs have been met."

Peachtree Doors and Windows, a Nortek company, has a state-of-the-art manufacturing facility in Gainesville, Georgia, with its headquarters, research and development, and product development facilities in Norcross, Georgia. A Peachtree Planning Center in Norcross is open to the public, allowing homeowners to personally select from a variety of entry doors, patio doors and windows for their homes.

Its forward-thinking approach to design has led Peachtree to be recognized as a leader in the industry. The company

(Far left) Decorative glass windows enhance *Southern Living*'s Dream Home.

"Image" windows welcome the Georgia sunshine.

has received prestigious awards from a wide variety of industry associations, including the Northwestern Retail Lumber Association's Industry Choice Award and *Today's Homeowner* magazine's Best New Products Award.

"We feel we have the best-looking, best-working products on the market," said Tremblay. "We deliver benefits today and offer solutions for the future. By continually seeking the newest materials and utilizing the latest technology, we feel we've earned our place at the top of our industry."

Citadel patio doors bring light and beauty to sunrooms.

Cates Construction and Development Companies

One could say without exaggeration that Atlanta's north side has been altered visibly over the years by the vision of Jerry and Gene Cates.

These twin brothers founded Cates Construction and Development Companies in the late 1950s. Gene, the engineer, and Jerry, the lawyer, combined their diverse talents to plan and develop home sites, apartments, office townhouses, specialty stores and even a hospitality business.

In the already high-risk business of land development, the Cates brothers added more risk by introducing formerly untried concepts for shops and offices. For instance, they created a grouping of tenant-owned boutique shops, which they called Cates Plaza. Emulating a European village, the clustering of small specialty stores was an idea that caught on with retailers and customers alike. The same plan was extended to Cates Center, also in Buckhead.

By 1980 the Cates brothers were at the forefront of an emerging popularity for townhomes, and they built Muscogee Place with the look and feel of a Savannah in-town neighborhood.

Another project, Lenox Pointe, is a nine-acre tract of 40 offices, but the visitor can't tell at first glance whether they are homes or offices. Driving through the curving streets, one passes under spreading shade trees, spots old-fashioned lampposts and notices the varying shades of old brick on the Georgetown-style buildings. Each building was individually sold and designed to the purchaser's requirements before being built. Each unit is occupied by its owner. These are touches that distinguish a Cates project from a high-volume, high-rise, one-size-fits-all approach.

It's no wonder that the 1984 Better Buckhead Award went to the Cates brothers for their work in providing beautiful and functional places in which to live, work and shop.

Two of Atlanta's landmark homes were owned by Gene and Jerry Cates: the Pink Palace (the former Andrew Calhoun estate) and Peacock House (the former Rushton home). Peacock House was a Decorator Show House and later became the Southern Center for International Studies. Cates Development sold portions of the land around these houses and developed them as high-end home sites, thereby saving the houses from the wrecking ball.

Jerry continues the business after Gene's sudden and untimely death in 1990. However, he is not alone. At one time or another he has had at least one of his six daughters working at his side.

This cluster of offices is in the heart of Buckhead, yet presents the classic appearance of 19th-century in-town residences.

Creativity is often the combining of two already existing but dissimilar concepts. That is what Cates has offered Atlanta in the creation of modern neighborhoods that look like 19th-century Charleston streets, offices that look like residences, a cluster of new shops that resembles a quaint European village, and a hotel that feels like a home.

Dargan, Whitington & Maddox

The roots of what is now Dargan, Whitington & Maddox can be traced back over 100 years to when Cliff Hatcher founded the Cliff D. Hatcher Insurance Agency in 1892. The agency's primary business was serving as the Atlanta mortgage correspondent for numerous insurance companies, including The Fireman's Fund, American Surety, and United States Casualty.

Milton Dargan's legacy with the firm began in the early 1900s when he joined Hatcher as a partner. Taking over after Hatcher's death in the mid-1920s, Dargan, with new partners Whitington and Conner, incorporated the company of Dargan, Whitington, and Conner in January of 1932. The firm was a charter member of the Atlanta Mortgage Bankers Association and served as mortgage correspondent for the Travelers Insurance Company for more than 75 years.

Cone Maddox III loves history and respects the past, especially the past of his beloved Atlanta. He respects the past so much that, after buying the commercial real estate firm of Dargan, Whitington, and Conner in 1966, it took him an additional 22 years before he made his name an official part of the corporate entity. That's because Milton Dargan, Walter Whitington and John L. Conner were respected business and social leaders who did their part in creating what is now metropolitan Atlanta; and Maddox believed he needed to prove himself worthy of having his name on the same line with such illustrious Southern gentlemen.

Since purchasing Dargan, Whitington, and Conner, Cone Maddox III, serving as chairman, continues to enhance the reputation of one of Atlanta's oldest and most prestigious commercial real estate firms by ensuring that the company maintains its focus — its heritage — as an intimate family-oriented business. Maddox's wife, Karen, a certified commercial appraiser,

is the president and chief executive officer and his three daughters, Virginia Maddox Lozano, Sharon Maddox Turner and Blanche Maddox Pearson, are vice-presidents; Karen's two sons, Jon and Robert Taunton, serve as directors.

Changing with Atlanta and reinventing itself to meet the needs of a dynamic market, Dargan, Whitington & Maddox evolved through a natural progression into a company that provides commercial and residential appraisals and a variety of appraisal-related services, including market, investment and use-value estimates, highest- and best-use studies,

The Dargan, Whitington & Maddox brain trust: Chairman Cone Maddox III and his wife, Karen, the president and chief executive officer of Atlanta's second-oldest commercial real estate firm

marketability and feasibility studies, and site location services. The firm has extensive professional expertise and experience in providing courtroom testimony in state and federal courts. While specializing primarily in the Southeastern United States, Dargan, Whitington & Maddox works with clients all across the nation.

With a lineage that is only several decades younger than the city it calls home, the commercial real estate firm of Dargan, Whitington & Maddox has been, in one form or another, developing, insuring, servicing and evaluating the concrete, clay, brick and steel of Atlanta since 1892. And despite numerous name and ownership changes during its history, the company continues to succeed by understanding that its business is simply the business of Atlanta.

Robinson-Humphrey

Atlanta was full of visionaries in 1894 — men who built railroads and mills, doctors, lawyers, bankers, opportunists. All were drawn to Atlanta for a stake in the city's rebirth as the apex of the new South. Into this flourishing economy came Roby Robinson, a young man with a dream of his own: to help the city prosper. He realized that in order to grow, Atlanta would need capital, and he vowed to meet that need through his one-man municipal bond firm.

His timing couldn't have been better. The following year, The Cotton States and International Exposition brought droves of visitors to Atlanta and promoted the city as a transportation and commercial center. According to historians, the exposition may have been the single most important factor in Atlanta's emergence as a major Southeastern city. In its wake, textile mills and industrial complexes sprung up along the rail lines, luring people from all parts of the South with promises of work while their wealthy owners built mansions and settled in Atlanta to raise their families.

By 1902, Robinson's reputation for funding civic projects had spread and *The Atlanta Journal* called him "a financial genius." That same year, William G. Humphrey, a professional bond trader, teamed up with Robinson. Originally called the English-American Trust Co., the new partnership was incorporated as The Robinson-Humphrey Company, Inc. It was later to become one of the top equity underwriters in the United States.

During the firm's early years, the Southeast was primarily agrarian but soon a retail and service economy emerged. As communities expanded, there was an increasing demand for capital to build roads, bridges, schools and other public projects. The small bond trading firm prospered and put its stamp on the growing economy.

Disaster stuck in 1921 when Roby Robinson died of pneumonia at age 50. The leadership of the firm fell into the lap of his young son-in-law, Henry B. Tompkins whose remarkable sense of humor and great intellect proved invaluable when the stock market crashed in 1929.

Unlike many other investment companies, Robinson-Humphrey[SM] not only held on during the Great Depression, but flourished under Tompkin's leadership. He managed to turn adversity into opportunity, and R-H[SM] emerged from those difficult times in sound financial condition. Once again, the fates dealt a bad hand and World War II absorbed virtually all of the country's capital, but the firm survived. As soon as the war ended, the South's economy, following the nation's lead, soared and created a huge demand for investment capital. R-H grew and developed expertise as full-service firm with a reputation for integrity and service.

In the mid-40s the firm began making primary markets in regional stocks using its own capital and, in 1947, opened its first full-service branch office in Columbia, South Carolina. When the firm purchased a seat on the New York Stock Exchange in 1951, R-H became the investment banker to many of the emerging companies in the region. Combined with the creation of a research department, R-H sealed its dominance in the Southeast.

Underwriting municipal finance projects like the MARTA transit system and Georgia Highway 400 underscores R-H's role in the region's growth.

The firm's research visibility and commitment was raised to a new level in the mid-70s when its leading Southeastern competitor was sold and virtually the entire research team moved to R-H. Simultaneously, the firm grew as an underwriter and distributor of new issues and other public offerings.

From its humble beginnings as a one-product municipal bond firm, R-H evolved into a full-service investment firm offering a wide range of investment products to meet clients' needs. Along with the shift in revenues, separate departments were created to give customers a far wider range of services.

After dramatic growth in revenues and profits in the 1970s, R-H attracted a number of corporate suitors and in 1982 the firm became a subsidiary of Shearson/American Express. Robinson-Humphrey continued to prosper, increasing revenues more than six-fold. In 1993, through its brokerage subsidiary Smith Barney Harris Upham, Inc., Primerica, Inc. acquired Robinson-Humphrey from American Express, along with the assets of the domestic retail brokerage and asset management business of Shearson Lehman Brothers, Inc. Today, Robinson-Humphrey is a wholly owned subsidiary of Salomon Smith Barney, Inc., a member of Citigroup.

In its 100-year history, there have been only six CEOs: Roby Robinson; Henry B. Tompkins; Alexander Yearley, IV; Justus C. Martin Jr.; Jerome D. Sands Jr.; and Thomas K. Tracy. Each has put his leadership stamp on the growth of the firm.

Corporate Philosophy

When Roby Robinson hung his shingle in 1894, he placed client needs above all else. As the firm has grown and expanded, so has its promise to provide all the products, information, services, opinions or resources necessary to solve virtually any financial problem. The range of products and services now extends from stocks and bonds to mutual funds and insurance, from education funding to retirement plans, from mergers and acquisitions to public stock offerings. The firm is a Top 20 equity underwriter in the United States (source: CommScan Equidesk) and has a leading presence in middle-market mergers and acquisitions. Internationally, R-H is recognized for its equity research and market-making abilities. With an outstanding distribution system, impressive research capability and superior banking skills, R-H offers unique competitive advantages to its corporate clients.

"Focused on Growth"[SM] is the firm's rallying cry and R-H has set a clear goal of even better service to its primary clients, the small and mid-cap companies with exciting growth potential in the financial, technology,

Survey for outstanding earnings estimate accuracy and stock-picking skills. Robinson-Humphrey senior analysts have more than a decade of experience on average and are committed to providing idea-oriented research as part of broad and continuing coverage in key areas. Not content to rest on past accomplishments, analysts continuously strive to improve their expertise as evidenced by industry recognition, professional designations and advanced academic degrees.

Analysts take pride in the depth of their personal relationships with corporate management and on their network of contacts with competitors, customers and suppliers. These strong relationships within the business community have helped extend their efforts beyond conventional analysis to the nuances and subtleties of industry trends and market dynamics.

health and business services sectors and investors in those sectors.

The firm views itself as being made up of four equilateral triangles representative of its key components of sales, trading, investment banking and research. Each of the operations is dependent upon the other to form a solid corporate team working together to bring some of the best possible service and expertise to clients.

It Begins with Research

Quality research is at the core of R-H's commitment to its individual, institutional and corporate clients. The firm's Equity Research Department offers a continuous flow of ideas on companies which are on the cusp of a growth curve in markets exhibiting exciting potential. The firm, which prides itself on its idea-oriented research, has been richly rewarded, receiving top honors for its equity research.

Instead of focusing on the macroeconomic factors, R-H recommendations are centered around individual stock selection. At the heart of this stock selection effort are the R-H research analysts. Respected by industry peers, the Equity Research Department has earned national recognition from the Annual Institutional Investor All-America Research Team and *The Wall Street Journal's* Annual All-Star Analysts

Corporate Finance — a Partner to its Clients

Partnering with their clients, R-H investment bankers use a relationship-based approach to develop innovative financial strategies that will help clients reach their objectives. Areas of specialization include equity and debt offerings, as well as merger and acquisition services.

Companies of all sizes need equity capital to achieve their growth objectives and to provide liquidity for their shareholders. To meet those needs, the Corporate Finance Group strives to help clients enhance shareholder value and achieve their strategic and financial goals. The Corporate Finance Group provides a full range of investment banking services including: initial public offerings, public offerings of debt and equity securities, private placements of debt and equity securities, mergers, acquisitions and divestitures, leveraged buyouts, and financial advisory services including fairness opinions, valuations and corporate restructuring. Robinson-Humphrey ranks in the Top 20 investment banking firms nationwide (source: CommScan Equidesk) in managing new and secondary equity issues and is a leader among regional investment banks.

The Corporate Finance Department works closely with emerging companies which require growth capital, more seasoned companies looking for expansion capital, and companies attempting to acquire other businesses. Robinson-Humphrey's expertise in these areas is of paramount value to the client.

Perhaps Robinson-Humphrey's greatest strength is a distribution network that spans the United States and international markets. The retail sales force is located in more than 50 retail offices and the Institutional Sales Group markets research to mutual funds, insurance companies, pension funds and investment advisors around the world. Robinson-Humphrey is an active trader in listed equity securities for companies in the R-H research universe and a market maker for over 300 NASDAQ stocks. After-market support includes sponsorship of industry seminars for investors, company presentations to select institutional accounts domestically and internationally, in addition to an annual April investors conference.

R-H's relationship-based approach helps clients develop innovative strategies to reach their objectives.

Corporate Client Group

The Corporate Client Group works in conjunction with Investment Banking professionals to help meet the nonfinance needs of corporations, executives and high net-worth individuals. The firm serves public and private companies by managing the proceeds from capital raising and merger and acquisition transactions. In addition, the firm provides a wide variety of services, including the design and implementation of 401(k) and other retirement plans, executive stock option exercise and stock purchase plans, restricted stock loans and sales, personal financial planning services, and hedging and risk management for low-cost-basis and restricted securities. Many of these services are offered in partnership with Salomon Smith Barney.

Capital Markets and Trading

Robinson-Humphrey is the largest and most active NASDAQ market-maker of any firm headquartered in the Southeast. It is frequently the primary market maker in a particular stock and commits capital and provides liquidity to ensure an active aftermarket for new issues. Robinson-Humphrey handles large block transactions in listed securities for institutional clients and offers priority to market-making activities for the securities of its investment banking clients. Institutional clients include mutual funds, insurance companies and investment advisors in the United States and abroad.

The R-H Institutional Sales team delivers equity research and sophisticated trading capabilities to institutional clients around the globe. They are recognized as a leading source of investment ideas for emerging growth companies in the Southeast and nationally, mid-cap growth stocks and companies in industries where R-H has acknowledged research expertise. Robinson-Humphrey communicates its recommendations through customized mailings on recent research, daily research briefings, formal conference calls, as well as several institutional investment conferences throughout the year. Rapidly changing markets require timely delivery of information. Its research Web site offers investors virtually instantaneous access to breaking news and commentary from its research analysts.

System, MARTA, Georgia Highway 400 and Emory University. The Municipal Bond Department is one of the largest in the region with a staff of seasoned professionals. Municipal research analysts who focus exclusively on Southeastern issuers provide a wealth of knowledge about Southeastern issuers.

As the region has grown, so has the firm's level of expertise and resources committed to Public Finance. The firm is the leading underwriter of general municipal and health care revenue bonds in Georgia, North Carolina and South Carolina (source: Securities Data Company, Inc.). Added to an expansive secondary trading market in bonds throughout the Southeast, the benefit to individual investors and municipal issuers is enormous in terms of both access to bonds and marketing capability.

Robinson-Humphrey's Annual April Institutional Investor Conference in Atlanta has showcased this effort for over a quarter-century. Each year nearly 200 publicly traded companies present their stories. The conference allows investors and potential investors from all over the United States and Europe to come to Atlanta to look "beyond the numbers" and meet directly with company principals. The conference program offers detailed business profiles and statistics on all participating companies and gives investors a unique "hands on" opportunity which is designed to help them meet the market and competitive challenges of the future.

The institutional sales force also works closely with skilled trading professionals who specialize in listed and NASDAQ issues. This expertise in more than 300 publicly traded NASDAQ securities and a position trading desk for listed issues, allows the sales and trading operations to better meet the needs of clients smoothly and efficiently.

Financing the Region's Growth

For more than 100 years, R-H has dominated the Southeast tax-exempt bond marketplace. The firm has underwritten bonds to finance everything from school facilities and jails to the University of North Carolina

Private Investors

Today's individual investor has unique needs and the R-H staff of professional Financial Consultants gives clients a complete array of strategies to address virtually any individual financial concern. As a subsidiary of Salomon Smith Barney, R-H offers everything from basic common stocks to the most sophisticated financial planning tools. Services include a complete monthly financial statement, free check writing, cash access via thousands of ATM machines worldwide, automatic dividend reinvestment as well as gain and loss accounting for tax purposes.

Robinson-Humphrey is dedicated to the growth of its clients' portfolios and financial position. It provides a wide range of services including equity research, retirement plans, portfolio management services, mutual funds and risk management for restricted shareholders. The Personal Financial Planning Department has more than a quarter-century of experience in personal financial planning assisting clients in all areas of asset allocation.

To keep at peak performance and to address client needs in a climate of continuing complexity in financial, tax and investment issues, R-H Financial Consultants consider ongoing training and development a key with regard to performance for their clients. Their goal is to ensure that each client's financial concern is addressed.

Giving Back to the Community

Now more than ever before, Robinson-Humphrey is committed to giving back to a community that has given it so much. Through individual effort and corporate sponsorship, R-H provides support for a broad base of charities that serve the Atlanta metropolitan area and throughout the Southeast. The firm focuses on organizations that strive to meet a pressing community need, especially projects that improve education or promote cultural, social or health services.

Robinson-Humphrey's commitment to its community is consistent and long-lasting. As a provider of local funding for "Wall Street Week," R-H is among the longest continuous corporate sponsors of Georgia Public Television. Meeting and exceeding the R-H criteria of promoting the arts, The Woodruff Arts Center is also a beneficiary of R-H's financial and hands-on support. Robinson-Humphrey employees serve on boards and volunteer their services to the center's High Museum of Art, the Atlanta Symphony Orchestra, and the Alliance Studio Theatre.

In addition, Robinson-Humphrey is one of the founding sponsors of The Atlanta Mile and 5K Run which benefits the Georgia Foundation of Athletic Excellence that helps Georgia's amateur athletes maximize their performance in their competitive and

With strong leadership and dedication to clients, Robinson-Humphrey is focused on a promising future.

working careers, the Scottish Rite Children's Medical Center and Shepherd Center Research Fund. Among others, R-H supports The American Cancer Society, Emory University and the United Way of Metropolitan Atlanta.

Focused on the Future

Robinson-Humphrey, a Southeastern leader, has a rich past and an even more promising future. Throughout its long history, the firm has proudly retained its original name and distinctive identity as the leading research, investment banking and brokerage firm in the region. Robinson-Humphrey has survived the test of time by taking a leadership position and is dedicated to help meet the ever increasing needs of the client, whether institutional or individual. Just as the firm focused on the city and region of its birth 100 years ago, R-H now boldly turns toward national and international markets to meet the future. With strong leadership, a commitment to increased market knowledge and service to its clients, Robinson-Humphrey is clearly "Focused on Growth."

In 1894 Roby Robinson founded Robinson-Humphrey to help meet the capital needs of Atlanta and the South.

Northwestern Mutual Life, The Goodwin Agency

The Civil War had been over for just four years when Dr. William White started a new venture: selling life insurance policies for the Wisconsin-based Northwestern Mutual Life Insurance Company. Founded in 1857, the company was developing new markets — a key factor in it becoming one of the largest life insurance businesses west of the Atlantic seaboard. Much of that growth took place in Atlanta, where in 1870 Dr. White became the first local agent for Northwestern Mutual.

The story of Northwestern Mutual in the South is intricately linked to the men who steadily worked to turn the fledgling Georgia agency into one of the company's largest. Following his father's lead, W. Woods White took on the challenge in 1880. In April of 1885, he was appointed the company's first general agent in Georgia. The agency sold $57,000 of life insurance protection in that first year. White wrote much of the business himself, but over time he also built an agency with offices in Macon, Augusta, Columbus and Athens as well as Atlanta.

When White retired in 1921, district agent Hamilton Yancey Jr. and Atlanta office manager Frank B. Lowe became partner general agents. Their partnership lasted just two years, and they were followed by Luther E. Allen, who led the agency for 30 years. Leadership then passed to John M. Law, CLU, a Northwestern agent who had built a strong district agency in Bluefield, West Virginia.

Under Law's direction, the agency's business dramatically increased, requiring a move from its original downtown location in the Healey Building to more spacious offices in Midtown. Law's enthusiasm and dedication to the industry were apparent in a company

Combining 47 years of leadership, John M. Law, CLU, (left) led the agency from 1953 through 1978; William O. Goodwin, CLU, ChFC, has presided since 1979.

newsletter in which he wrote, "To me, it is a 'he-man's' business. It is only for the strong in heart."

In 1975 the general agency split into north and south Georgia operations. Four years later, William O. Goodwin, CLU, ChFC, succeeded Law as the general agent for Atlanta and South Georgia. Under Goodwin's leadership, the agency has built a model organization that has received national acclaim for agent retention and productivity. Goodwin's work was acknowledged in 1996 when he became only the 33rd person to be inducted into the Agency Management Hall of Fame by the General Agents and Managers Association.

In 2000, Northwestern Mutual's $86 billion of assets made it the fifth-largest life insurance company in America, and The Goodwin Agency, based in Buckhead, is one of its 102 general agencies. Though the agency has enjoyed profitable growth for more than a century, perhaps no period has been so successful as the last two decades. Goodwin credits this growth to "discriminating buyers who become loyal policy owners when superior products are backed by quality service and the financial strength of Northwestern Mutual." The agency currently has more than $13 billion of life insurance in force.

Northwestern Mutual has always received the highest possible rating from the major rating services — Moody's, Standard & Poor's, A.M. Best, and Duff & Phelps. Additionally, the company has always ranked No. 1 in the industry in *Fortune* magazine's "America's Most Admired Companies." During the agency's 115-year history in Georgia, Goodwin is only the fifth general agent to head the organization. That kind of continuity is emblematic of the strength and stability that have made Northwestern Mutual the "policy owner's company."

The Coca-Cola Company

More than 100 years ago, the world's best-kept commercial secret started in Atlanta. Behind this secret is the story of a local pharmacist, an Atlanta banker and several enterprising businessmen who turned a local fizzy beverage into the world's most popular soft drink — Coca-Cola.

The legend begins in the backyard of John Stith Pemberton, an Atlanta pharmacist. On May 8, 1886, Dr. Pemberton stirred up a caramel-colored syrup in a three-legged copper kettle and was so delighted by the taste that he shared it at the local soda fountain at Jacobs' Pharmacy. There, a bubbly drink made its debut, selling for five cents a glass.

The new product needed a signature name. "Coca-Cola" was suggested by Dr. Pemberton's partner and bookkeeper, Frank M. Robinson, who thought "the two Cs would look well in advertising." He then created the enduring Coca-Cola trademark, penning the words Coca-Cola in the now familiar Spencerian script. On May 29, 1886, the first advertisement for Coca-Cola appeared in *The Atlanta Journal*, inviting locals to try "the new and popular soda fountain drink."

Although the Coca-Cola business would later become known for its successful advertising and marketing innovations, the first year of sales averaged just nine drinks per day. Dr. Pemberton would never have imagined that his local drink would become the heart of a global business in nearly 200 countries around the world.

But Asa G. Candler, an Atlanta businessman, saw great potential for the soft drink. He acquired Dr. Pemberton's interests in the business venture until he had sole ownership in 1891 for a total investment of $2,300. Using his business savvy, Candler increased sales of Coca-Cola syrup with many innovations, such as the first-ever coupons and celebrity endorsements. To further promote Coca-Cola, Candler and his business partners formed a new Georgia corporation in 1892 — The Coca-Cola Company.

While Candler was expanding business operations, a candy store owner was pondering a way to spread Coca-Cola throughout the nation. In 1894, Vicksburg, Mississippi, merchant Joseph A. Biedenharn installed bottling equipment in the back of his store to keep up with the demand for Coca-Cola. He began selling cases of Coca-Cola up and down the Mississippi River, becoming the first Coca-Cola bottler.

Large-scale bottling began in 1899 when Benjamin F. Thomas and Joseph B. Whitehead of Chattanooga, Tennessee, bought the rights to bottle and sell Coca-Cola nationwide from Candler for one dollar. Together with other entrepreneurs, they built a powerful network of bottlers, which remains the backbone of The Coca-Cola Company's soft drink operations today.

The Candler era came to a close when Atlanta banker Ernest Woodruff and an investor group purchased The Coca-Cola Company in 1919 for $25 million. At that time the company was reincorporated in Delaware and 500,000 shares of common stock were publicly sold for the first time at a price of $40 per share. Today, a single share of stock purchased in 1919, with dividends reinvested, would be worth nearly $7 million.

In 1923 Woodruff's son, Robert, took over day-to-day operations as the newly elected president of The Coca-Cola Company. With this new post, Robert W. Woodruff would begin a remarkable six decades of leadership for the company, breathing new life into the business and making Coca-Cola an international icon.

With Woodruff at the helm, The Coca-Cola Company became the first truly global consumer

The late Coca-Cola Chairman and CEO Robert Goizueta (left) with longtime Coca-Cola Chairman and mentor, Robert W. Woodruff

products company and established the Foreign Department. During the early 1900s, bottling operations were under way in Cuba, Puerto Rico, the Philippines, Guam and France.

Coca-Cola strengthened its international reach by forming an alliance with the Olympic movement, which is now a more than 70-year-old partnership. In 1928 a freighter headed to the Olympic Games in Amsterdam carried 1,000 cases of Coca-Cola and the U.S. Olympic team.

At the outbreak of World War II, Coca-Cola was bottled in 44 countries. During the war, Woodruff sought to put a Coca-Cola "within an arm's reach of desire." From the mid-1940s to 1960, the number of countries with bottling operations doubled.

Woodruff made an indelible mark on The Coca-Cola Company and on Atlanta itself. He channeled millions of philanthropic dollars into Atlanta and its institutions. Woodruff insisted on making his donations anonymously, but his generosity made him the most famous anonymous donor in Atlanta and a lasting legacy. His support of education — with more than $230 million in contributions to Emory University alone — is an ongoing focus of giving for The Coca-Cola Company.

In 1981 the Cuban-born Roberto C. Goizueta succeeded Woodruff as chairman and chief executive officer. Formerly a chemist with The Coca-Cola Company's office in Havana, Goizueta sharpened the company's focus on capturing growth in the beverage industry. He pioneered the concept of shareowner value, delivering unprecedented return on shareowner investment. His leadership boosted the company's market value from $4 billion to $145 billion.

Goizueta also continued the company's tradition of giving in Atlanta, establishing The Coca-Cola Foundation in 1984. Today, The Coca-Cola Foundation is one of the nation's leading corporate foundations, contributing $100 million in the decade of the 1990s and supporting education at more than 500 universities, schools and organizations in Atlanta and around the world.

Upon Goizueta's death in 1997, his protégé, M. Douglas Ivester, was elected chairman and chief executive officer. A 19-year veteran of the beverage business, Ivester previously served as the company's president,

Jacobs' Pharmacy (c. late 1800s) in downtown Atlanta, where the soft drink was introduced at the soda fountain on May 8, 1886, is located near the present Coca-Cola International Headquarters.

chief financial officer and head of its U.S. and European operations. Ivester retired from the company at the end of 1999. In February 2000 the board of directors named Doug Daft, a 30-year veteran of the company, chief executive officer and the 11th chairman of the board in the company's history. Daft, an Australian native, has taken swift, bold and decisive actions in order to make The Coca-Cola Company a more nimble and competitive organization as it embarks upon the 21st century. He assembled a new senior management team and led a transformation of the company by decentralizing its operations through a global realignment that has pushed resources, responsibility and accountability to the business units in the more than 200 countries where it operates.

Perhaps nowhere else in the world has a simple local product turned into such a global icon and economic engine. Surveys consistently call Coca-Cola the most recognized brand name in the world. The Coca-Cola Company employs more than 30,000 people worldwide, with more than 5,000 of those jobs in Atlanta. Researchers have shown that each job in the Coca-Cola system creates up to 10 other jobs among suppliers and customers in the larger economy.

In addition to stimulating local economic growth, part of what distinguishes The Coca-Cola Company is its longtime tradition of giving back to the communities it serves. From Trees Atlanta to the city's premier cultural center, The Woodruff Arts Center, to the Atlanta University Center and the elementary schools where Coca-Cola employees volunteer, most Atlantans can quickly name a community project touched by The Coca-Cola Company. City leaders attest that it is this community involvement that helped build Atlanta into the bustling economic center it is today.

National Service Industries

The marble rotunda of the National Service Industries building in Midtown soars over an enormous bronze sculpture that depicts a runner in three stages of a race. The first figure is crouching at the starting block; the second is pushing toward the finish; and the third is thrusting his arms high in triumph. The 16-foot-long, 11.5-foot-high work entitled "Winning" is not only decorative — it represents the history and philosophy of this industry giant.

Though the National Service Industries (NSI) title didn't come along until 1964, this $2.5 billion company has roots that stretch back to the days following World War I. As the story goes, founder I.M. Weinstein spent some time in a French hospital after being shot in the chest and leg. His observation of the enormous amounts of towels, linens and crisp uniforms used in war hospitals inspired him to create a company that would take over the incredibly labor-intensive job of cleaning and pressing those items. In 1919 his Atlanta Linen Company began renting an assortment of textiles

"Winning," the bronze sculpture in the lobby of the National Service Industries building, represents the company's commitment to excellence.

to Atlanta businesses. Soon branches were springing up in cities across the South, and the name changed to National Linen Service.

After years of success, National Linen Service faced what could have been a major setback in 1956 when the Justice Department alleged monopolization in the Southeast. As a result, the company began to sell off several plants and accounts. At the same time, Weinstein looked for new ways to grow and recapture the lost business. By the 1960s, he'd found the key: diversification. By purchasing other businesses, the company expanded dramatically, and National Service Industries was born. Through the years, some companies were sold off while others merged into the mix. In 1999 the financially strong NSI corporation still included National Linen Service, the country's largest linen rental firm that processes almost 2 billion pieces of laundry each year. Five other strong businesses are part of the NSI family: Zep Manufacturing Company, Atlantic Envelope Company, Selig Industries, Lithonia Lighting, and Enforcer Products.

NSI's first acquisition, Zep Manufacturing Company, began making cleansers and lubricants in 1937. That was the year founder Mandle Zaban borrowed against his life insurance policy to start his own business. The company's name was created from some of its first investors: Zaban, William Eplan and Saul Powell. After World War II, Zaban turned the reins of the business over to his son, Erwin, who led the company's expansion across the country.

In 1961 Zaban heard from an old friend, Milton Weinstein, the son of National Linen Service's founder. Weinstein offered to purchase Zep, and as part of the deal, Zaban became an executive vice president and board member of NSI. After working his way up to CEO, Zaban retired in 1996, but not before marking several milestones, including the company's first billion dollars in 1984 and the $2 billion mark just 12 years later. He also oversaw the move of NSI headquarters from its outdated facility at 14th and Peachtree streets to its present location just a few blocks away at the corner of Peachtree and West Peachtree. His reputation and business acumen helped attract some of the Southeast's most respected executives to the NSI board.

Atlantic Envelope Company (AECO), an NSI family member since 1964, began with the now bygone art of making envelopes by hand. Founder Sigmund Guthman tapped that talent to create the company in 1893, but by 1904 he was using machines to turn his home-grown business into the $200 million operation that today produces not only envelopes, but also paper products and office supplies, including the envelopes used by Federal Express. In 1962 the name changed from Atlanta Envelope to Atlantic Envelope to reflect the company's expansion along the East Coast. Two years later, AECO® merged with NSI.

The second-oldest NSI affiliate is Selig Chemical Industries, created by Simon Selig in 1896 when he was only 16 years old. The $30 million company manufactures an array of environmentally safe cleaning products. Among its first offerings were disinfectant soaps and insecticides, including the continually best-selling Se-fly-go®, which does just what its name implies. The company developed a reputation for products that not only were effective but also had amusing names, among them, Gosh it Cleans!™, an all-purpose cleaner, and Nothing™, for windows. Selig became part of NSI in 1968.

Shedding light in unusual places is the expertise of NSI's Lithonia Lighting division, founded in 1946. Founder Sam Freeman started the business in Lithonia, Georgia, about 20 miles east of Atlanta, when the small town was the only one to answer his queries about factory space. With the financial backing of two cousins already in the lighting business, Freeman began making fixtures. His first year in business brought in about $287,000 — a figure that soared by 134 percent the next year. The company joined NSI in 1969 and has proved to be one of its best performers, generating almost $1.5 billion in revenue. As the largest manufacturer of commercial lighting fixtures in North America, Lithonia Lighting dispels darkness around the world, from the Georgia International Horse Park outside of Atlanta to the Sphinx. Each year, thousands of distributors and contractors visit the company headquarters in Conyers, Georgia, the next town east of Lithonia, to check out the array of commercial, industrial, institutional and residential lighting fixtures. Another 25 plants are situated around the United States, Canada, Mexico, England, Spain and Australia.

In 1997 NSI purchased Enforcer Products, which became the first NSI division to sell directly to retail customers. Weed killers, wasp and hornet sprays, flea traps, rat killers and flea and tick shampoos are some of the items listed in the Enforcer inventory.

The success of NSI, though closely bound to the strength of its individual companies, is just as tightly tied to the success of its employees. Jim Balloun, who stepped into the chairman's role in 1996, has placed great emphasis on making the company an attractive place to work as well as a draw for investors. NSI's belief in the excellence of each individual in the organization is best summed up in the plaque that hangs near the "Winning" sculpture at the Midtown headquarters. "At National Service Industries, winning is one of our strongest motivating forces," it reads. "Winning means setting difficult goals, and meeting them... concentrating our efforts on the business we know best to produce superior returns for our shareholders... having a corporate culture that fosters innovation, embraces change and encourages employees to reach their full potential. As the company builds strength upon strength, we remain dedicated to serving the needs of our customers and maintaining the highest standards of excellence."

The rotunda at the headquarters of National Service Industries looks out over Atlanta's Peachtree Street.

Snapper, Inc.

It's always been about blades. Whether honing blades to cut down Georgia pines or developing revolutionary lawn mower blades, Snapper's roots cut deep into the Georgia soil.

William R. Smith, Snapper's founder

The Snapper story began before the turn of the last century when most lawn mowers were livestock. Frank Ohien and Clarence Chaffe founded what is now Snapper, Inc. in 1890. Incorporated as Southern Saw Works on November 1, 1894, by then owner Isaac Boyd, the company made circular saws for the growing Georgia lumber industry. For almost 60 years, as lumber prospered so did Southern Saw.

But by 1949, saw making was an industry in decline. William R. Smith, who then owned Southern Saw, watched as green lawns replaced towering pines. Smith, seeing opportunity, made an insightful decision to enter the lawn mower industry. He purchased the patents of "Snappin' Turtle" mowers, one of the first rotary mowers, then being built in Florida. Actual Georgia production began in East Point in January 1951, when 16 of the unique mowers were shipped. By the end of 1951, a total of 3,975 mowers were manufactured and delivered throughout the United States. Several of these first mowers are on display at the Smithsonian Institute in Washington, D.C., and the Atlanta History Museum.

In the early 1950s, lawn mowers were a "growing" business. Although the first mowers were English-made push reel mowers, Americans took the design one step further, adding newly developed small engines to reel mowers. During the 1950s and 1960s, as lawn sizes grew from the postage lots in the city to the half-acre or more lots of the suburbs, homeowners were spending more of their recreation time mowing grass. Power reel mowers, though widely available, were expensive, heavy and awkward to handle. Their open reels made safety a continuing concern.

On January 16, 1951, Snapper introduced its "Snappin' Turtle," the first self-propelled rotary mower. It's smaller, lighter engine and safe, covered blade revolutionized the industry. A lower, more compact body made with new, less expensive yet stronger materials brought the price to a reasonable level. The rotary mower became as common as a garden spade.

As the mower business grew, the saw business waned. Soon, lawn mower manufacturing replaced saw production in the plant. Even so, by 1954 the East Point plant could grow no further. The decision was made to merge Southern Saw Works and the McDonough Foundry & Machine Works and move the entire operation to McDonough in Henry County. McDonough Foundry & Machine Works, a supplier to Southern Saw, had been organized in 1946 to produce iron castings and textile machinery. The merger of the two manufacturers created a new company known as McDonough Power Equipment.

Snapper mowers were leading a new revolution in lawn care equipment, and McDonough Power was growing with this revolution. Innovations in power mowers and accessories, many designed by Snapper, fueled the growth of rotary mowers and McDonough

New technology takes Snapper into the next generation with the Yard Cruiser

Power's line of consumer products. In fact, Snapper owns 44 patents for innovations in safety, deck design and transmissions.

As lawns got bigger and leisure time got shorter, even self-propelled walk-behind mowers couldn't cut it fast enough. So Snapper engineers designed and produced one of its most lauded innovations, the Snapper rear-engine-riding mower. A hybrid of sorts, it gave consumers a machine priced between a walk-behind mower and its more expensive cousin, the lawn tractor. The Snapper was built with an engine behind the operator so as not to obstruct the view of the mowing area and to keep the hot engine behind rather than in front of the operator. In its early production the Comet — named in the midst of the space race — replaced the traditional steering wheel with handlebars similar to those on a bicycle. Consumers loved them, and even today the company gets letters from homeowners who still proudly own and operate those mowers. At one time, Comet sales were more than 80 percent of McDonough Power transactions.

The success of the Comet and other products made Snapper an attractive acquisition, and in 1967 Snapper was purchased by Atlanta-based Fuqua Industries. The alliance provided Snapper with the capital to expand to a second manufacturing plant in Texas and continue the development of new and innovative additions to its product line, including lawn tractors in 1982 and rear-tine tillers and snowthrowers in 1983. Building on its growing product and name recognition, McDonough Power was renamed Snapper Power Equipment in 1982.

Between 1982 and 1987, Snapper was growing almost twice as fast as the industry. During 1985 the McDonough plant was building a mower every 52 seconds to keep up with demand. Commercial equipment was added to the Snapper mix in 1987 and the company used its years of creativity in the residential market to redefine the standards for commercial mowers.

But a downturn in the economy coupled with a nearly nationwide drought as well as the success of mass merchandisers and discounters caused difficulties

Today's version of the Rear Engine Rider

for Snapper. As a result, sales stalled in the late 80s and early 90s. As the decade progressed, Snapper developed inventive products such as the hydrostatic rear-engine rider and tractor and the Ninja® mulching system to answer consumer demands for better and more earth-friendly mowing systems.

On the administrative side, Metromedia International Group purchased Snapper's parent, Fuqua. But changes in the front office did not stop changes to the product line. In 1997 Snapper introduced its biggest innovation yet — the Yard Cruiser®. A variation of the rear-engine rider, the Yard Cruiser is a zero-turn radius mower providing the ultimate in comfort with single-hand, joystick steering and the best of the Snapper mowing tradition.

After almost 50 years, the company has grown to be a leader in the industry, with approximately 900 employees housed in nearly 1 million square feet of facilities in McDonough, Georgia. Major distribution centers outside of Georgia are located in Texas, Nevada and Ohio. Snapper products are sold nationwide and abroad through over 5,000 servicing dealers.

What started with a commitment to innovation and quality has persevered through the good and tough times. Now Snapper is prepared to start its second half-century with a renewed dedication to the ideals that have brought it to the new millennium. One might say, Snapper is "Born To Mow."

ADVERTISING AIDS
TO HELP YOU SELL
SNAPPIN' TURTLE
AMERICA'S FINEST LINE OF ROTARY POWER MOWERS!
for **1959**

Early advertising for Snapper's innovative "Snappin' Turtle" products

Atlanta Marriott Marquis

The glass tube elevators shine, the fountains sparkle and the marble floors gleam in the grand lobby of the recently renovated Marriott Marquis, one of Atlanta's premier hotels. But what completely captivates first-time visitors as well as returning guests is the soaring 50-story atrium, encircled by balconies that extend almost to the skylights in the ceiling.

Designed and completed in 1984 by Atlanta architect John Portman, the Marquis was the third hotel built in Portman's Peachtree Center complex in the heart of downtown. Today, the Marquis remains a landmark of stunning architectural scope that causes most who enter through its glass front doors to stand in wonder with their heads tipped back and mouths wide open.

With one look, it's clear that Portman achieved his goal of creating a hotel that showcased the open atrium style — a style he helped popularize. At the same time, he aided the city's redevelopment efforts by placing the hotel downtown, in a location that caters to visiting conventioneers and tourists. Perhaps in part because of its strategic location, the Marquis was chosen as the headquarters for the International Olympic Committee and guests from around the world during the 1996 Olympics. Today, the Marquis commemorates this historic event with the inscription of names of former Olympic host cities and the Olympic rings on the lobby walls.

The main level of the Marquis is luxurious, with marble floors and burgundy carpets. But the room's main attraction is overhead, where the streamers of a gigantic, pale pink kite drift down from the ceiling's skylights. Marquis guests and visitors are invited to step into the sleek elevators, outlined in lights, which shoot up the sides of the lobby to the 10th-floor Skyline level where spectacular city views await. Some of the best vistas in town are from the hotel's top eight floors, where frequent Marriott guests are pampered with card-accessed elevators, private conference rooms, honor bars and concierge lounges that offer breakfast. But from almost any balcony, guests may peer down into the lobby and get a sense of the atrium's Coca-Cola-bottle shape.

With 1,675 guest rooms, including 68 suites, and more than 1,200 employees, the Marriott Marquis is the company's second-largest hotel facility, trailing the only other Marquis, in New York City. The hotel caters to business travelers and conventioneers who flock to Atlanta year round. The guest rooms are arranged with their needs in mind and are dubbed "rooms that work," with ergonomic chairs at each desk, outlets for laptop computers and high-speed Internet access. Other features include coffee makers, mini refrigerators, ironing boards and irons, hair dryers and entertainment armoires.

The two lowest levels of the Marquis comprise the heart of the hotel's state-of-the-art convention center. With 120,000 square feet, the convention space is one of the largest in the state, with banquet rooms and ballrooms that host more than 1,000 groups and 1 million people each year under its glittering chandeliers. A 38,000-square-foot exhibit hall can be divided to accommodate two events at one time. Huge freight

Streamers from a pink kite tied to the Marriott Marquis' 50-story ceiling float over the hotel's atrium lobby.

elevators, big enough to carry cars (which they have been called upon to do), can be loaded with whatever props exhibitors bring. A secondary entrance at the rear of the hotel is designed so that tour buses can pull up right to the door and guests may enter directly into the convention area or take escalators to the lobby elevators. (This arrangement is particularly popular with many sports teams that stay at the hotel; players can head directly to their rooms without parading through the lobby!)

On the weekends, the hotel bustles with visitors enjoying overnight stays while visiting nearby restaurants and professional sporting venues. In some cases, guests combine work and pleasure. The hotel works with its guests to put together packages of rooms with tickets to various happenings, from a football game at the Georgia Dome to the arts events in the area.

Throughout the building, four restaurants provide an array of dining selections, from an early-morning blueberry muffin and Starbucks latte in the Atrium Express, to an oversized sirloin with all the trimmings in the Marquis Steakhouse. Champions is the recently renovated sports bar; Allie's American Grille is a 200-seat casual cafe that serves breakfast, lunch and dinner in a dining room surrounded by enormous glass windows overlooking patios and fountains. The Grandstand Lounge on the hotel's mezzanine serves evening cocktails. In addition, room service operates 24 hours.

Along with multiple dining options, the Marquis boasts concierge services, a gift shop, 24-hour business and fitness centers, a spa and sauna, masseuse services, and an indoor-outdoor pool under a glass dome. In addition, hotel guests enjoy visiting privileges at the nearby Peachtree Center Athletic Club. Covered walkways connect to MARTA, Atlanta's subway system, and other restaurants, shops and offices in the Peachtree Center complex.

"Our location is one thing that truly sets us apart from other cities," says Mark Vaughan, the Marquis' marketing director. "We have a multitude of dining and entertaining options, but we're also accessible to MARTA, which goes to the airport and to Buckhead's entertainment district. And we're close to the Georgia World Congress Center, the major convention center in Atlanta."

The Marriott Marquis sits amid the skyscrapers of downtown Atlanta and the Peachtree Center complex.

Guests of the Marriott Marquis also enjoy a full range of complimentary destination services. The Marquis staff will plan their transportation, off-site meetings, meals or an entire package.

No matter where in the city they may be attending an event, Marquis guests benefit not only from the hotel's central location but also from its architectural grandeur. When guests enter the building, they have something dramatic to look up to. It happens every day when people walk in. They just look up and exclaim, "Wow!"

The view from the top of the Marquis' 50-story atrium follows the trail of a gigantic pink kite anchored to the ceiling.

Château Élan Winery & Resort

The 16th-century French-style Château Élan Winery & Resort

Nestled in the foothills of North Georgia's pine mountains, only a few miles removed but seemingly a world away from the commercial cacophony of metro-Atlanta, is a place where French provincial and Southern comfort mingle. Château Élan Winery & Resort in Braselton, Georgia, is perhaps the one place in the world where the humble muscadine abides with Cabernet Sauvignon.

When Château Élan was founded in the early 1980s, Atlanta was on the cusp of international prominence. Today, both the city and the resort have gained national and international recognition.

To the accidental tourist, a first glimpse of the 16th-century French-style château from Interstate 85 north of Atlanta is quite a surprise. Yet, among the rolling hills in what used to be rural cotton country, the château seems a natural part of the landscape.

The challenging bunkers and terrain of the par-72 Woodlands course

Château Élan Winery & Resort is the fruit of a labor of love that began during an impromptu visit to a roadside fruit stand. The winery's founders, pharmaceutical entrepreneur Dr. Donald Panoz and his wife, Nancy, had stopped to pick up a fruit basket on their way to a dinner party. While perusing the fresh fruits, which included plump, sweet muscadines (a wild grape indigenous to the Southeast), the couple's interest in growing vinifera was sparked.

The notion of a winery in the North Georgia foothills was met with considerable skepticism from other winemakers and from the surrounding rural communities. North Georgia was fertile soil for the South's king crop: cotton. But wine grapes?

Donald Panoz consulted California winemaking experts to determine whether the soil and climate could sustain a vineyard. A small test vineyard was planted behind the Panoz's pharmaceutical plant in nearby Gainesville. Themselves agricultural novices, Donald and Nancy Panoz consulted a representative from the Georgia Department of Agriculture, who suggested a tried and true Native American method of placing a fish in the ground along with the grape vines. "They grew like gangbusters," recalls Nancy Panoz.

However, heavy clay content in the Braselton soil prevented the vines from flourishing as they did on the land behind the pharmaceutical plant. But the couple persisted until they found a patch of suitable land that previously had been used to grow cotton. The renowned Panoz persistence prevailed, and four years later Château Élan released its first wines, a 1984 vintage Johannisberg Riesling and Chardonnay. Not long after, Château Élan was opened to the public. Today Château Élan boasts the largest production and distribution of any Georgia winery on its nearly 200 acres of rolling pinstriped vineyards.

The winery produces nearly 20 varieties of wine that have garnered more than 250 awards. Visitors can taste and purchase white, red, blush and port wines, plus a collection of Georgia specialties that combine the distinctive taste of muscadine grapes with other flavors such as raspberry, strawberry and peach.

The Château, which houses the winery, Art Gallery, Wine Market, and adjacent Paddy's Irish Pub, is now a familiar landmark to Atlanta natives. The Art Gallery is home to a variety of fine works created predominately by emerging local artists. A recent addition to the Château's collection, and a favorite of Nancy Panoz, is Florida sculptor Bradley Cooley's "Dancing in the Grapes," a twice-life-size bronze statue of a woman crushing grapes with her feet. The Wine Market offers a wide selection of wines and related merchandise including gourmet foods, apparel and unique gifts. Paddy's is an authentic Irish pub that features traditional Irish fare and weekend entertainment.

Visitors to the winery's complimentary tours and tastings began to inquire about overnight accommodations. Responding to that need, The Spa at Château Élan and The Inn at Château Élan were built. Having spent a number of years in Europe, the Panozes endeavored to create an atmosphere that bespoke of Southern hospitality with a European flair. To that end they have incorporated fine cuisine, wine, art, recreation and world-class accommodations into a Mobil Four-Star resort and meeting destination. Taking advantage of the resort's 25,000-square-foot, state-of-the-art conference center, corporate meetings and retreats comprise the majority of the hotel's business.

The Inn has 306 rooms featuring country French decor, including 23 suites and a 2,000-square-foot presidential suite. Two of Château Élan's seven restaurants are located at The Inn. The Versailles Room, situated in the Inn's expansive glass atrium, offers dining in a patio-style atmosphere. The menu includes a variety of entrees prepared with a South of France flair. L'Auberge, a lounge overlooking the Inn's atrium, offers food and spirits in a causal setting.

Spa guests may choose from one of 14 theme-decorated rooms, such as the Greek Room featuring marble flooring and Greek columns. The Spa offers a variety of spiritually and physically revitalizing services: facial treatments, fitness programs and specialized body treatments including Hot Stone Therapy Massage. The Fleur-de-Lis dining room offers Spa guests a selection of healthy gourmet spa cuisine.

Land determined unsuitable for growing grapes was put to use for another of Donald Panoz's passions. In 1989, The Château Élan Golf Club was created, featuring 63 holes of championship golf on four courses. Amenities include two clubhouses, two professional golf shops, two restaurants and a covered tournament pavilion. Professional instruction is offered April through October. Two- and three-bedroom Petit Château Golf Villas line the 15th fairway of The Château course.

The Château, a public golf course designed by Dennis Griffiths, was the first to open in 1989. Seven years later, Griffiths also designed The Woodlands, a stunning course with green fairways year round. The crown jewel of Château Élan Golf Club is The Legends, a private, members-only 18-hole course designed by golf Hall of Fame greats Gene Sarazen, Sam Snead and Kathy Whitworth. A nine-hole, par three executive walking course is conveniently located behind the Inn.

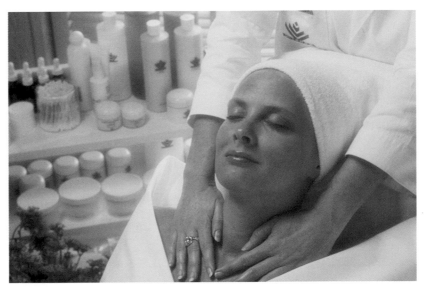

Guests of The Spa enjoy treatments that soothe the mind and body.

The resort also features an equestrian show center that plays host to a number of championship equestrian events throughout the year as well as a world-class tennis complex designed by Stan Smith. And for those who find the lure of Château Élan too enticing to leave behind, there are several residential communities featuring homes and estates. Whether visitors come to Château Élan for a day trip or for a lifetime, the melding of Southern hospitality and European flair makes their stay an experience like no other.

Embassy Suites Hotels

Atlanta has come a long way since General William Tecumseh Sherman and his Union troops left the city in flames in 1864. Appropriately adopting the mythical Phoenix as its symbol, Atlanta rose from the ashes to become a sprawling, urban megalopolis, a city that wears the crown as the Capital of the New South. And, Embassy Suites Hotels has been a proud resident of Atlanta since 1985.

World-famous for its award-winning atriums, Embassy Suites Hotels offers Atlantans and their out-of-town guests a safe harbor from the rushed, tumultuous pace of big-city life. With four hotels strategically located

throughout metro Atlanta, everyone can experience the soothing, relaxing feeling of visiting a tropical paradise while still enjoying the conveniences of a major metropolitan city.

Consistently perched near the top of *Consumer Reports'* Customer Service Satisfaction Survey for upscale hotels, Embassy Suites Hotels, created by Hervey Feldman in 1983, has, in its relatively brief existence, become an innovative leader in the hospitality industry. Besides being the first full-service all suites hotel, Embassy Suites Hotels was also the first

hotel chain to offer complimentary made-to-order breakfasts and complimentary two-hour evening manager's receptions.

Every Embassy Suites Hotel offers a spacious two-room suite with a king or two double beds and a large living room with a dining and work area for four including an easy chair and sofa bed. A wet bar, microwave, refrigerator and coffee maker are also provided along with two remote-controlled televisions, two telephones with voice mail and data port, an iron with ironing board, hair dryer and an alarm clock radio.

Value-added services for guests with disabilities, including roll-in showers and beds on frames with no obstructions are also offered, as are smoking or non-smoking accommodations, complimentary newspapers delivered to the door, a game room and indoor/outdoor pool, sauna, whirlpool and exercise facilities.

Embassy's Atlanta flagship property is the Embassy Suites Buckhead. Located on historic Peachtree Street, the hotel resides in the heart of Buckhead, the ritzy upscale section of Atlanta that is the city's most prestigious neighborhood for dining, shopping and business. Featuring 317 spacious two-room suites overlooking a spectacular 16-floor tropical atrium, the Embassy Suites Buckhead mingles perfectly with its surroundings, an area called the "Beverly Hills of the South." The renowned reputation of the Buckhead area also makes it one of the most desirable locations for businesses and organizations to host their functions and, with over 3,800 square feet of flexible meeting/banquet space, the Embassy Suites Buckhead can accommodate business or social functions from three to 300 people.

While offering free shuttle service to area office complexes and shopping malls, the hotel is centrally located, only one block from the MARTA Rapid Transit Station and only three blocks from Lenox Square Mall and Phipps Plaza. Centennial Olympic Park, Turner Field, the Georgia Dome, World Congress Center, CNN Center and The World of Coke are all less than 10 miles away and are easily accessed by MARTA.

There's an old saying that a person traveling to heaven must first change planes in Atlanta. The busiest airport in the world, Hartsfield International serves as a stopping off point for millions of frequent flyers each year. Weary travelers to Atlanta, looking for a respite from the stress of air travel, are only minutes away from the soothing peace and quiet of the Embassy Suites Atlanta Airport hotel in College Park, Georgia.

Five stories and 233 suites surround another impressive atrium. The hotel's restaurant, Moniker's Grille and Sports Bar Grille, features continental cuisine, prime steak and fresh seafood and offers the exhausted journeyer much needed rejuvenation. And, with over 7,500 square feet of flexible meeting space, businesses and organizations have more than adequate space for meetings and banquets. Travelers staying at the Embassy Suites Atlanta Airport who are looking to explore the city are only a mile and a half from the airport MARTA station, providing accessible, reliable transportation to downtown Atlanta and beyond.

Located near the junction of I-285 and I-75 on Akers Mill Road in northwest Atlanta, the Embassy Suites Hotels Atlanta-Galleria is ideally situated across the street from the Galleria Convention Centre and two major malls. Its location, allowing ease of ingress and egress onto two major interstate systems, provides accommodating access by car to many of Atlanta's most popular destinations — White Water Park is only an eight-mile drive while downtown Atlanta, Six Flags over Georgia, Turner Field, Centennial Olympic Park and the Georgia Dome are less than 15 miles away.

After spending a few minutes in the Galleria's nine-story tropical atrium, guests will quickly forget the fast pace of the city just beyond the front door. All of the 261 two-room suites offer a luxurious retreat from the urban pressures. Jamie's Restaurant and Lounge, specializing in casual American cuisine in a comfortable setting, is another reason for relaxing indoors while the big city continues to move at such a hectic speed.

Serving the northern section of the city is the Embassy Suites Atlanta-Perimeter Center. Domiciled on Crown Pointe Parkway in the Perimeter Center Office Park, the Embassy Suites Atlanta-Perimeter Center is optimally located in one of the fastest-growing high-tech areas of Atlanta. Oracle, SAP and IBM are a few of the many nearby companies that frequently take

advantage of the Embassy Suites Hotels Atlanta-Perimeter Center's hospitality. A Nordstrom Department Store and the other shops that comprise the upscale Perimeter Mall are located less than a half-mile from the hotel, as is the Dunwoody MARTA station. Don't feel like walking? Don't worry. Complimentary transportation is offered within a three-mile radius of the hotel.

Embassy Suites Hotels Atlanta-Perimeter Center showcases another tropical utopia encased in 10 stories with 241 two-room suites. The spacious suites include six handicap suites, four executive conference suites, one presidential suite and meeting/banquet facilities for up to 150 people. The hotel's recreational facilities include an indoor heated pool, whirlpool, two saunas, and an outdoor sun deck and fitness center. Close by is access to golf, tennis and a jogging track. And when guests get hungry at Embassy Suites Hotel Atlanta-Perimeter Center, there's Alexander's Restaurant and Lounge, a charming, in-house café featuring American cuisine for lunch, dinner and in-suite dining.

Historians have debated for years General Sherman's true motivation for burning Atlanta. One spurious legend contends that Sherman torched the city in disgust when he could not find suitable accommodations during his two-month stay. Imagine if Embassy Suites Hotels had been in existence and operating in Atlanta in 1864. A rested, less stressed William Tecumseh Sherman probably would have ridden out of town whistling "Dixie" and Atlanta would have escaped his terrible retribution.

John Smith Co.

John Morton Smith, born in Ireland in 1835, first appeared in Atlanta's city records in 1870. But a year before that, the enterprising businessman had already put his stamp on the reviving post-Civil War city as the proprietor of a small business that would grow into one of Atlanta's finest carriage companies.

JOHN M. SMITH,
MANUFACTURER OF

PHAETONS, BAROUCHES, SURREYS, T CARTS.

VICTORIAS, CABRIOLETS, ROCKAWAYS, LANDAUS

85 BROAD AND 78 FORSYTH STREETS,
ATLANTA, - - - GEORGIA.

An early business card of John Smith, the city's premier manufacturer of carriages and coaches in the decades following the Civil War

The John Smith Company put the Atlanta police department on wheels in 1932 with the sale of 10 Chevrolet automobiles.

From a modest blacksmith's shop on Broad Street, Smith began turning out carriages and coaches for Atlanta citizens, building the foundation for one of the oldest businesses in the community. Owning a carriage built by the John Smith Company soon became a mark of distinction and wealth — prices ranged from $150 for a surrey to more than $2,500 for a brougham. Smith's attention to detail and comfort was soon recognized beyond Atlanta and he won a total of 45 awards for his fine carriages. He was famous for the quality of his carriages constructed with, as Atlanta historian Franklin Garrett put it, "Every bolt of steel and every spoke of hickory." Among the accolades were "Best Family Carriage" in 1877, given by the Georgia State Agriculture Society; a Certificate of Award from the 1881 Cotton States and International Exposition for carriages and buggies; and the 1887 Piedmont Exposition "Best Victoria" award.

In 1895 the organizers of the Cotton States and International Exposition gave Smith a special recognition for his display of horse-drawn firefighting equipment. It was also a John Smith Brougham that carried President and Mrs. Grover Cleveland to that fair, held in Atlanta's Piedmont Park.

The following year, Smith's son, John E., graduated from the Georgia Institute of Technology and went on to complete additional courses of study on carriage design in New York. Nicknamed Cap'n John, he joined his father in running the company, and together they continued to cultivate a distinguished clientele from their expanded factory on Auburn Avenue.

In addition to a keen carriage-making skill, John E. Smith was sensitive to future trends. By the early 1900s, he began to tinker with "horseless carriages" and he eventually built one gasoline-powered and two electric cars. By 1906 it appeared that the automobile would supplant the carriage as the preferred mode of transportation, and so in that year he sold his first automobiles. Again, Cap'n John was a transportation leader.

In 1913 the John Smith Company captured the city's attention by burning its stock of phaetons, victorias

and sulkies — valued at well over $30,000 — which symbolically marked the end of the carriage era. *The Atlanta Journal* noted that the "carriages were chopped up, piled in heaps, and burned as so much trash" so that the building where they were stored could be cleared to make way for cars. That same year, John M. Smith died, marking the end of a leadership era as the company passed into the hands of his son.

Three years later, Atlanta's automobile market was booming and consumers had their pick of more than 34 models. In the early years the Smith dealership carried a variety of cars, including Reos, Pierce-Arrows, Hudsons, Chandlers, Chalmers, Saxons, Hatfield High Wheelers and Apperson Jack Rabbits. Records of the day estimated that more than 6,000 cars, with an average price of $700, were chugging along Atlanta roads. It was not long before Cap'n Smith, long noted as the city's official General Motors Buick dealer, again found the need for bigger quarters. In 1921 the company moved to a new location on West Peachtree Street, where for 55 years it anchored the block with one of the Southeast's largest indoor new car showrooms.

In 1924 Smith shifted his allegiance exclusively to Chevrolet. In an interview with *The Atlanta Journal,* he explained the switch: "Our acquisition of the Chevrolet franchise (comes) after careful consideration. We are convinced that the field for a small car, economical in operation, low in upkeep-cost and with a low initial price, holds the widest scope of operation." At the time Chevrolets were the second-largest selling cars in the world, and Smith had them priced to sell from $583 to $930.

Smith soon became a national figure in the auto industry. He was one of the first members and leaders of the National Automobile Dealers Association. In 1935 he took a seat on the first President's Dealer Advisory Council of General Motors. His son, Hal Smith, joined the family firm and was later selected by GM to a seat on that council.

The first "air wheels" rolled out of the John Smith Company showroom in 1931.

John E. Smith II joined his father, Hal, in 1962 and was elected president in 1974. It was a crucial time in the company's history, as the dealership found itself in the path of the city's expanding subway system along West Peachtree Street. The decision was made to move the business to one of the metro area's booming suburbs, and in 1976 the John Smith Co. opened its doors on Cobb Parkway on an 8.5-acre site a few miles north of the city limits. Thirteen years later, another three acres were added to the Cobb site.

Through the years, the dealership has been led continuously by members of the Smith family — quite a remarkable feat for any company to boast. John E. Smith II represents the fourth generation of Smith family members to guide the company. Like his father and grandfather, John E. Smith II is a graduate of Georgia Institute of Technology and is a past president of the Metropolitan Atlanta Automobile Dealers Association. He has also followed the lead of his predecessors by involving his company with a variety of philanthropic causes, among them the YMCA, the United Way and the Atlanta History Center.

In the late 1990s the organization and its more than 100 employees continued their strong showing as one of the area's major retailers of new and used General Motors and Chevrolet products. Among long-time Atlantans, the company's nickname, "the Old Reliable," still applies.

JW Marriott Hotel Lenox

The designers of the JW Marriott took on a challenging task in 1990 when the renowned chain acquired a property in the heart of Atlanta's most fashionable neighborhood. The 24-story building, with its mirror-glass windows and unusually angled walls, sported an assortment of nooks, crannies and asymmetrical public rooms, as well as a lusterless past. But that was about to change. The top priority of the makeover was to create a facility with the sophistication and elegance synonymous with Marriott's luxury hotels within the confines of a building bearing the thumb prints of two previous owners.

Constructed in 1988, the structure hugging the corner of Lenox and East Paces Ferry roads initially was managed by a company that never opened its new doors. Within months of its completion, the building changed hands and operated for two years as a Westin Hotel. Then, Marriott stepped in with the goal of creating an upscale facility in Buckhead, Atlanta's ritziest community, noted for its fine dining, nightlife and shopping. One of just two luxury hotels in the vicinity at that time, the twice-owned building was about to become the JW Marriott Hotel Lenox.

The JW Marriott Hotel Lenox sits in the heart of Buckhead, Atlanta's premier entertainment and shopping district.

Marriott executives and their designers agreed that the look of the hotel had to reflect the level of service and style customers have come to expect from the company. The initial plans were to incorporate a popular Southern theme borrowed from *Gone With the Wind*. But the designers sought to rise above the architectural cliches and quickly convinced Marriott executives that their Buckhead flagship should evoke more than the "moonlight and magnolia" theme romantically linked to Tara. Instead, they took their sketch pads to the Swan House, one of the city's most historic homes and the embodiment of residential glamour and sophistication that today serves as the showplace of the Atlanta Historical Society.

The Marriott crew borrowed heavily from the color schemes and architectural style of the Swan House and incorporated those elements throughout the hotel's lobbies,

dining areas and 371 guest rooms. Visitors notice the first and most striking comparison to the Swan House in the hotel's lobby, where the gold, green and burgundy marble floors sport a star motif copied from the Swan's foyer. Carved mantelpieces around the fireplaces of the lobby and restaurants were inspired by the house. The hotel's floor coverings are reproductions of the mansion's colorful and intricate Oriental patterns, and the first-floor restaurant borrowed a garden theme from the Swan House solarium. A very pale shade of green, known as celadon, found in the home's Chinese porcelain collection, is the color of choice for most of the hotel's walls.

Luxurious touches inspired by the great house are also found in the green Brazilian marble of the ballrooms, baths and the lobby elevator, as well as the crystal chandeliers surrounded by ornate plaster moldings in the meeting rooms. A backlit tray ceiling in the lobby is sumptuously coated in silver leaf.

As a final *pièce de résistance*, artists from around the city and state were called upon to produce original art works for the building. One painter, taking his lead from the hotel's theme, created detailed watercolors of Atlanta's historic homes for the walls of the guestrooms, suites and public rooms.

One of the few deviations from the Swan House style was incorporated into Ottley's, the hotel's restaurant. Furnished in gleaming dark woods and decorated with equestrian-themed paintings, the restaurant took its name from the Ottley family, the original landowners who once operated a horse farm on the hotel site.

In creating the city's only JW Marriott, the company upheld a solid commitment to luxury and service that is still emphasized today. For guest comfort, the building boasts a glass-covered, heated indoor lap pool; a complete health club with saunas and a steam room; and a whirlpool and massage service. There is a restaurant and lobby bar with a baby grand piano; a gourmet coffee, sandwich and snack shop; and 24-hour room service. The hotel's top three floors feature key-accessed guest rooms and a concierge lounge stocked with a continental breakfast each morning, soft drinks throughout the day, hors d'oeuvres in the afternoon and cordials and desserts in the evening. The hotel's concierge staff also arranges baby-sitting and business services. Terrace suites on the top floors feature spacious balconies with sweeping city views. In-room amenities include marble baths, separate showers, king-size beds, terry bathrobes, mini-bars, coffee makers, irons and ironing boards, hair dryers and in-room movies.

The hotel has cultivated a reputation for catering to corporate clients who gather in the 17,000 square feet of meeting space. Meeting and function rooms, named after

Southern state capitals, host events from high-powered corporate board meetings to citywide conventions ranging from 10 to 1,000 guests. On an average day, as many as 300 guests check into the hotel, the bulk of which are business executives arriving from all over the world.

Weekends at the JW Marriott take on another dimension. Rooms are usually occupied by getaway guests who enjoy a short stroll along an enclosed promenade from the hotel to Lenox Square Mall. Guests are also within walking distance of several other upscale shopping districts, as well as the Buckhead entertainment and restaurant district, and are across the street from MARTA (Atlanta's subway) for convenient transportation to Hartsfield Atlanta International Airport and all of the city's professional sports venues.

The hotel is also a standout among the company's many noted facilities. It continually garners high marks from both business and leisure guests as well as meeting planners, who rank this Marriott hotel among the nation's finest for customer satisfaction and service. Through years of extending exceptional service and hospitality, the JW Marriott has turned a building with a shaky start into one of the city's most respected and sought after hotels.

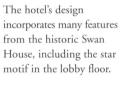

Eleven individual meeting rooms, providing the utmost in privacy and luxury, accommodate mid-size groups of 15 to 200 people.

The hotel's design incorporates many features from the historic Swan House, including the star motif in the lobby floor.

Suburban Lodges of America, Inc.

David E. Krischer, Chairman & Chief Executive Officer of Suburban Lodges of America, Inc.

Talk about building a better mousetrap. Atlanta entrepreneur David E. Krischer didn't create the extended-stay hotel concept; he just perfected it, making it more affordable for everyone. That's the reason his Suburban Lodges has become, during its relatively brief existence, the largest economy, extended-stay hotel brand in the country.

Krischer, the founder, chairman and chief executive officer of Suburban Lodges of America, was born with a keen entrepreneurial business acumen. Realizing Atlanta was a progressive, growing city with a fertile business environment, he and his wife, Jill, relocated to "The Hub of the South" in 1973 after he earned his law degree with honors from Boston College Law School. Practicing law for the next 13 years, Krischer watched and waited for the right opportunity to fulfill his lifelong dream of creating his own successful business. When that opportunity came along in 1986, Krischer made his move. It was a move that would revolutionize the lodging industry.

Traditionally, hotels had always served consumers' nightly needs while apartments fulfilled longer-term needs of a year or more. But Krischer recognized that a very large segment of consumers — including business-people on temporary assignment and families relocating to new areas — were unable to find economically priced temporary lodging. And while extended-stay hotels (lodging that includes a regular hotel room together with a kitchen, for stays that average a week or more) had recently entered the marketplace, they resided at the upper end of the price chain and were cost prohibitive for most people.

Krischer believed that by doing business just a little bit differently, he could reduce operating costs and pass the savings on to the guest in the form of lower nightly and weekly rates. Restaurants, lounges, swimming pools and large staffs make up a major portion of a traditional hotel's operating costs. Krischer reasoned that by eliminating or reducing these unnecessary high-cost items he could still offer consumers virtually everything they needed at very affordable rates. Suburban Lodge hotels could be effectively managed by a staff that would be half the size of a typical hotel. A nice-sized guest room with a functional kitchen, essential amenities and friendly customer service would be offered.

Krischer broke ground on the first Suburban Lodge hotel in the summer of 1987 in Forest Park, Georgia. Opening on March 4, 1988, the hotel was a tremendous success and, after opening two more Atlanta properties that were equally successful, Krischer decided to test the regional waters by opening a Suburban Lodge hotel in Alabama and another in

Kitchens, great rates and comfortable accommodations make Suburban Lodges one of the best lodging values.

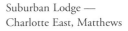
Suburban Lodge Extra — Atlanta North, Sandy Springs

channels, personalized voice mail and a dataport are also provided in each guest room, and laundry facilities are available on site.

Imitation is truly the highest form of flattery. Since Krischer pioneered the economy extended-stay hotel concept, it has become the fastest-growing segment in the hotel industry with every major hotel company, along with numerous start-up companies, racing to grab a piece of this lucrative pie. By 1998, the extended-stay segment had its own committee in the American Hotel & Motel Association with Krischer as its founding chairman. But, with occupancies that consistently outpace industry norms, a 97 percent guest satisfaction rating, and more

South Carolina. Slow, methodical regional expansion was Suburban Lodges' strategy during its infancy, but explosive national growth and industry leadership have been the norm since Krischer took his company public in 1996. By early 2000 Suburban Lodges had over 140 hotels open or under development in 20 states, including over 20 locations in the Atlanta area.

Suburban Lodge hotels are perfect for extended-stay guests during relocation, temporary work assignments and business or leisure travel. Each guest room includes a fully equipped kitchen with refrigerator, stove-top, microwave, coffee maker, sink, cookware and dishware. Cable television with premium

Suburban Lodge — Charlotte East, Matthews

Suburban Lodge — Houston, NASA Space Center/Six Flags

hotels opening every month, Krischer's Suburban Lodge hotel chain is without question the standard by which everyone is measured.

Despite the fierce competition, Suburban Lodges maintains its leadership role by offering an above-average experience for a below-average price and by continuing to follow David Krischer's simple but straightforward corporate mandate, "Provide our guests with high-quality accommodations and courteous, professional service at incredibly affordable rates."

Bone's Restaurant

In 1978, just as Atlanta's Buckhead community was taking shape as an upscale nightlife and shopping district, Susan DeRose and Richard Lewis opened a neighborhood eatery destined to become an institution dedicated to a service style superior to a private club, yet open to the public. Bone's became almost instantly Atlanta's answer to New York's 21 Club.

DeRose and Lewis' vision grew to a 250-seat, two-level restaurant on Piedmont Road. Upstairs, the eatery's look is indeed reminiscent of a gentlemen's club, with dark paneled walls, beamed ceilings, plush carpeting, brass fixtures and high-backed leather chairs. Downstairs, hardwood floors, linen-topped tables, red-leather chairs, etched-glass dividers and globed ceiling fans invoke the feel of a chic supper club. The walls are crowded with photos and caricatures of the city's leading citizens. Private dining rooms, perfect for intimate gatherings, are lined with exposed brick walls.

Since it opened its doors, Bone's has established itself as one of the city's leading venues for high-powered business meetings, a comfortable place where the service is impeccable and the guests are free to concentrate on business. It's the place where Ted Turner and his colleagues celebrated the purchase of MGM; where the 1996 Olympic Committee came to mark the naming of Atlanta; where people in the community bring their best friends for special occasions. For many, dinner at Bone's is a family tradition passed down through three or four generations.

The finest food simply prepared was part of the strategy that has helped the restaurant thrive. The menu stars are the selection of USDA prime aged beef cuts, from an 8-ounce petit filet mignon to the massive 26-ounce T-bone. Veal chops, crab cakes, salmon and live lobsters flown in daily from Maine share the spotlight. Southern influences surface in the black-eyed pea soup, roasted corn and tomato chow-chow, shrimp and crawfish etoufee, grit fritters and sinfully sweet pecan pie.

But Bone's is more than a dining destination noted for superb steak and seafood. The restaurant staff, from bartenders to busboys, includes professionals with a combined total of 450 years in the fine-dining business. They are committed to and pride themselves on meticulous personal service, remembering their customers' names and preferences and making guests feel welcome.

Bone's, an internationally acclaimed restaurant in the heart of Buckhead, is an "in" spot for many of Atlanta's movers and shakers. Its clubby atmosphere, award-winning cuisine and a 10,000-bottle wine cellar make it an ideal spot for business meetings as well as special occasions.

"We're not just selling food; we're creating a sense of community," says Lewis. "We have dishwashers who have been here for 20 years, and waiters who have been taking care of people for so long they know not only how they like their food cooked and which tables they prefer, but also when they're having babies."

Such commitment to excellence has earned accolades from national and local publications. "It's all part of our Southern hospitality that makes us one-of-a-kind," says Lewis. Bone's is an institution in Atlanta, and happy to be part of the city's history.

Buckhead Life Restaurant Group

During Atlanta's continuing boomtown quest to define itself, restaurants and restaurateurs tend to pop up like wildflowers and last as long, often simply gone with the wind after a brief flourish. And then there is Pano Karatassos' Buckhead Life Restaurant Group, a nationally acclaimed dynasty of high-end dining establishments in Atlanta. Karatassos has been the dominant force in changing Atlanta's image to a world-class place to dine. In effect, he has revolutionized the city's restaurant scene. In the process, Pano, as he is known locally, has become more recognized than most city fathers.

"Turning Atlantans onto fine food was about as easy as getting Scarlet to give up Ashley," wrote the *Atlanta Journal-Constitution*. "If any credit is due, it goes first to the team of Pano Karatassos and Paul Albrecht (a former colleague) who pooled their savings, left Lake of the Ozark, Missouri, and opened Pano's and Paul's in January 1979…"

Atlanta Fish Market opened next in 1981 at Lenox Square and then expanded to larger quarters on Pharr Road with its landmark 65-foot copper fish. 103 West opened in 1982, followed by 11 other restaurants through 1999. Other Buckhead Life establishments include the Buckhead Diner; Chops and The Lobster Bar; Pricci; Veni Vidi Vici; Buckhead Bread Company and Corner Café; and Nava. The most recent additions are The Club, a private jazz and cigar club, and Bluepointe, an Asian-influenced seafood eatery.

Buckhead Diner, with its gleaming chrome and steel exterior and plush decor, was described by a California newspaper as "the ritziest diner in the country." It has consistently been voted in "Best of" features as Atlanta's favorite restaurant for both visiting celebrities and locals. Buckhead Diner and Chops were selected as two of six prototypes for the EuroDisney complex in France.

There is no hint of a chain operation with the Buckhead Life Restaurant Group. Each restaurant is individualistic in style, decor and cuisine, and the themes include Continental, American, modern and rustic Italian, Southwestern, seafood, steaks, and cafe cuisine.

A colleague attributes Karatassos' success to attention to detail and quality. A Savannah native who grew up in the restaurant business, Pano was educated at The Culinary Institute of America in Hyde Park, New York. His career path led him to assignments in Europe and the United States and a long list of culinary awards.

Karatassos also has earned many local and national charitable and civic honors. Through the Atlanta Food Bank, he launched the first U.S. program channeling freshly prepared hot meals — not just

Lobster Bar at Chops

surplus canned goods — to the hungry. As a longtime Atlanta chairperson of the national Share Our Strength (SOS) Taste of the Nation event, he helped raise millions for hunger relief agencies, consistently making Atlanta first in the nation in that effort.

Through the quality of his restaurants and his personal impact on the community, Pano Karatassos has become a contemporary Atlanta tradition and his restaurants have become a culinary legacy.

Delta Air Lines

Delta's goal is to become the No. 1 airline in the eyes of its customers, flying passengers and cargo from anywhere to everywhere. Passengers already fly Delta more often than any other airline in the world. The airline offers more than 5,299 flights each day to 362 cities in 58 countries on Delta, Delta Express, Delta Shuttle, the Delta Connection carriers and Delta's Worldwide Partners. Delta is a founding member of the SkyTeam global airline alliance, which provides customers with extensive worldwide destinations, flights and services.

But, barely more than seven decades ago, Delta was only a dream. When C.E. (Collette Everman) Woolman founded Delta Air Service in 1928, he was combining three of the things he loved most — people, airplanes and the American South. The company had actually begun four years earlier, in 1924, as Huff Daland Dusters, the first commercial crop-dusting operation in the nation and a subsidiary of a New York airplane manufacturer. Huff Daland started out with two Army issue Jennys, the backing of the U.S. Department of Agriculture Extension Service, and the hopes of a people whose cotton crops were being decimated by the boll weevil, a tiny airborne insect that had emigrated from Mexico. Headquartered first in Macon, Georgia, and then in Monroe, Louisiana, Huff Daland operated two dusting seasons annually under Woolman's

Delta founder C.E. Woolman at his desk in 1959, holding a model of the DC-8, the first of three planes Delta was to introduce to the world
Delta Air Transport Heritage Museum, Inc.

field management — summers in the Southeastern United States. and winters in South America. Woolman, neither military ace nor wealthy flyboy but an agricultural engineer, thereby entered commercial aviation through an unusual path in the 1920s — agriculture rather than private air races or military service.

The first year Woolman charted Huff Daland's flights marked the 10th anniversary of the first scheduled air service in the United States (begun in Florida in 1914). It also predated Western Air Service's first airmail deliveries by two years, and Pan Am's service between Key West and Havana by three years. Commercial crop dusting was a rarity at the time; however, airmail routes were becoming well established, especially in the populous Northeastern and boundless Western regions of the country. Airplane instrumentation was still primitive. Sometimes night flying was facilitated through beacon-lit runways, and passenger service seemed like a probability, if not yet a profitable one, on the airmail routes.

For Woolman, however, neither airmail routes nor passengers seemed likely until the Air Mail Act of 1925 and the Air Commerce Act of 1926 opened the doors to the creation of private, nonmilitary, commercial air services. At that time, Huff Daland had the largest privately owned aircraft fleet in the world (18 planes) and an ambitious vice president and field manager who saw an opportunity. Woolman had already had overseen the sale of Huff Daland's airmail routes and dusting interests in South America, and now he saw his chance. With borrowed money, a handful of personnel and "sweat equity," a name derived from the region it served, Woolman created Delta Air Service.

In the next year Delta flew its first passengers. On June 17, 1929, a Delta Travel Air S6000-B, the monoplane then known as the "limousine of the air," carried five passengers and 150 pounds of cargo at a speed of 90 mph from Dallas, Texas, to Jackson, Mississippi, with stops at Shreveport and Monroe, Louisiana. Delta's passenger service nonetheless ended in 1930

when a predecessor to American Airways received the Southern airmail route. Delta, like the other budding commercial airlines, relied on airmail to subsidize its minuscule passenger income and to stabilize its other air transport operations. For the time being, instead of expanding through airmail, Delta increased its dusting operations.

The South at this time had already suffered a decade of economic depression and the entire region was not competing successfully in industry, commerce and manufacturing. But there were signs of progress, especially in the urban areas — Dallas, Birmingham and Atlanta — and Woolman was patient and persistent. In one fell swoop, the minute he had the chance, C.E. Woolman connected these Southern cities and lined them all up behind Delta Air Service. Twelve Southern cities supported Delta's bid for mail service for years, but to no avail.

Then in 1934, under the Black McKellar Act, Delta finally got the airmail route it pioneered. That route ran from Dallas to Jackson, Birmingham, Atlanta and Charleston. Dubbed the "Trans-Southern Route" by Delta, it became the foundation for Delta's future passenger service, its reputation for "service and hospitality from the heart," and its economic importance to the South. The Trans-Southern carried Southern air mail, passengers and cargo, and it knit the region

together in the air just as the railroads had done a century earlier on the ground. On October 29, 1945, Delta Air Corporation officially became Delta Air Lines.

Until the United States entered World War II, Delta flew the Trans-Southern route with only a few additions to it, chiefly to Cincinnati — its first non-Southern destination — and Savannah, a second major coastal town. Route expansions accompanied other improvements and changes for the airline. First came Delta's purchase of the Douglas DC-3, the plane that made commercial passenger travel profitable in aviation. And second came the headquarters move from Monroe, Louisiana, to Atlanta, Georgia.

Donald Douglas had actually introduced the DC-3 in 1936. Commodious by the standards of the day, the DC-3 seated 21 passengers comfortably, even luxuriously. Douglas Aircraft utilized all the technological advances of the day; in fact, the plane was so well designed and constructed that DC-3s still fly commercially today — four decades after they were introduced. Delta received the first four of its first five DC-3s in 1940. The first, the "City of Atlanta," served as a pilot trainer, and the second, now known as "Ship 41," had its inaugural flight on Christmas Eve.

A number of factors coalesced to make Delta's move from Monroe to Atlanta not only propitious but also advisable. For one thing, Delta's newest two routes

(Dallas-Charleston and Cincinnati-Savannah) intersected at Atlanta. Atlanta was now the geographic "center" of the route system, making it the most efficient site to conduct aircraft maintenance. For another, the federal government had made Atlanta regional headquarters for several national government offices, including the post office and the Federal Reserve Bank, which in turn gave Atlanta Airport a national status. Beginning with the WPA and CWA projects under President Roosevelt, and then with greater acceleration under the war preparedness program, the Atlanta Airport received more than $1 million in federal subsidies for improvements and expansions. Delta moved its headquarters into a hangar and small administrative building right behind the Quonset hut terminal that served the Atlanta Airport until 1948 when the hut gave way to a new, state-of-the-art control tower and classically styled waiting room.

The onset of World War II slowed commercial passenger traffic, but situated in the midst of one of the nation's biggest recruitment centers, Delta could serve military transport and otherwise contribute to the war effort. Woolman, ever extemporizing, directed his company's efforts to modify more than 1,000 aircraft for military use, overhaul engines, install new instrumentation and train new pilots and mechanics for the Air Transport Command.

The Delta wing at the Atlanta new municipal airport as it looked in 1965; airline services grew so fast that this facility was replaced altogether by Hartsfield International less than 20 years later. *Delta Air Transport Heritage Museum, Inc.*

In 1945, when Delta officially changed its name to Delta Air Lines, 90 percent of its male employees were war veterans, and Woolman could count on their expertise to accept new growth and challenges. Delta added cargo to its services, and in 1946 the airline celebrated its 1 millionth passenger. In the post-war years Delta began establishing an impeccable record of safe flying, receiving its first award in 1947. By 1961 Delta had flown 11 billion miles without a single fatality.

Growth occurred in the 1950s through the revitalization of passenger service and also through merger. A union with Memphis-based Chicago & Southern Airlines brought Delta new service into the Heartland and into the Caribbean. The two airlines had complementary routes and uncommon corporate compatibility, which made the merger smooth and relatively easy. Delta flew as Delta C&S for two years and then dropped C&S from its livery. Delta was now more than a regional carrier, with routes to Chicago, then New York City as well as eight additional cities before the end of the decade.

World War II had not only trained a generation in aviation, but it also introduced the jet engine, though it would be almost 15 years before jets found their way into commercial use. When they did, Woolman pursued their acquisition with the vigor of Atlanta's own Mayor William Hartsfield, who insisted a new airport be built to accommodate them. Hartsfield convinced the city, the county and the state to invest in his airfield, and Delta made a $10 million investment in its first jet planes. Delta turned for its jets to the Douglas Aircraft Corporation, which, under the leadership of Woolman's lifelong friend Donald Douglas, was manufacturing the DC-8.

On September 18, 1959, Delta placed the first Douglas DC-8 into regularly scheduled service, a "proud occasion" according to Woolman. Delta then went on to introduce two more jet types to the world: the Convair 880 in 1960 and the Douglas DC-9 in 1965. Delta is the only airline to have introduced three jets to air service, and it pioneered the transition from prop planes to jet aircraft without using any turbo-props in between.

Following this giant step into jet service were three decades filled with tremendous growth and equally impact-laden challenges. Woolman lived to see his airline become a transcontinental carrier in 1961 with service to Los Angeles and other major West Coast cities. When he died in 1966, he had successfully transformed a company with 14 employees into one with more than 10,000 personnel. After his death, Delta stopped crop dusting but it did not stop growing. It added wide-body jets, most notably the Lockheed 1011-Tristar, and also kept buying Douglas aircraft from the newly merged McDonald Douglas Aircraft Corporation. Nor did Woolman's death stop the company from serving its customers with his impeccable dedication to safety and hospitality. The year 1971 marked the first of 17 straight years in which Delta received the highest customer-satisfaction ratings as determined by the Department of Transportation. Delta did indeed love to fly, and it showed.

In 1972 Delta merged with Northeast, bringing new service into New England and Canada and additional service into Florida. Delta launched its maiden transatlantic service to London in 1978 and maiden transpacific service to Tokyo in 1979. In 1984 it established the first-ever code sharing agreement, with ASA (Atlantic Southeast Airlines), which has since merged into the parent corporation. In the largest union to date, Delta merged with Western Air Lines in 1987, from which Delta emerged as the fourth-largest airline in the United States and the fifth-largest in the world. This merger brought Delta a large route network in the Western United States, new service into Mexico and additional service to Hawaii. Delta added service to London, Frankfurt and Tokyo, and in 1991 it acquired most of Pan Am World Airways' North Atlantic routes and its JFK and Frankfurt hubs, which turned Delta overnight into an important global carrier.

This growth has taken place in the midst of, in spite of, and some times because of, the changes in the commercial aviation industry. In 1978 Congress elected to deregulate the airlines. The Airline Deregulation Act opened business to newcomers, and the number of carriers suddenly mushroomed from 36 to 123. Routes grew and fares plummeted. Frenzied growth among the airlines killed some of them while others, like Delta, acted more cautiously, if not always prudently. During a downturn in the economy in the early 1980s, Delta employees, in an incomparable act of company loyalty and confidence in 1982, purchased through payroll

"The Spirit of Delta," Delta's first Boeing 767, was purchased by the employees and presented to the company on December 15, 1982, with great corporate confidence and loyalty.
Delta Air Transport Heritage Museum, Inc.

deductions the company's first Boeing 767, the "Spirit of Delta."

It was Pan Am in 1991, however, that stretched the company to its limits and forced stringent economic measures in the early 1990s. Leadership 7.5, as it was known, returned the company to profitability by the end of 1994, but at the cost of some customer service and employee morale. Service and morale both lifted during the Olympics of 1996, with Delta serving as the official airline and a rededicated "Spirit of Delta" carrying the Olympic flame from Athens to Atlanta.

The company has since rebounded under the leadership of new CEO and President Leo Mullin. In 1997 Delta made history by serving more than 100 million passengers in a single year, 2 million a month in Atlanta alone. Delta has introduced new services such as BusinessElite™, new alliances such as with Air France, and has expanded services in Latin America. In 1998 *Air Transportation World* named Delta the Global Airline of the Year and in 1999 *Aviation Week* named it the best-managed airline.

In the same year, Delta unveiled the symbol of its new spirit, a "better than new" DC-3, the original "Ship 41" that had flown Christmas Eve in 1940, and signaled new growth and a new hometown for the airline. The plane was found in 1992 in Puerto Rico and restored with such precision and integrity that it earned top honors at the 2000 Oshkosh air show. This gleaming silver bird symbolizes Delta's true heritage now and in the future, resting as it does on a historic reputation for service and incomparable maintenance, and a corps of dedicated people.

BellSouth Corporation

Only 30 years after the railroads founded the city of Atlanta, telecommunications stepped in to spur the city's growth. In 1877 the first telephone was installed in the city's new Western and Atlantic Railroad Depot, which was built to replace the station Sherman had burned in the Civil War.

Customer satisfaction is a top priority at BellSouth. For the fourth consecutive year, BellSouth has captured the highest ranking in the J.D. Power and Associates Local Residential Telephone Service Satisfaction Study.

BellSouth is providing telecommunications, wireless communications, cable and digital TV, directory advertising and publishing, and Internet and data services to over 37 million customers in 19 countries worldwide.

A year later, James M. Ormes of the fledgling Bell Telephone Company traveled to the Southeastern states to survey the potential for telephone expansion. He found "the people of the South so alive to the advantages of the telephone and the field of business so promising," that he negotiated the famous Ormes contract requiring Western Union to withdraw from the telephone business in the Southern territory. On December 20, 1879, Ormes formed the Southern Bell Telephone and Telegraph Company, which covered the seven states of Kentucky, Tennessee, North Carolina, South Carolina, Georgia, Florida and Alabama. In 1892 Southern Bell constructed its first of many buildings in Atlanta at 78 Pryor Street to house the main switchboard of the Atlanta Exchange.

Firmly rooted in the birth of the telecommunications industry and in Atlanta, Southern Bell grew to become part of the national Bell System held by AT&T. Today's BellSouth was formed with the divestiture of that system. BellSouth began operations in 1984 as the largest of seven regional Bell holding companies, consisting of South Central Bell, Southern Bell, BellSouth Advertising and Publishing Company and BellSouth Mobility, Inc.

BellSouth's innovation, vision, community service and financial success have made it a major contributor to the rapid growth of the Southeast. In 1998, Standard and Poor's/DRI valued BellSouth's nine-state economic impact at nearly $200 billion in its first 15 years.

From the beginning, Southern Bell and its affiliates put the Southeast at the heart of the communications revolution. It activated the first cellular systems in Florida in 1984 and was the world's first company to hit the 500,000-customer mark in 1990. "The decision to pursue wireless communications aggressively was a visionary, not an obvious choice," said Jere Drummond, vice-chairman, BellSouth. "Industry leaders projected that there might be a million cellular customers by 2000. The actual figure is around 76 million."

In 1985 the company formed BellSouth International, Inc. to manage the company's overseas expansion, a move that has grown to provide wireless and other communications services to 19 countries in Latin America, Europe and the Asia/Pacific region.

At the same time, the company streamlined operations by unifying Southern Bell and South Central Bell under one company name. BellSouth was the new identity emblazoned on 2,576 buildings, 26,000 vehicles, 181,351 pay phones and 8.5 million calling cards.

The industry may have started with the telephone, but it has moved far beyond as the world relies more upon data transmission fueled by the Internet. Businesses and individuals need phone numbers and fax lines, ADSL (high-speed) Internet access, interactive pagers, RAM mobile data communications and e-commerce solutions... and BellSouth is providing them. As early as 1985, BellSouth began laying the groundwork to meet the growing demand for high-speed, reliable connections over which computers could move data. The company installed more than 72,000 miles of fiber-optic cable and launched five new high-speed, high-capacity data services. Today, that network has grown to over 3 million miles of fiber.

Atlanta is arguably the most heavily fibered city in the world. The fiber-optic network that BellSouth installed for the 1996 Olympic games delivered real-time voice, video and data from every Olympic venue to 1.5 billion people worldwide and remains a strong foundation for the city's economic growth.

"During the Olympics, BellSouth transmitted an unprecedented 3,862 hours of uninterrupted, digital-quality video without a single blip. At the same time, we handled over 1 billion telephone calls in the metro-Atlanta area without any difficulty. In ACOG's problem log, the BellSouth page is blank and that makes me extremely proud," said Drummond.

Since Congress's Telecommunications Act of 1996 to increase competition in the industry, BellSouth has faced new competitors and industry convergence as communications providers seek to provide customers a complete bundle of services. Through new business agreements and technologies, BellSouth is gaining a national presence in the market. In the midst of this industry transformation, the company has won the national J.D. Power and Associates Award for telephone customer satisfaction four years running.

By putting its customers and communities first, BellSouth has become a $25 billion international communications services company, providing telecommunications, wireless communications, cable, digital TV, directory advertising and publishing, and Internet and data services to nearly 37 million customers in 19 countries worldwide. Since its 1984 initial stock offering, BellSouth shareholders have enjoyed more than 1,800 percent return on their investment.

The company's three-pronged strategy for future growth is: first, to continue to bring the best services and products to its core market, the Southeast; second, to penetrate new markets with its wireless services; and finally, to increase its international operations. In Atlanta, construction is under way to consolidate 13,000 employees from 75 suburban sites into three new urban office complexes along Atlanta's public

In a marketplace driven by technological advancement, BellSouth strives for excellence through innovation. The new mobile computing platform for BellSouth's 15,000 service technicians was honored with the 1999 SUPERQuest "Best Built Operations Support System" award.

transportation lines, MARTA. Taking into consideration the city's concerns for traffic, for energy conservation and for a strong city center, company leaders felt that it was the right decision.

Being a caring and active corporate citizen has been a company hallmark from the beginning. Since 1986, the BellSouth Foundation has given over $46 million in grants to further education in the region. Individual employees have invested their time, money and expertise in community organizations (valued at over $2 billion) through individual efforts and the BellSouth Pioneers, a volunteer organization of active and retired employees with over 94,000 members.

"Over the years, I've had the opportunity to work side by side with BellSouth employees in Atlanta and in neighborhoods across the country. I've witnessed firsthand their commitment to community," said Jimmy Carter, former president and chairman of the Carter Center.

BellSouth will continue to uphold its heritage by creating the most effective and innovative communications technologies for the communities it serves.

Epps Aviation

Like other regions around the country, the South welcomed the return of their World War II heroes, particularly embracing the daring pilots. But commercial flight was still in its infancy and winging through the sky was still deemed purely recreational. By the 60s, the "sport" had emerged as a fast, efficient alternative to ground transportation and satellite airports cropped up across the country. Along with these outlying airports came legions of entrepreneurs eager to turn their avocations into vocations. It took grit, tenacity and hard work and only a few of these fledgling businesses survived and prospered.

One that not only survived but also thrived was Epps Aviation, whose owner, Pat Epps, graduated from Georgia Tech in 1956. After graduation, he married his high school sweetheart, Ann Hailey, and took a job with Boeing Airplane Company in Seattle as a flight test engineer on the prototype 707. In 1958 he completed Air Force pilot training, serving until 1963 as a transport pilot on several different multi-engine models. He tried engineering in Huntsville, Alabama, for 18 months but his addiction for airplanes and flying drew him into the flying business part time selling for Mooney Aircraft. By 1965, he decided to try aviation full time and opened

Epps Aviation's charter fleet stands poised for the next flight in front of Epps' main hangar.
Photo by Clint Rodgers

the hangar doors of Epps Aviation at DeKalb Peachtree Airport, just nine miles from downtown Atlanta.

As Hartsfield International Airport became the busiest in the nation, DeKalb Peachtree took its place as an important "reliever" airport and hub for private corporations and recreational fliers. Epps Aviation played a large role in that growth and is the airport's longest-operating Fixed Base Operation (FBO), celebrating its 35th anniversary in 2000.

The small company that began by selling fuel and providing aircraft maintenance has evolved into a 21-acre complex, adding charter service, aircraft sales, aircraft management, avionics service, parts, five corporate hangars, 40 T-hangars and tie-down space for local and visiting aircraft.

Today, the company, stronger than ever, is an industry leader. "In recent times, the air transportation industry has seen the introduction of aircraft management companies and the invention of fractional ownership companies," says Epps. "The fractional ownership program has expanded the market tremendously and more growth is expected."

The heart of this business is customer support and Epps provides "red carpet" treatment. Fuel service, including catering, ground transportation, car rentals and hotel reservations, is available around the clock. Epps' Charter offers a fleet of Learjets and King Airs to take busy executives wherever they want to go, when they want to go. With over 200 years of combined experience and over 100,000 hours of combined flying time, Epps' pilots can land at virtually any airport anywhere, domestically as well as internationally. Epps also transports time-sensitive documents with its fleet of 11 Mitsubishi MU2s in the Northeast.

Epps maintains an extensive parts and equipment inventory, in addition to a vast research library. With over $1 million of test equipment and spares, the company is an authorized service center for Cessna, Mitsubishi and Pilatus and for all the major avionics manufacturers.

But the love of the business stems from Pat's initial introduction to flight. He inherited his devotion from his father, Ben T. Epps, who became Georgia's first pilot in 1907 when he built his first "airship" out of wire, fabric, bicycle parts and a two-cylinder, 15-horsepower Anzani engine. Ben Epps went on to design a total of eight aircraft but the hobby was in its infancy and flight was fraught with mishaps. A takeoff crash took his life in 1937 at the Athens, Georgia airport, which was subsequently named in his honor. Despite the death of her husband, Pat's mother, Omie Williams Epps, an eternal optimist, supported the efforts of her nine children to fly. Eight became pilots.

Epps also inherited his father's pioneering spirit, resourcefulness and perseverance — traits that led him through many an adventure. The "granddaddy" of those adventures was The Greenland Expedition that located and retrieved a World War II vintage P-38 fighter plane that had been buried 265 feet beneath the ice cap for 50 years. Epps was the organizing force behind that adventure.

He had long been intrigued with the legend of the six lost P-38s awaiting rescue beneath the Greenland ice cap, and when a visiting pilot mentioned that he'd always wanted one, Epps couldn't resist the challenge. What began as a lark to locate "The Lost Squadron" of Greenland soon became his dream and his obsession — encompassing 11 years and seven expeditions to the top of the world. When Epps and three others embarked on the mission with "hokey sleeping bags, a four-man tent that slept one and a half and a shovel," they omitted all the essentials, including a spare gas tank and radio! Epps calls his naiveté on that first excursion "astounding."

As the expeditions spanned the years, the preparations and equipment were refined from very primitive to high tech and Epps' determination increased tenfold. Of the six P-38s that ran out of gas in a blizzard in 1942 and were forced to land on a remote ice cap, only "The Glacier Girl" has been rescued. The remaining five P-38s still lie frozen beneath the ice awaiting other visionaries.

In 1999 Pat Epps was honored by his peers when he received the "American Spirit Award" from the National Business Aviation Association (NBAA). He was cited for his "courage, pursuit of excellence and service to others in the aviation community" and recognized as the organizing force behind the Greenland Expedition, his ownership of Epps Aviation and his involvement in the NBAA. In addition, the company received two of the industry's biggest honors. Epps Aviation is the only company in Atlanta routinely named to *Professional Pilot Magazine*'s list of best Independent Fixed Base Operators (FBOs) in the United States (Epps was No. 4 in 2000). It also made the nation's top 50 list of Independent and Chain FBOs and was called by *Business to Business Magazine* "the South's premier corporate and general aviation facility."

Pat Epps on the Greenland icecap in 1990 in front of the DC3 used during The Greenland Expedition.

The legacy continues and Epps' love of flying has not diminished over the years. He is still flying his signature red, white and blue aerobatic Beechcraft Bonanza in local air shows. The passion for flight he inherited from Ben has been passed on to his three children, Patrick Jr., Marian and Elaine, who are all pilots. Marian Epps Tharp is the company's CFO and one of her most enlightening childhood memories is of her father handing out business cards good for one free airplane ride. "He is the industry's biggest fan," she says, "and many of our employees share his passion. Out of 150, nearly 50 percent are licensed pilots and many have remained with us from the beginning."

The last 35-plus years have seen many changes in the fast-growing DeKalb city of Chamblee and Epps Aviation has been a guiding force in that growth, helping bring industry, opportunity and prosperity to the community. The future of Epps appears just as bright.

MARTA

"At MARTA, It'smarta" is the phrase that gets everyone going! It gets the buses rolling and the trains moving. It epitomizes the Olympic success of the Metropolitan Atlanta Rapid Transit Authority (MARTA) and promises stellar achievements for the new millennium. Often described as "Atlanta's world-renowned public transit system," MARTA is committed to making a difference in Atlanta's quality of life by providing safe, reliable, cost-effective and affordable public transportation.

Since its inception, MARTA has made a significant impact on transportation infrastructure in metropolitan Atlanta. As early as 1952, the regional planning guide recognized the importance of mass transit to regional

MARTA took a bow for its outstanding performance as the Official Provider for Spectator Transportation for the Centennial Olympic Games.

growth. In 1954, the Metropolitan Planning Commission noted the need for rapid transit "within a few years." In April 1962 the Metropolitan Atlanta Transit Study Commission was formed to study programs and report on the need, advisability and economic feasibility of rapid mass transportation.

The Georgia General Assembly passed the Metropolitan Atlanta Rapid Transit Authority (MARTA) Act in 1965, creating an independent, "single-purpose" authority to plan, build and operate a rapid transit system within the metropolitan Atlanta area — specifically within Fulton, DeKalb, Clayton, Cobb and Gwinnett counties and the city of Atlanta. The act,

however, required local referendum in the five counties and the city of Atlanta before the agency could actually begin operations. From 1965 to 1971, the necessary referendums were passed and ratified in the two participating counties and the city of Atlanta.

In January 1974 the first architectural and engineering design consultant teams were selected. In February 1975 groundbreaking ceremonies were held on the East Line, and three years later the first of 100 new rail cars arrived. On June 30, 1979, amid many fanfares, MARTA began rail service on the East Line connecting with seven stations running from the Avondale Station to the Georgia State Station. Six months later, service began on the West Line extending service to the Hamilton E. Holmes Station (formerly called Hightower Station).

The South Line opened in 1981, extending service from Five Points to Garnett, and in 1982 service began on the North Line with service expansion to the Arts Center Station. Continued expansion extended service to the current terminal stations: on the South Line, Hartsfield International Airport in 1988; on the Northeast Line, Doraville in 1992; on East Line, Indian Creek in 1993; and on the North Line, Dunwoody in 1996. Construction is also underway for two additional stations on the North Line — Sandy Springs and North Springs — both scheduled to be completed by December 2000.

In 1996, just 30 years after its inception, MARTA took a bow for its outstanding performance as the Official Provider for Spectator Transportation for the Centennial Olympic Games. Atlanta brought the Olympic torch to the South, while MARTA shone the spotlight on mass transit. As the first local transit agency to partner with an Olympic Committee, MARTA offered 24-hour rail service for 17 days and transported 1.5 million passengers daily totaling more than 25 million customers during the games. The Atlanta Committee for the Olympic Games Chief Billy Payne said, "Atlanta could not have won the

transports more than 560,000 passengers daily. By the year 2005, MARTA expects to carry 200 million riders annually. This increase reflects the predicted growth in the region, which will undoubtedly call for additional transportation solutions. MARTA embraces the new millennium as an opportunity for service expansion and excellence.

In the 21st century, Atlanta is on the verge of creating a state-of-the-art regional transportation system — one that will change the very face of Atlanta. With the introduction of transit-oriented development (TOD) around select MARTA rail stations, MARTA is contributing to an improved quality of life in metropolitan Atlanta. For example, at MARTA's second-busiest station, Lindbergh Center, a 48-acre TOD site of residential, commercial and retail spaces is under construction to encourage transit use. By the completion of the project in 2005, MARTA estimates more than 2 million new riders to the Lindbergh Center Station alone.

In addition to the innovative development plans around various rail stations, a cooperative effort among MARTA, Delta Air Lines and Hartsfield International Airport created a unique transportation partnership — "The Train, the Plane, the World." Focusing on providing convenience and quality customer service to its shared customers, Delta Air Lines has opened a ticketing and baggage counter located in the lobby of the MARTA Airport Station. As the first of its kind in North America, MARTA is still making history in Atlanta while making a transportation difference for metropolitan Atlanta.

Games had it not been for MARTA and the Games would not have been the success they were had it not been for MARTA."

With over 4,700 employees, MARTA is one of Atlanta's largest employers and prides itself on its internal resources. MARTA is a successful organization because it has a committed, experienced work force dedicated to providing quality customer-focused service. From bus and rail transportation to government relations and marketing, MARTA covers all bases of mass transit. To meet the demands of patrons' various daily commute destinations, MARTA's busiest station, Five Points, serves more than 30,000 passengers daily. Whether transferring from the South Line to the airport or transferring from the West Line to visit the Georgia Dome, the Georgia World Congress Center or Phillips Arena, MARTA provides public transportation to many Atlanta landmarks. Other MARTA-accessible locales include the Carter Center, Underground Atlanta, the High Museum of Art and the Martin Luther King Jr. Center to name a few.

As in its genesis, MARTA continues to play a significant transportation role in the region. With more than 700 buses covering 150 routes operating 30 million miles of bus service annually, and with 240 heavy rail cars trekking 46 miles of track between 36 stations traveling 52 million miles a year, MARTA is the seventh-largest transit system in the nation. Operating in the city of Atlanta and DeKalb and Fulton counties, MARTA

Buckhead Coalition, Inc.

*Buckhead is unique in that it is an unincorpo-*rated community of 28 square miles with official boundaries, but it is not a political entity. It is a neighborhood of homes, schools and places of worship located directly in the center of Atlanta's bustling corridor to the outer northern suburbs and home to glass office towers, hotels, restaurants and shopping meccas.

In August of 1988, 14 Atlanta businessmen met to discuss the growing concern that their Buckhead neighborhood was changing faster than anyone could control. Left to chance, the commercial and residential parts of the community could become more clogged with traffic, plagued by deteriorating property values and inevitably ugly.

These businessmen formed the Buckhead Coalition to address their common concerns. By working together they could meld their managerial expertise, vision and economic power to influence the changes that Buckhead was about to endure. Three tasks were identified: to plan for the community's future, to provide marketing tools and to serve as a citizen's advocate.

The community planning function involves funding and commissioning studies on long-range land use, traffic management and the need for sidewalks and beautification. A significant accomplishment was the successful backing of the extension of the Georgia 400 toll road into Buckhead. This multi-lane highway connects Buckhead to Paris by giving

A statue of the buck that gave Buckhead its name is entitled "The Storyteller" and suggests the retelling of legends that surround the creation of the community.

residents a quick route to Atlanta's international airport. Another milestone was the creation of the "Buckhead Blueprint," an extensive professional study costing a quarter of a million dollars and outlining recommendations for land use, public safety and preservation of the environment.

The Coalition provides marketing services by publishing a guidebook: a compilation of facts and statistics about Buckhead's retail centers, office buildings, educational institutions, social services, meeting facilities, major employers, population, household income, proposed real estate development and much more. The guidebook is an invaluable one-source reference document for those thinking of relocating to the area, contemplating a marketing campaign to residents or opening or expanding a hotel, restaurant or other business.

Advocacy for citizens is not a well-advertised function of the Buckhead Coalition, but nevertheless reflects the vision of the founders — to give back to the community and improve its quality of life. The Coalition has placed "instant 911" telephones in heavily used commercial sections, making residents and visitors safer while deterring crime. It has also placed low-cost defibrillators in some public buildings as a first response to those experiencing heart attacks.

Membership in the Coalition has risen to a self-imposed maximum of 75, comprised primarily of chief executive officers who join by invitation only and contribute an annual dues assessment of $5,000. This provides the organization with its funding, although some city planning efforts are financed through governmental grants.

This part chamber of commerce, part visitor's bureau, part town hall and part citizen's ombudsman is unique in its vision, purpose and function. As Buckhead continues to grow and change its profile, the Buckhead Coalition will help guide that change for the benefit of its residents, visitors, shoppers and business owners.

Partners in Atlanta

King & Spalding

The law firm of King & Spalding has from its modest beginnings risen to become a nationally renowned institution with a substantial practice not only in the city of Atlanta, but across the country and around the world. After more than 115 years of service, King & Spalding is today ranked among the top 50 law firms in the world. King & Spalding has more than 600 attorneys in four offices, representing clients in 48 practice areas. The firm's mission is to draw from its history of premier quality legal work, client service and community stewardship while incorporating technology and business innovations for the 21st century.

The Firm's History

Alexander King and Jack Spalding formed their lasting partnership in 1885, at about the same time the city of Atlanta was recovering from the Civil War. Atlanta had a population of 50,000 residents, Georgia Tech was a foundling institution and the Coca-Cola formula was still a year away from being introduced.

Former U.S. Senator and Partner Sam Nunn; Chairman of the Policy Committee and Managing Partner Walter W. Driver, Jr.; Senior Litigator Chilton Davis Varner; and Former Managing Partner and Senior Litigator Ralph B. Levy

For two years Alex King, a great legal scholar with a memory for detail, and Jack Spalding, an extremely adept businessman with extraordinary financial acumen, managed their firm by engaging primarily in commercial practice and title examination. The addition of Pat Calhoun as a third partner in 1887 led the firm to become involved in and nearly consumed by railroad and power-generating interests. Calhoun had a profound interest in railroads and much of the firm's business involved corporate powers and leases and contracts with various railroad lines. Following the panic of 1893, King & Spalding began a 40-year involvement in railroad receiverships, with over 30 cases during that time period. Much of the work with railroads involved unifying the railroad system and rejuvenating the South to its former dignity and economic health.

King & Spalding's legendary involvement in civic affairs extends as far back as its contribution to help build Atlanta's street railways and Georgia's hydroelectric plants. Then as now, the firm espoused the common benefit of working for the entire community. In its early years, the firm was deeply interested in building up and promoting not just Atlanta, but the entire South to rival the North in industry and trade. In 1895, when the Cotton States and International Exposition was looking for a site, Jack Spalding stepped forward to advocate the attributes of Piedmont Park as a potential location. He not only convinced leaders to situate the Exposition there, but also later contributed to Piedmont Park's rescue from its pending conversion to a mill village.

Through partner changes and physical relocations in the early years, King & Spalding remained focused on its commitment to clients and the community. Long-standing relationships with two of its clients exemplify the firm's client commitment. King & Spalding's representation of The Coca-Cola Company began soon after it faced the company in litigation as counsel for the opposing Coca-Cola Bottling Company, in an effort to cancel a 20-year-old contract. The Coca-Cola

Company was so impressed with the legal skills of the attorneys that it hired the firm to become the company's primary outside counsel in the 1920s. To date, four of The Coca-Cola Company's general counsel have come from the ranks of the King & Spalding partnership, including the current General Counsel Joseph L. Gladden. Founded by the Woodruff family, SunTrust Banks, Inc. became a firm client in 1931 when Ernest Woodruff pulled the predecessor of SunTrust Banks, Inc. out of a merger with the First National Bank of Atlanta. SunTrust Banks, Inc. joined a syndicate to purchase the capital stock of The Coca-Cola Company from the Candler family in 1919. SunTrust Banks, Inc.'s shares of The Coca-Cola Company received as compensation for that financing still remain in the SunTrust Banks, Inc. vault, along with the secret formula for making Coca-Cola.

By the 1940s, King & Spalding had been through 12 name changes, seven relocations and three generations of partners, yet still maintained a strong sense of continuity in the face of new growth. As postwar advancements in all aspects of life began to emerge, the firm's partners remained resolute in their determination that the firm provide the best possible service to its clients, while agreeing it was vital that a business law firm monitor significant developments in local and national politics. As if to emphasize that point, the firm was enlisted to propose legislation to authorize cities and counties to create hospital authorities and to levy taxes for building and operating hospitals for citizens who otherwise could not afford health care. This legislation was eventually passed into law. Perhaps the most important achievement during this period, however, was the firm's activity to help guarantee the continuation of Atlanta's public school system when it was in danger of closing permanently under the strain of civil unrest in the 1950s and 1960s.

The decade of the 1960s also witnessed the firm's first organized hiring and recruiting campaign, which proved to be a highly successful tactic. With an increasing emphasis on political issues, in 1962 the firm hired its first legislator and prominent statesman, Charles L. Gowen. It was about this time, following various firm name changes that accompanied the addition or departure of partners, that the firm re-established its original name of King & Spalding.

Former U.S. Attorney General and Partner Griffin B. Bell; Senior Litigation Partner Larry D. Thompson; and Former Partner and Current Senior Vice President and General Counsel for the firm's client Emory University, Kent Alexander

In 1974, sensing a need for more structure and direction than ever imagined by the firm's founders, a Long Range Planning Committee was set up to appraise the firm's future and compile a report on various management and organizational options for the future. Administration was restructured, and the firm began to function as a *business*, with needs that could be projected well into the future. All members firmly believed that trust and respect among themselves and pride in the firm were absolutely essential to providing the best client service and community involvement possible.

In 1979 King & Spalding opened a Washington, D.C. office in direct response to a request from its longtime client The Coca-Cola Company. Partners in Atlanta and Washington, D.C. soon built a federal tax practice that was later ranked by *Euromoney Magazine* survey to be among the best in the nation. The success of the Washington, D.C. office prompted expansion into the New York market in 1992 and the opening of a Houston, Texas, office in 1995.

King & Spalding Today

King & Spalding began the new millennium by celebrating its 115th anniversary. The firm is acutely aware of its heritage of excellence, characterized by an outstanding record of prosperity and equilibrium, a

stimulating practice of national and international scope, and a high degree of collegiality and institutional loyalty. It is now focused on the next 100 years.

Premier Quality Legal Work

The clients served by the firm are its proudest achievement and perhaps most convincing credential. With over 600 attorneys practicing in 48 specialized areas, the range and scope of the firm's services and activities is comprehensive. King & Spalding's diverse client base encompasses U.S. and foreign corporations and individuals, businesses, industry associations, nonprofit organizations and coalitions of clients with parallel interests. The firm currently represents more than 250 public companies, including nearly half of the Fortune 100. King & Spalding also represents hundreds of emerging and mid-sized companies in a number of industries including e-commerce, health care, technology and telecommunications. The firm's historical legal practice of corporate law and litigation is the foundation upon which King & Spalding built its current practice.

King & Spalding is unique because of the quality of its people. To continue to provide the highest caliber legal services for its clients, the firm strives to attract the brightest attorneys. Some of the firm's notable past and present partners include former U.S. Attorney General Griffin B. Bell, former U.S. Senator Sam Nunn and former Georgia Governor George D. Busbee. The partnership also includes two former U.S. Attorneys for the Northern District of Georgia as well as two past presidents and an additional nine members of the American College of Trial Lawyers, two past

presidents of the American Health Lawyers Association and three past presidents of the National Association of Bond Lawyers.

Client Service

Working in partnership with its clients, King & Spalding strives to develop relationships that are productive, mutually beneficial and collegial. A high degree of collegiality is the hallmark of its partnership and serves as a testament to the firm's internal culture and stability. Its client base benefits by having both the full resources of a large, multifaceted law firm and the personal attention of an experienced group of dedicated men and women.

At King & Spalding, the focus on client service begins with attorney training and development. K&S University is the firm's continuing legal education program and the Link Program provides an internal structure where new attorneys are mentored by older attorneys. Another recent innovation is the firm's on-premises courtroom that allows its attorneys the opportunity to sharpen their skills in a realistic setting and permits them to experience the cutting-edge technology frequently used during trial. This courtroom helps fulfill the firm's commitment to its lawyers and clients, a continuing legal education and a preparatory advantage.

As technology has become more and more integral to the practice of law, the firm chose a partner to become Director of Information & Technology. King & Spalding has also kept pace with the introduction of its third-generation Web site. The Web site is easy to use and includes attorney biographies and photographs as well as a virtual law library to highlight articles written by King & Spalding attorneys on selected topics. The firm's other technology initiatives include video-conference facilities in all offices, an attorney laptop program, a firm-wide contact management database, a widely used internal Intranet and an Extranet connection for partnering and efficient communication with clients. With the help of technology, King & Spalding continues to integrate its offices in support of its "one firm" philosophy and multidisciplinary team approach.

Community Stewardship

Moving into the 21st century, King & Spalding still holds community stewardship to be an important mission. The firm contributes to the community through time and resources on a firm-wide basis, and through the individual activities of its attorneys and staff.

King & Spalding encourages its lawyers to provide pro bono legal services to individuals, groups and organizations who are of limited means or seeking to protect their civil rights, civil liberties or public rights. The firm also provides pro bono legal services to a number of nonprofit organizations including Atlanta Habitat for Humanity, Families and Advocates for Immigrant Rights, Trees Atlanta, Big Brothers Big Sisters, Phoenix Theatre Academy and Goodwill Industries. Some examples of King & Spalding's ongoing pro bono support include the handling of over 30 cases for the Atlanta Saturday Lawyer Program each year; representing clients referred by the Washington Legal Clinic for the Homeless; serving as *guardians ad litem* for abused and neglected children; representing children in truancy proceedings; and accepting adoptions through the Houston Volunteer Lawyers Pro Bono Project.

The firm's lawyers serve on over 200 boards for civic, charitable and educational organizations. Its aggressive efforts to promote the city of Atlanta helped ensure Atlanta's selection as host of the 1996 Summer Olympic Games, much as the efforts of co-founder Jack Spalding helped ensure Atlanta's selection as the site of the Cotton States and International Exposition 101 years earlier. In the mid-1990s, King & Spalding was one of the first law firms in the country to establish the position of Director of Community Service, to organize the firm's efforts and assist individuals in their volunteer efforts.

King & Spalding has always been a leader in giving. In 1999, the firm received an American Bar Association award for donating 500 used computers to legal aid organizations. The firm is the leading law firm contributor to the United Way in Atlanta, significant because all donations are made by individuals rather than the partnership.

By focusing on the basic precepts of premier quality legal work, client service and community stewardship, King & Spalding continues to prosper. Building upon these foundations with technology and business innovation ensures that the firm will continue to thrive in the new millennium.

(Opposite page) Director of MIS Jamie Usher; Partner and Director of Information and Technology Thomas B. Gaines Jr.; and End User/Applications Support Manager Paula McDonald.

As part of King & Spalding's community stewardship, a number of the firm's attorneys and staff work together to build a house for Atlanta's Habitat for Humanity.

Blackshaw, Olmstead, Lynch & Koenig, LLC

Given today's tight labor market where demand for strong senior leadership and high-level executive talent is great, the executive search field is experiencing significant growth and increasing competition. Among those players, Blackshaw, Olmstead, Lynch & Koenig, LLC set itself apart from the rest of the field through the continuous day-to-day, hands-on account involvement of the senior partners.

In executive search, as much as any other field, the ability to develop intimate one-on-one relationships and negotiate with the finest talent allows Blackshaw, Olmstead to achieve superior product delivery in a highly competitive environment.

Founded in the mid-1970s, the firm currently leverages its expertise and experience to fill top echelon jobs at many of America's most recognized and renowned corporations.

"Company decision makers view us in the same vein as they do their attorneys or CPAs. Today, as dynamic and bottom line-oriented as business is, the key to success is having the best talent on your team. Every CEO needs to have a relationship with at least one search firm," advises partner Brian M. Blackshaw.

In 1979 the firm became Blackshaw, Olmstead, soon after which it was sold to an international search firm. The firm's principals reopened an independent boutique firm named Blackshaw, Olmstead & Atwood in the late 1980s. The following decade was marked by growth in the firm's client base and the addition of four new partners, including Lynch and Koenig.

By the mid-1990s, the Atlanta-based firm had acquired clients from California to New York and Boston, as well as throughout the Southeast region. The Los Angeles office specializes in entertainment, diversity recruiting, engineering and manufacturing, while the firm's Greenwich office specializes in Wall Street/financial services and venture capital representation. Membership in TranSearch, a global retainer executive search organization, gives its principals access to executive talent worldwide in 43 countries.

The firm's client list reads like a who's who of blue-chip corporate America: BellSouth, Blockbuster Entertainment, Cendant, The Equitable Companies, General Electric, Kimberly-Clark, Morgan Stanley, Mitsubishi, Simon & Shuster, The Walt Disney Companies, Siemens, Seagram and Okabashi.

From entertainment to financial services to health care and, most recently, e-commerce, the common denominator among Blackshaw, Olmstead clients is a desire for top-notch, discreet search fulfillment. These companies seldom have the time, talent and expertise to conduct a successful in-house executive search.

The research-intensive process of identifying top talent often includes shopping the competition and luring top performers away from their present situations. In a highly competitive job market, every head is fair game, and Blackshaw, Olmstead, Lynch & Koenig has the inside track on the nation's most sought-after talent.

(Left to right) Joel Koenig, John Lynch, George Olmstead and Brian Blackshaw in 1998 at the Henry Silverman Dinner in New York

Life University

Life University, located in bustling Cobb County just 15 minutes northwest of downtown Atlanta, began as one man's dream and continues to flourish under the protective wings of its charismatic founder and president, Dr. Sid Williams.

Life University's inauspicious birth in 1975 took place in a rented warehouse across the street from Lockheed and Dobbins Air Force Base. Originally established as a college of chiropractic, it only signed up 22 students for the first class. In spite of pessimistic predictions by critics, the school overcame tremendous odds and blossomed into its present prestigious standing as a full-fledged, accredited university. Today, some 4,000 students pursue a rich variety of undergraduate and graduate degrees on the beautiful wooded campus.

As home of the world's largest college of chiropractic, Life University has graduated nearly 12,000 doctors of chiropractic who are now practicing their profession throughout the world. Life University, through the auspices of its daughter organization, Life International, has taken the lead in introducing

chiropractic to the world. Working with top officials in dozens of countries to build clinics, mobile health care and educational facilities, Life has established an awareness and appreciation of chiropractic on every continent of the globe.

Responding to Dr. Williams' penchant for perfection, Life has also gained national acclaim for its phenomenal achievements in sports. In all, the university has won more than a dozen NAIA national titles in sports and has more than justified the title of "School of Champions."

Dr. Sid, as friends and associates call him, was born in Rome, Georgia, and spent most of his early years within an hour's drive of Atlanta. As related in his autobiography, *LASTING PURPOSE: A Mindset for Success*, Dr. Sid had the good fortune of developing habits of self-discipline early in life, which included believing in his vision, focusing on the task at hand and always persisting.

Young Sid Williams decided in his sophomore year that he wanted to be a football star. Within just a few weeks, he became a star player on Atlanta's Tech High varsity team, which was one of the South's most competitive.

Later he played football for nearby Georgia Tech. In spite of numerous injuries, his competitive spirit reigned and he helped his championship football team win the Orange Bowl game in 1952. The young athlete's prowess and tenacity prompted Coach Bobby Dodd, when interviewed by the *Atlanta Journal*, to say, "Sid Williams is the best end for his size in America." In 1999 Coach Dodd's opinion was permanently affirmed by Dr. Sid's election to the Georgia Tech Athletic Hall of Fame.

Initially planning to pursue a medical degree, and already accepted for his graduate studies, a serendipitous event diverted the young Sid Williams in another direction that has remained unaltered for nearly five decades. When a football injury seriously interfered with his stamina and agility and did not respond to extensive medical treatment, a friend introduced him

Dr. Sid E. Williams, Founder and President of Life University

to chiropractic. Fully restored to good health and vitality, Sid Williams was back in Tech's starting lineup and on his way to changing the course of the world's health care history.

He shared his enthusiasm for chiropractic with his sweetheart, Nell Kimbrough, and the couple married in 1953. Instead of taking a typical honeymoon, they pooled their meager resources and headed for Davenport, Iowa, where they both enrolled in the Palmer Chiropractic College.

After earning their doctor of chiropractic degrees, Drs. Sid and Nell Williams returned home to practice. Beginning with a clinic in Austell, they soon owned and operated 19 chiropractic clinics throughout the Southeast.

Not satisfied with only providing care for patients, Dr. Sid also wanted to train others in the profession. He founded Dynamic Essentials International to educate chiropractors, students and the public in the practices and philosophy of chiropractic. The four-day quarterly seminars, which began in 1964, are still being held today and now attract thousands of participants.

In 1966 the two established Life Foundation, Inc., a nonprofit organization dedicated to service, education and research in the chiropractic field. The foundation initially published a newspaper, *Health for Life*, which was distributed to patients by their chiropractors. Under the umbrella of the Life Foundation, a mobile health clinic was started in Atlanta that provided chiropractic care by the clinic's staff. Dr. Williams also

Founded with an enrollment of just 22 students in rented warehouse space, the campus now features modern, state-of-the-art buildings on 125 acres.

founded and published *Today's Chiropractic* magazine, the leading journal in the profession which now has a worldwide circulation of more than 70,000.

For many years, Dr. Sid dreamed of establishing a chiropractic college in the Southeast. It was only through unrelenting persistency and a fervent belief in the value and possibility of his vision that the little school quickly grew to become one of Atlanta's largest universities and a leader in the chiropractic profession.

As the student body grew in size, academic diversity and its firm reputation for quality, Life Chiropractic College changed its name to Life College. By 1997, the institution had accumulated all the credentials to earn accreditation as a university.

A large percentage of Life University's 4,000 students are seeking a doctor of chiropractic degree. The rigorous graduate program, which has attracted students from all 50 states and 45 other countries, takes three and a half years to complete beyond undergraduate requirements. Most entrants have undergraduate or postgraduate degrees.

Life also offers a chiropractic technician diploma and 29 degree programs in business, nutrition, dietetics, the sciences, and several associate-level degree programs. An important part of the curriculum is the master of sport health science degree in the School of Graduate Studies.

In addition to the specific course offerings and granting of degrees, a unique philosophy underpins Life's successful approach to higher education. Dr. Sid founded the institution on the principles of his guiding philosophy, Lasting Purpose, which requires practitioners "to love, to serve, and to give" out of their own abundance. It reflects a belief in the "law of just returns" that

The Life University Learning Resources Center is one of several new structures created during an extensive campus expansion program.

will always be in effect and help them to win success in their personal life and in their chosen profession. Education at Life University recognizes and respects the innate recuperative powers of the body. It is built on the principle that the body can heal itself when provided with the proper environment, which includes regular chiropractic care.

Life University's campus is comprised of more than 20 modern buildings situated on 125 acres in Marietta along the banks of historic Rottenwood Creek. An authentically restored 19th-century village along the creek, including an operating water-powered mill, attracts year-round visitors who enjoy walking the trails and relaxing beside the waterfall.

With its growing reputation as a sports leader, Life University had the unique honor of hosting international track meets in 1995 and 1996 in which athletes from many nations gratefully utilized the Life campus and its training facilities to train for the 1996 Summer Olympic Games held in Atlanta. Following the Olympics, Dr. Williams created the International Sports Training Center. Coaches and athletes from other nations travel to the campus to participate in the university's Dynamic Essentials for Lasting Peak Performance (DELPP) program. This program, an outgrowth of the Dynamic Essentials program, combines the philosophy of chiropractic with high-level physical training, mental discipline, nutrition and sports health science.

The superb sports facilities at Life University, along with its expertise in sports chiropractic, have made it a worldwide focus for many efforts concerning human performance. There are two gymnasiums, wellness facilities, a five-mile cross-country trail and a track-and-field stadium. These training facilities, the coaches and the trainers have made Life University a center for research on endurance, sports health and peak performance.

Life has taken the leadership in a host of international initiatives, including the low back pain study conducted in conjunction with the World Health Organization (WHO) and completed in 1999. This work has produced a groundbreaking report by the WHO on low back pain that brings chiropractic to the forefront. As a result of collaboration and involvement with this respected international organization, WHO has joined with the university in a major research effort to study the global burden of the subluxation and other musculoskeletal disorders.

Life University's relationship with WHO has gained the chiropractic profession new and greater respect and recognition among the health care leaders and government officials throughout the world. It has resulted in the university serving as host for a major Pan-American Conference on WHO's Tobacco Free Initiative in April 2000.

Beginning in the 1950s with the catalyst of successful chiropractic care for one player's football injuries, and culminating in the creation of a university in Cobb County, the evolution of Life University has been a natural journey to its present success.

Life University's history serves as a testimonial to what can come of one person's dream when that mission is fueled by love for all human beings and concern for their well being. Dr. Sid's passion for chiropractic and his unfettered belief in its potency as a major contributor to world health is boundless and reflected in his life, his career and the institutions that he has created.

Shepherd Center

Shepherd Center's founding was inspired by an accident that occurred when 22-year-old James Shepherd suffered a paralyzing injury while body surfing in Rio de Janeiro. His parents, Alana and Harold Shepherd, rushed to his side and arranged for his return to Atlanta when he was medically able to travel. Upon their return, the family was dismayed to discover the lack of medical care and rehabilitation services available for people with spinal cord injuries in Atlanta and the entire Southeastern region of the United States.

After extensive rehabilitation in Colorado, James regained the ability to walk with the aid of a cane and leg brace. For the Shepherd family and their friends and supporters, James' accident became the catalyst to create a spinal cord injury center in his hometown that would serve others in need of specialized treatment.

With support and financial backing from the local business community, Shepherd Spinal Center was founded in 1975 as a six-bed unit operating out of leased space in an Atlanta hospital. The Shepherd family, Medical Director David F. Apple Jr., M.D., and countless supporters worked tirelessly to provide for further expansion. This dream became a reality in 1982 when a freestanding, 40-bed facility opened on Peachtree Road. Just 10 years later, Shepherd reached another milestone with the opening of the Billi Marcus Building, a $23 million addition that more than doubled the hospital's size, expanded outpatient services and provided a home for the Multiple Sclerosis Center. Finally, to reflect this ever broadening array of services and unprecedented growth, Shepherd Spinal Center changed its name to Shepherd Center in its 20th anniversary year.

Today, Shepherd Center has grown into a 100-bed, state-of-the-art catastrophic care hospital treating patients with spinal cord injuries and disease, acquired brain injury, multiple sclerosis and a range of neuromuscular and urological disorders. Shepherd houses the largest model spinal cord injury program in the country, is designated an official Multiple Sclerosis Center by the National Multiple Sclerosis Society-Georgia Chapter, and is part of the Georgia Model Brain Injury System. In addition to inpatient medical and rehabilitation services, Shepherd Center provides outpatient services at its main facility on Peachtree Road and also at Shepherd Pathways, a community-based ABI outpatient services, day program and residential rehabilitation center in Decatur, Georgia.

Serving the Southeast since 1975, Shepherd Center is a private, not-for-profit hospital specializing in the care of people with spinal cord injury and disease, acquired brain injury, multiple sclerosis and other neuromuscular disorders, and urological problems.

As a founding sponsor of the 1996 Atlanta Paralympic Games, Shepherd Center was the guiding force behind bringing more than 3,000 world-class athletes with disabilities from 104 nations to the city for Paralympic competition.

Shepherd Center prides itself in being more than a medical facility. It serves as an advocate for all people with disabilities and works to help make communities more accessible to wheelchair users. As one of the largest private, not-for-profit specialty hospitals in the United States, Shepherd Center is dedicated to helping people with disabling injuries and illnesses rebuild their lives with dignity, independence and hope.

Atlanta Falcons Football Club

On June 30, 1965, a little-known Georgia insurance executive, Rankin M. Smith, bid a winning $8.5 million to bring Atlanta its first and only NFL football franchise. It was the start of an enduring relationship: the Falcons remain a one-city, one-family-owned ball club to this day. At his first press conference, Smith immediately endeared himself to football enthusiasts by asking: "Doesn't every adult male in America want to own his own football team?"

The question struck a chord with Atlanta fans, who had been rooting for the Washington Redskins as the closest pro team but, clearly, were ready for a team

(Far right)
Rankin Smith — Atlanta Falcons founder and devoted Atlanta civic leader

Taylor Smith and Dan Reeves — Team President and Head Coach proudly display the George Halas NFC Championship Trophy.

of their own. Embraced warmly, the new franchise was able to set an NFL record for season tickets sold by a new club — 45,000 in only 54 days. In turn, the team would change the face of the emerging metropolis, enliven its hospitality industry and help to create the worldwide sports reputation that Atlanta enjoys today.

Smith's NFL bid was no whim. An Atlanta sports pioneer since the 50s, he had worked steadily to bring professional sports to the city. He was a leader of Major Sports, Inc., the catalyst that helped build the $18 million Atlanta-Fulton County Stadium — a lure that would draw both the Milwaukee Braves Baseball Team and the new NFL franchise to the city within a year.

Officially, the Atlanta franchise was titled "Five Smiths, Inc." for Smith's five children (all who would

play an active part in the team's history), but by contest, fans chose the nickname "Falcons." A teacher's winning entry wrote, "The Falcon is proud and dignified, with great courage and fight... and has a great sporting tradition." The team would live up to its name.

Fan interest continued to mount in 1966 as Smith signed Tommy Nobis as the first player. A Texas linebacker, Nobis was the most coveted college player in the nation and the NFL's first draft pick. "I always wanted to play in the NFL and playing for a brand-new franchise was like a dream — new uniforms, a new stadium and the most supportive and patient fans. Atlanta was a younger city and an NFL franchise carried a lot of prestige. Those were exciting days," said Nobis, who played 11 seasons, was named outstanding player twice and made five Pro Bowl appearances before joining the Falcons' front office staff.

In black jerseys adorned with a Falcon crest, the first team took the field in 1966. There were more losses than wins in the first years, but on December 19, 1971, with 40 seconds left on the clock, the offense scored to beat New Orleans, 24-20, and give the Falcons its first winning season. Inspired by head coach Leeman Bennett (the coach with the most wins in the club's history), the Falcons' "Gritz Blitz" defense set an NFL record for the fewest points allowed in a season in 1977. Opponents scored only 129 points in 14 games, an average of 9.2 per game.

Fans got an early Christmas present on December 24, 1978, when the team won its first playoff game against the Eagles, 14-13. In 1980, powered by three Steve Bartkowski touchdown passes, William Andrews' sixth 100-yard game, behind an offensive line led by Jeff Van Note, and a rugged defense, the team beat the 49ers to clinch the Falcons' first-ever NFC Western Division title. To date, the team has made six playoff appearances and won two division titles and one conference championship.

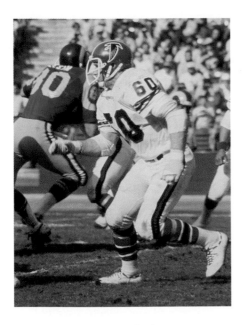 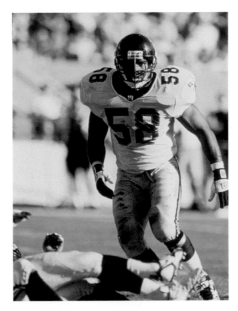 

The Falcons really began to soar when Georgia native and NFL's "Winningest Active Coach," Dan Reeves, became head coach in 1997. In only his second season, Reeves led the team to the NFC Western Division title with a 14-2 regular game season, including a heart-stopping win (30-27) in the NFC championship game over the 16-1 Minnesota Vikings in overtime. Propelled by Jamal Anderson, Chris Chandler, Bob Whitfield, Morten Anderson, Jessie Tuggle, Ray Buchanan, Terance Mathis and Chuck Smith, the team was awarded its first George Halas trophy as National Football Conference Champions and a berth in Super Bowl XXXIII. They fell to the Broncos in future hall-of-famer John Elway's last NFL game.

Over the years, Smith turned down numerous overtures from other cities to move his franchise, despite low revenues from a shared football/baseball stadium. Instead of leaving, Smith spearheaded construction of a new world-class stadium, convention and event facility for the city. The Falcons' 20-year agreement to become the Georgia Dome's major tenant helped clinch the project. A sold-out crowd of 70,000 fans watched the Falcons beat the Philadelphia Eagles, 20-10, in their inaugural game in their new stadium in August of 1992.

More than a stadium, the Dome became a major player in the international sporting community. Atlanta's professional sports tradition and the Dome were critical to gaining the 1996 Olympics, bringing "Dream Team" basketball, gymnastics and world attention to the city. Smith was a driving force behind landing two Super Bowls (1994 and 2000), the Men's Final Four Basketball Tournament (2002) and other major sporting events for Atlanta. "It was a rare and universal respect that Rankin enjoyed... and when he pitched his city's qualities, people knew he meant it," said Indianapolis Colts President Jim Irsay. Within the league, he was known as an NFL man first and always. He worked tirelessly to bring new Southeast franchises to Charlotte and Jacksonville.

He was also a devoted backer of his native city and state, serving on major civic boards and leading the campaign for the $43 million Fernbank Museum of Natural History. His quiet generosity was made formal in 1985 with the founding of the Atlanta Falcons Youth Foundation. Through this nonprofit organization, Falcon players, coaches and staff shine off the field as well as on. Team players average over 250 community appearances a year and the foundation has given over $1 million to benefit nearly 100 state youth organizations. The foundation's success inspired the Atlanta Hawks and Braves to start their own charitable organizations.

Smith was inducted into the Georgia Sports Hall of Fame in 1995, and at his death in 1997, the Falcons passed to the capable hands of his son, Taylor Smith, who grew up holding many staff positions. Under his leadership, the club is building a new $18 million, 26-acre, state-of-the-art training center — proof that the Falcons intend to be part of Atlanta's vitality and growth for years to come.

(Left to right)

Tommy Nobis, "Mr. Falcon," dominated the gridiron for the Falcons from 1966-1976.

William Andrews ran over and slashed through defenses for five years until suffering a devastating career-ending injury in 1984.

Jessie "The Hammer" Tuggle from Spalding, Georgia, has terrorized opposing running backs for 14 seasons.

Atlanta History Center

The Atlanta History Center is dedicated to presenting the stories of Atlanta's past, present and future in a variety of engaging and exciting ways through interactive exhibitions, fun and educational programs, collections representing the diverse heritage of the city, and research resources for area residents and visitors. Operated by the Atlanta Historical Society, which was

The modern Atlanta History Museum was added to the other features of the Atlanta History Center in 1993. The 30,000-square-foot museum features state-of-the-art exhibitions tracing the unique history of the region as well as traveling exhibitions highlighting historic themes of national importance.

founded in 1926, the center is today comprised of two historic homes, a modern 30,000-square-foot museum and a research library/archives all located on a 33-acre campus made up of five distinctive and beautiful garden landscapes. The center is a cultural resource for residents and students, as well as a popular attraction for visitors and conventioneers. Each year nearly 160,000 people visit the site located in Buckhead, which is noted for its beautiful residences, burgeoning office towers and exciting nightlife, about 15 minutes north of downtown.

Atlanta History Museum

Through its award-winning exhibitions, the museum tells the story of all Atlanta's people from Indian settlements to the international city of today. Classical details enhance the interior public spaces; the atrium is reminiscent of an early railroad station, evoking Atlanta's beginnings as a transportation center. The museum features four permanent exhibitions: "Turning

Point: The American Civil War," "Shaping Traditions: Folk Arts in a Changing South," "Metropolitan Frontiers: Atlanta 1835-2000" and "Down the Fairway With Bobby Jones." In addition to its permanent exhibitions, the History Center includes a full schedule of rotating temporary exhibitions created by staff curators from local collections as well as traveling exhibitions from prestigious museums around the nation. Also included in the museum building is a shop featuring unique artwork and crafts of the region, hard-to-find and popular books, and a variety of memorabilia based on museum exhibitions. Visitors can relax and grab a bite to eat in the quaint surroundings of The Coca-Cola Café, a re-creation of a 1950s-style diner.

"Turning Point: The American Civil War" — DuBose Gallery

The Civil War was a critical turning point in United States history. Few events have so profoundly affected Americans, changed their lives and the country. In 1865, at a staggering cost in death and destruction, Northern victory established an indivisible nation, ended slavery and set the United States on a course that would broaden democratic freedoms for all Americans. This dynamic 9,200-square-foot exhibition features more than 1,400 objects primarily from the renowned DuBose Civil War Collection, but also includes the Thomas Swift Dickey Civil War Ordnance Collection and other holdings. Visitors experience the war through the eyes of both Confederate and Union soldiers who fought on the front lines as well as civilians who struggled to survive at home.

"Shaping Traditions: Folk Arts in a Changing South" — Goizueta Folklife Gallery

This exhibition traces the unique and evolving attributes of Southern folk culture through antique and contemporary objects as well as oral and musical traditions. Developed from the Atlanta History

Center's John A. Burrison Folklife Collection, it features 500 examples of handcrafted pottery, woodwork, basketry, weaving, quilting and metalwork, and explores the lives of several master folk artists.

"Metropolitan Frontiers: Atlanta 1835-2000"

From Indian settlements and the coming of the railroads through the Civil War, cotton fields and *Gone With the Wind*, to civil rights and the city's growth into an international metropolis worthy of the 1996 Olympic Games, Atlanta's story is a fascinating one. Visitors travel through time in this groundbreaking exhibition with hundreds of rare artifacts, antique clothing, historic photographs, original documents, video presentations and special areas for hands-on exploration.

"Down the Fairway with Bobby Jones"

From the phenomenal story of golf legend Robert Tyre "Bobby" Jones Jr. to the rolling green fairways of Augusta National and the Masters, Georgia has led the way in the development of golf as one of the nation's best loved sports. "Down the Fairway with Bobby Jones" traces Georgia's incredible golf story from course development and tournament play to women in the game and the integration of public courses.

At the center of the exhibition is the story of the man considered to be the most important golfer in the history of the sport, Bobby Jones. Photographs and personal artifacts follow his life through his incomparable number of tournament wins, family, successful business career and ongoing dedication to the game. Other sections feature items such as an 1800s feathery ball, 18th-century clubs, replicas of four grand slam trophies, rule books from St. Andrews, golf clothing and shoes, one of the coveted Master's tournament green jackets, original papers from desegregation proceedings, scorecards, badges and junior golf artifacts.

Historic Houses

Swan House, an elegant classically styled mansion, is listed in the National Register of Historic Places and has become an Atlanta landmark. Built in 1928 for the Edward H. Inman family, heirs to a cotton brokerage fortune, the house was designed by well-known Atlanta

architect Philip Trammell Shutze and contains many original antique and reproduction furnishings. Swan House depicts the lifestyle of a wealthy Atlanta family in the early 20th century. It also houses the Philip Trammell Shutze Collection of Decorative Arts.

The 1928 Swan House mansion is a popular feature of the Atlanta History Center. The elegant home, built by one of Atlanta's premiere families, is open for daily tours and special events.

Tullie Smith Farm is an 1845 plantation-plain farmhouse surrounded by outbuildings including a separate open-hearth kitchen, blacksmith shop, smokehouse, double corncrib, pioneer log cabin and barn complete with animals, as well as traditional vegetable, herb and flower gardens. Tullie Smith offers a taste of rural life in Atlanta before the Civil War. The house is listed in the National Register of Historic Places.

Gardens

Thirty-three acres of beautiful gardens, woodlands and nature trails show the horticultural history of the Atlanta region. Gardens include the Mary Howard Gilbert Memorial Quarry Garden, with native plants, wildflowers, bridges and a stream; The Tullie Smith Farm gardens, featuring formal boxwoods and classical statuary; Swan Woods Trail, labeled for nature study; the Garden for Peace, home of the Soviet Georgian sculpture "The Peace Tree;" the Frank A. Smith Memorial Rhododendron Garden, blooming with dozens of species of rhododendrons and azaleas; and the Cherry-Sims Asian-American Garden, where species from the Southeastern United States and their Asian counterparts are cultivated.

Library/Archives

The library/archives staff answers more than 7,000 reference requests a year. Through the library/archives, researchers and media can purchase copies of photographs as well as images of items from the society's collections. The Cherokee Garden Library, founded by the Cherokee Garden Club in 1973, offers an extensive gardening and horticulture research collection. The library/archives are located in McElreath Hall, which also houses staff offices.

Blue Cross and Blue Shield of Georgia

Atlantans driving along Peachtree Road years ago may remember passing a narrow red-brick office building just south of Lenox Square and on the far side of the street. Most people probably never noticed it because it was cramped between its neighbors and blended right into the structural landscape of Buckhead.

That nondescript building was headquarters for Blue Cross and Blue Shield of Georgia. The new headquarters, now on that same site, sends quite

Blue Cross and Blue Shield of Georgia's headquarters in the heart of Buckhead

another message to Atlantans: "We're updated, streamlined, and not to be ignored as you pass by."

The new look in Blue Cross and Blue Shield's home is emblematic of what has changed inside: a new corporate and financial structure, new products and a new purpose, all with the same recognizable strength and dependability of an organization that has been in business a long time.

In small communities throughout Georgia, residents sometimes refer to their "Blue Cross" policies when, in fact, they are insured by another company. To some, it seems, Blue Cross and Blue Shield is synonymous with health insurance.

The Birth of "The Blues"

In time and space, the glass and marble of this new building is far from the mines and forests of the Pacific Northwest — where the story began. "The Blues," as it is fondly known, began in the early 1900s when the employers of miners and lumberjacks wanted to provide medical care for their employees for a flat monthly fee. This led to physicians later banding together into medical service bureaus, the first of which was formed in 1917. These bureaus became the foundation for the Blue Shield Plan, which started in California in 1939.

The Blue Cross Plan originated in Dallas, Texas, in 1929 and offered public school teachers guaranteed 21 days of hospital care for $6 a year. The plan gained popularity quickly and spread to other employers.

The two "blue" organizations evolved separately, both of them undergoing growth and changes in name, structure and affiliation. It wasn't until 1982 that the two merged, forming The Blue Cross and Blue Shield Association.

Blue Cross and Blue Shield in Georgia

Only eight years after the founding of the school teachers' program in Texas, Georgians could purchase low-cost health insurance from either Blue Cross or Blue Shield. From those Georgia beginnings in 1937, the state's largest insurer of health benefits has emerged.

The genesis of the "Georgia Blues" was an act of the state legislature that created the Atlanta Blue Cross Plan, founded with a loan of $5,000 from local hospitals. It provided only one plan: single-member hospitalization insurance. The premiums were an unbelievable 90 cents a month. In 1954 the Atlanta Blue Shield Plan was created to cover physician services.

Similar plans sprouted in Savannah and Columbus, and in 1985 they combined with Atlanta's plan to form Blue Cross and Blue Shield of Georgia.

Georgia Blue had operated as a not-for-profit company throughout its history but found itself facing formidable competition from national insurers who were heftily funded. It could not raise capital, as competitors could, through the issuance of stock. This severely limited its ability to keep premiums low and, at the same time, fund technology and other forms of innovation and growth. Thus it appealed to the Georgia General Assembly to gain for-profit status. This was granted in 1995 through an act of the General Assembly and approval by the state's Insurance Commissioner.

Cerulean Companies, Inc. (cerulean means "deep and lasting blue") was subsequently formed as the holding company for Blue Cross and Blue Shield of Georgia and its affiliate companies.

From humble beginnings and the single, uncomplicated health care insurance policy of yesterday, Blue Cross and Blue Shield of Georgia exploded into the modern world and now offers a wide array of more than 12 products to meet the diverse needs of its customers. These include the well-known traditional indemnity product, a more price-sensitive health maintenance option, and preferred provider plans.

Georgia Blue's presence in Atlanta offers much more than its products and jobs for Georgians. From spearheading the Georgia Caring Program for Children to starting a workplace domestic violence awareness program called SAFE!, to serving as a Partner in Education with a local elementary school, to sponsoring such events as the Walk for Juvenile Diabetes, Blue Cross and Blue Shield has prided itself on leading and participating in initiatives that enhance Georgians' quality of life.

Blue Cross and Blue Shield of Georgia now covers more than 1.7 million Georgians. Of every household in Georgia, one in three has at least one member insured by the Georgia Blues. As that number continues to grow, Blue Cross and Blue Shield of Georgia will continue to fulfill its mission of providing quality, affordable health coverage to as many Georgians as possible.

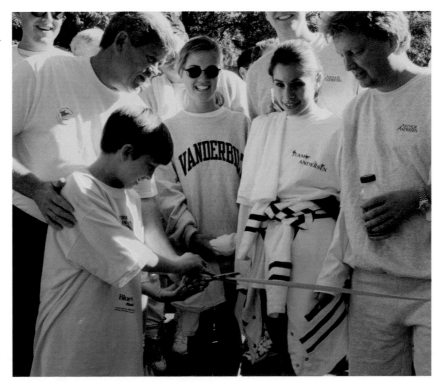

Blue Cross and Blue Shield of Georgia President and CEO Richard Shirk helps cut the ribbon to start the Walk for Juvenile Diabetes.

Six Flags Over Georgia

Atop poles as tall as full-grown pine trees, six brightly colored banners fly high over the gates of Six Flags Over Georgia, the Southeast's premier family thrill park. The flags of Spain, Britain, France, the Confederacy, the state of Georgia and the United States represent Georgia's past and help bring to life events which shaped it.

When throngs of excited visitors first passed through the beautiful Six Flags gates in 1967, they were captivated by the high-flying flags, wide vistas, lush shade trees and wide variety of family entertainment. With more than 100 rides, shows and attractions providing spine-tingling thrills and gentler pleasures, a day in the park is a treat for children up to 100.

Some come for the excitement, others for entertainment; but it's the roller coasters that visitors remember most. Nestled amid trees or surrounded by cool lakes, the coasters offer breathtaking views from staggering heights. Six Flags' first, the Dahlonega Mine Train, has been in continuous operation since the park opened. Resembling a runaway mine train straight from Georgia's gold rush days, it thrills "miners" with plunges, twists and turns on winding tracks during the park's longest ride.

The Georgia Scorcher® is one of the world's tallest and fastest stand-up roller coasters. Rising 107 feet and reaching speeds of 54 mph, it sends riders racing head-over-heels through 3,000 feet of contorted twisting, looping and spiraling purple and gold track — while standing up!

Batman, The Ride®, combines thrill-ride technology with blockbuster Batman movie magic. Ski-lift-style trains are suspended from the track above and riders fly at intense speeds over the outside of hairpin turns, vertical loops and corkscrews. At zero gravity, the floor drops out from beneath guests' feet. The faint of heart had best not ride!

Remaining one of the world's longest and tallest wooden roller coasters, The Great American Scream Machine® rises more than 100 feet above the ground. Featured in the 1975 Guinness Book of Records, it is a Six Flags "must do."

Ninja®, the Black Belt of Roller Coasters®, is the only steel coaster of its kind in the Southeast and features five inversions. Passengers describe hair-standing-on-end excitement while hurling 52 mph on the tallest coaster at Six Flags.

When it premiered, The Mind Bender® was America's first triple-loop coaster. This unique thrill ride catapults passengers through three loops — two of them vertical. The Viper®, called the "Coaster That Strikes Twice," propels riders from zero to 57 mph in less than six seconds, shooting them through a 360-degree loop, up a 70-degree incline and back again.

Roller coasters are only a portion of the fun at Six Flags. There are rides designed for the very young, games, restaurants, shops, strolling cartoon characters and even a parachute jump. A family tradition year after year, the fun never ends at Six Flags.

Despite premiering new attractions nearly every year, Six Flags employees still take time to give back to the Atlanta community. Each year the park sponsors a Pet Parade benefiting the Atlanta Humane Society. Entrants compete for prizes and all proceeds go directly to the Humane Society. Six Flags Over Georgia is owned by Premier Parks Inc., the world's largest regional theme park company, which hosts more than 40 million guests each year and serves the United States' largest metropolitan areas plus six locations in Europe.

Georgia Scorcher — Put your feet to the fire!

American Software

In 1970 Jim Edenfield and Tom Newberry launched a new company — American Software. From their two-room office suite in Colony Square they began marketing a groundbreaking computer software program that enabled companies to forecast demand for their products and order the precise amount of raw material needed to fill anticipated orders.

The program was an instant hit with major manufacturers and American Software emerged as a world-class player whose mission is to help manufacturers and distributors achieve a competitive advantage in the global marketplace.

Delivering the Vision

In addition to establishing itself as a key player in the high-tech history of Atlanta, American Software also has a history of anticipating the needs of companies in the global marketplace. With Edenfield and

American Software
co-founders
Thomas L. Newberry
and James C. Edenfield

Newberry at the helm, American Software has grown and prospered, offering a myriad of programs designed to help manufacturers and distributors find new and better ways to respond quickly to changing market conditions. They are designed with the advanced technology global enterprises need to make more informed business decisions and compete in a global economy. Following its initial public offering in 1983, American Software went international, establishing offices in London, Paris, Melbourne and Singapore. In

the late 1990s, through its subsidiary Logility, the company was the first to launch an Internet/intranet collaborative forecasting application. This groundbreaking solution allows manufacturers to work with their suppliers and customers to optimize their supply chains. No one knows what the future holds, but one can bet American Software will be right there — pushing the envelope, anticipating the needs of an ever-changing marketplace.

Giving Back to Atlanta

Just as its commitment to manufacturers has always been top priority at American Software, so has its commitment to the Atlanta community. Outreach projects usually begin with an individual employee, then gathering momentum, become annual events with companywide support.

Employees have been delivering meals for Project Open Hand since 1994. Year after year, they have assumed more responsibility and they now take over regular delivery routes. Initially begun by a single employee, the project provides an essential service for homebound patients with AIDS. American Software employees also turn out in large numbers for the annual AIDS Walk Atlanta.

The company initially began fund raising for the Juvenile Diabetes Foundation in 1997. To garner interest, company divisions competed against one another by sponsoring breakfasts and lunches. The winning division was the one raising the most money through the combined efforts of these projects and the walkathon. Through the years, the project has grown and nearly 100 percent of those who sign up for the walkathon participate or sponsor someone to walk. The good-natured rivalry between divisions has resulted in higher and higher goals and increased camaraderie among the staff. Other favorite charities include the Margaret Mitchell House, the Atlanta History Center, the American Cancer Society, SCI-TREK and the Children's Institute.

MAPICS, Inc.

Like a fast-growing youngster, MAPICS *has* matured from a small group within IBM to an independent, successful company specializing in Enterprise Resource Planning (ERP) software for discrete and batch process manufacturers. Originally rolled out as a manufacturing solution with IBM in 1978, MAPICS possessed striking features that covered operational and planning areas as well as financial and order handling. In 1993 the young adult moved away from the parent IBM — and then went public in 1997 as MAPICS, Inc. (MAPX on the Nasdaq National Market).

The company's technology now features 49 integrated applications available in up to 19 languages for customers in 70 countries — making it one of the largest installed bases of manufacturing customers in the industry. Manufacturers aided by the company's software include AP Technoglass, Schlumberger, Goodyear Tire & Rubber Co., Honda Motor Co., Ltd., SANYO Energy, Trans-matic Manufacturing, Inc., Volvo Construction Equipment, Weber Aircraft, and York International. As one customer said, "If you can count it, it was made utilizing MAPICS software."

Developing software for the future and for a customer base around the world, MAPICS creates programs that meet the requirements of pragmatic customers. The original software package was the first of its kind to be fully integrated. Today MAPICS is still manufacturing success. And long before other software firms thought about solutions, MAPICS provided free Y2K upgrades to its customers and was ready for the Euro.

The company has received kudos: named No. 1 in customer satisfaction and in implementing results from Advanced Manufacturers Research; and named highest overall in industry and product knowledge by software analyst The Gartner Group, Inc.

MAPICS technology allows clients to grow and change without losing the equity they have built in their systems. Its modular design lets customers add software applications and users simply, while lowering costs dramatically. Because the modular design is easy and cost effective, manufacturers "go live" faster and reap a quicker return on investments.

Listening to customers is key to MAPICS's success. Manufacturers want to shorten lead times, reduce inventories, increase plant efficiencies, and synchronize and streamline business processes. MAPICS responds by developing groundbreaking solutions for customers around the globe, which are supported by more than 80 independent organizations called Affiliates. These local experts understand local manufacturers and provide experienced support during the sell-cycle, implementation and beyond. Three call centers — in Georgia, the Netherlands, and Kuala Lumpur, Malaysia — respond to customers 24 hours a day, seven days a week. Online Web-based services include customer e-mail and a problem-solving staff.

As a company, MAPICS believes in being locally active and globally responsible. Employees have a history of community involvement and they participate in volunteer projects where they live and work worldwide. As MAPICS grows, so do its contributions of employee time, in-kind giving and board associations.

The company that began as a development group within IBM became a leader in its industry. MAPICS plans to remain in the forefront by responding to customer needs and developing innovative software solutions to solve the most complex manufacturing problems.

Globes in production using MAPICS technology

Bibliography

Ivan Allen, Jr. and Paul Hemphill, *Mayor: Notes on the Sixties.* Athens: University of Georgia Press, 1978.

"Atlanta Grows Up," special issue of *Atlanta Magazine* (on the occasion of the 150th anniversary of the city), June 1987.

Clarence A. Bacote, "The Negro in Atlanta Politics," *Phylon*, XVI (1955), 333-50.

Meta Barker, "How Decatur Escaped the Iron Horses," *Atlanta Historical Bulletin* (November 1936), no. 9, 12-18.

Laura and Ken Barre, *The History of Doraville, Georgia.* Roswell: Wolfe Publishing, 1995.

Joseph L. Bernd, "White Supremacy and the Disfranchisement of Blacks in Georgia, 1946," *Georgia Historical Quarterly* (Winter 1982), 503-509.

Betsy Braden and Paul Hagen, *A Dream Takes Flight: Hartfield Atlanta International Airport and Aviation in Atlanta.* Athens: University of Georgia Press, 1989.

Bridges-Cobb County Inc., *Marietta: Touchstones to the Past.* Marietta: Bridges-Cobb Inc., 1975.

O.E. Carson, *The Trolley Titans.* Glendale, CA: Interurban Press, 1981.

Edward Young Clarke, *Atlanta Illustrated.* Atlanta: J P Harrison & Co., 1881.

Lois Coogle, *Sandy Springs, Past Tense.* Atlanta: Decor Master Co., 1971.

Walter G. Cooper, *Official History of Fulton County.* Atlanta: Walter Brown Publishing Co., 1934.

Charles Crowe, "Racial Massacre in Atlanta," *Journal of Negro History* (1969), 150-173.

Elizabeth Lockhart Davis and Ethel Warren Spruill, *The Story of Dunwoody: Its Heritage and Horizons, 1821-1975.* Atlanta: published by the authors, 1975.

[East Point Historical Society], *Early History of East Point, Georgia or "A Historical Sketch of Pioneer Days."* East Point: printed by the Society, 1984.

A. Hollis Edens, "The Founding of Atlanta," *Atlanta Historical Bulletin, Part 1,* IV (July 1939), no. 18, 203-231.

_____, "The Founding of Atlanta," *Atlanta Historical Bulletin, Part 2,* IV (October 1939), no. 19, 275-290.

_____, "The Founding of Atlanta," *Atlanta Historical Bulletin, Part 3,* V (January 1940), no. 20, 65-85.

James C. Flanigan, *History of Gwinnett County, Georgia, 1818-1943.* Vol. I. Hapeville: published by the author, 1943.

_____, *History of Gwinnett County, Georgia, 1818-1960.* Vol. II. Hapeville: published by the author, 1959.

Allen Philip Francis, *A Compilation of Fact and Legend Pertaining to the History of Norcross in Gwinnett County, Georgia.* Norcross: Sponsored by the Norcross Womans Club, 1967.

Fulfilling the Promise: A Region comes of Age (the Counties of Butts, Carroll, Clayton, Coweta, Fayette, Harris, Heard, Henry, Lamar, Meriwether, Pike, South Fulton, Spalding, Talbot, Troup, Upson). Atlanta: Lindsey Publishing Company, Inc., 1990.

Franklin Garrett, *Atlanta and Environs.* 2 vols. Athens: University of Georgia Press, 1954.

The Georgia Annual: a Compendium of Useful Information about Georgia. Atlanta: A B Caldwell, Publishers, 1911, 1912.

George R. Gilmer, *Sketches of Some of the First Settlers of Upper Georgia.* Baltimore: Genealogical Publishing Co., 1970.

Henry Grady, *The New South.* New York: Robert Bonner's Sons, 1890.

Truman Hartshorn, *Metropolis in Georgia: Atlanta's Rise as a Major Transaction Center.* Cambridge, MA: Ballinger, 1976.

John D. Humphries, "The Organization of DeKalb County," *Atlanta Historical Bulletin*, VIII (December 1947), no. 32, 17-30.

Viola L. Jensen, "Higher Education for Negroes in Atlanta," *Atlanta Historical Bulletin*, VIII (October 1948), no. 33, 106-111.

Clarece Martin, *"A Glimpse of the Past: the History of Bulloch Hall and Roswell, Georgia."* Roswell: Historic Roswell, Inc., n.d.

Elizabeth Hanleiter McCallie, "Atlanta in the 1850s," *Atlanta Historical Bulletin*, VIII (October 1948), no. 33, 93-106.

Lois McMichael, comp., *History of Butts County, Georgia.* Atlanta: Cherokee Publishing Co., 1978.

Edwin Milton, *History of Hapeville, Georgia.* Alpharetta: Hapeville Historical Society and Hapeville Centennial Committee, 1991.

Eugene M. Mitchell, "Atlanta During the 'Reconstruction Period'," *Atlanta Historical Bulletin* (November 1936), no.9, 18-24.

Kay Mixon, "The Mountain of Controversy: A History of Stone Mountain" [booklet]. Stone Mountain: published by the author, 1970.

Harvey K. Newman, "Piety and Segregation," *Georgia Historical Quarterly* (1987), 238-251.

The People of Smyrna. Published by the city of Smyrna, 1972.

Howard L. Preston, *Automobile Age Atlanta: The Making of a Southern Metropolis, 1900-1935.* Athens: University of Georgia Press, 1979.

Robert Rainer, *Henry County, Georgia: the Mother of Counties.* Atlanta: published by the author, 1971.

Bradley R. Rice, "If Dixie Were Atlanta," *Sunbelt Cities: Politics and Atlanta Since World War II.* Richard Bernard and Bradley Rice, eds. Austin: University of Texas, 1983.

Darlene Roth and Andy Ambrose, *"Metropolitan Frontiers: A Short History of Atlanta."* Atlanta: Longstreet Publishing Co., 1996.

Vivian Price Saffold, *Past Memories, Present Progress, Future Dreams: A History of the Community and City of Chamblee.* Chamblee: Keystone Press, 1983. A 75th anniversary publication.

Lee Sayra, "Keeping the Promise: Agnes Scott College, 1889-1989," [paper]. Atlanta Historical Society, January 1989.

Norman Shavin and Bruce Galphin, *Atlanta: Triumph of a People.* Atlanta: Capricorn Corporation, 1985.

Adiel Sherwood, *A Gazetteer of the State of Georgia.* Athens: University of Georgia Press, 1939 [reprint of 1827 publication].

The State Capitol of Georgia [undated booklet]. Atlanta History Center, subject files.

Sarah Blackwell Gober Temple, *The First Hundred Years: A Short History of Cobb County, in Georgia.* Atlanta: Walter Brown Publishing Co., 1935.

U.S., Dept. of the Interior, NPS, National Register Nominations, for Clayton, Cobb, DeKalb, Fayette, Fulton, Gwinnett, and Henry counties, Historic Preservation Division, GA DNR.

U.S., WPA, *Georgia: The WPA Guide to its Towns and Countryside.* Columbia: University of South Carolina Press, 1990 [reprint of 1940 edition].

George White, *Statistics of the State of Georgia.* Savannah: W. Thorne Williams, 1849.

Otis White, "A Tale of Two Georgias," *Georgia Trend* (April 1986), 46-50.

Index

Partners & Web Site Index

Corporate profiles also appear on bookofbusiness.com

Patrons

Serologicals Corporation

Computerized & Advanced Technologies (CATCO)

Photo by Darlene Roth

Photo by Darlene Roth